SATHER CLASSICAL LECTURES

Volume Fifty-five

Christianity and the Rhetoric of Empire

St. Antony and St. Paul the Hermit in the desert. Italian school, seventeenth century. (Private collection. Photograph: Courtauld Institute of Art)

Christianity and the Rhetoric of Empire

THE DEVELOPMENT OF CHRISTIAN DISCOURSE

Averil Cameron

University of California Press

BERKELEY · LOS ANGELES · LONDON

University of California Press
Berkeley and Los Angeles, California

University of California Press, Ltd.
London, England

© 1991 by
The Regents of the University of California

First Paperback Printing 1994

Library of Congress Cataloging-in-Publication Data

Cameron, Averil.
    Christianity and the rhetoric of empire : the development of
Christian discourse / Averil Cameron.
        p.   cm.—(Sather classical lectures ; v. 55)
    Includes bibliographical references and index.
    ISBN 0-520-08923-5 (alk. paper)
    1. Christian literature, Early—Greek authors—History and
criticism.   2. Theology—Early church, ca. 30–600.   3. Christianity
and other religions, Greek.   4. Christianity and other religions,
Roman.   5. Greece—Religion.   6. Rome—Religion.   7. Church
history—Primitive and early church, ca. 30–600.   I. Title.   II. Series.
BR67.C26   1991
270.1—dc20   90-39376
                                                                    CIP

Printed in the United States of America
9   8   7   6   5   4   3   2   1

For Han Drijvers

The silence of eternity
Interpreted by love.

Contents

Illustrations

Preface

An invitation to give the Sather Classical Lectures confers both a great sense of intellectual responsibility and a heady amount of freedom. No restrictions are placed on the subject, so long as it somehow concerns the classical world, and while the discipline of six weekly lectures, delivered at eight in the evening to an extremely discerning and varied audience, may be daunting, it can, as so many others before me have discovered, also be an exciting and stimulating experience. The first lecture, one learns on arrival, is a major social event in the university calendar; in my case it coincided with the February storms—rain of a torrential quality not experienced in the traditionally rainy England—but the prospect of the Sather reception proved, somewhat to my surprise, enough of an attraction to counteract the deluge. One is fed with dreadful stories of dwindling audiences after that beginning, and it is true that the atmosphere changes and notably becomes much more informal with the subsequent change of room. But I like to think that Jane Sather, whose severe portrait looks down on all Sather lecturers from the walls of the Sather office, would not have been displeased to see another woman giving the lectures, only the third in the seventy-three series until this one, and that she would have been satisfied with the audience who came faithfully week after week to hear her.

The discussion that follows each lecture is traditionally informal and conducted in the hospitable surroundings of faculty houses and apartments. A lecturer naturally tends under such circumstances to want to relax rather than to explain or justify, but I am grateful not only for the generous hospitality offered so freely, but also for the many helpful comments and reactions, which often led me into unsuspected territory, particularly when they came, as they often did, from colleagues in disciplines outside the classical field. Here Randy Starn, Howard Bloch, and Svetlana and Paul Alpers immediately spring to mind. Within the classical field itself, I was particularly helped and encouraged, and often also entertained, by Leslie Threatte, Erich Gruen, Tony Long, Ron Stroud, Donald Mastronarde, Robert Knapp, Crawford H. Greenewalt, Charles Murgia, and Danuta Shanzer. I owe a special debt of friendship to Thomas Rosenmeyer and J. K. Anderson for their kindness throughout my stay. Other new friends who helped us in various ways as a family during our stay in the Berkeley community and the Bay Area are too numerous to list in full, but I should like particularly to mention the Herr family and the Humphrey family; finally, Kay Flavell helped us in many practical ways. I am not least grateful to Daniel and Sophie for disrupting their own lives to come with me to Berkeley.

Dinner table talk at Berkeley tends to center on two topics: food and the imminence of the next big earthquake. The latter sadly made itself felt in 1989. But in 1986, several months in this environment, detached from one's usual duties, was a stimulus as well as a privilege. During that time, and while I have been preparing the lectures for publication, I have had many opportunities to revise and refine my original ideas, although the chapters in this book still represent substantially the lectures as they were delivered. I should like to pay a particular tribute to the members of my graduate seminar at Berkeley, in particular Scott Bradbury, Maud Gleason, and Judith Evans-Grubbs, for their continuing friendly interest and their very useful observations. Many others generously offered information, help, and ideas, among them David Blank, Ann Bergren, Peter Brown, Elizabeth Clark, Trudi Darby, Caroline Dewald, Hal Drake, Han Drijvers, Raoul Mortley, Michael Nagler, Karen Jo Torjesen, Kathleen O'Brien Wicker, William Wuellner, and Froma Zeitlin. It is immensely comforting to know that so many others are interested in the problems I have been trying to confront. I was able to present some material in other places during my stay, notably at Princeton University; Scripps College, Claremont, California; the University of California, Santa Barbara and Los Angeles; Duke University, Durham, North Carolina; and at the South-West Branch of the American Academy of Religion meeting at Chattanooga and previously at the Triennial Meeting of the Hellenic and Roman Societies held in Cambridge in July 1985. All these audiences without exception provided useful and often unexpected comments.

This is an ancient historian's book about early Christianity. It is also highly personal, in that it reflects a set of particular recent interests and reacts against particular ways of interpreting the role played by Christianity in the Roman empire. Its range is deliberately wide, in that I have sought quite consciously to connect for my own better understanding the late antique or early Byzantine society on which most of my other writing has focused with its roots in the Roman empire. Thus it is informed by a preoccupation with the problems of transition, and with historical change in general. I am as much concerned with the problem of how a historian can explain change as with what might actually be thought to have happened.

Many other thanks are due in addition for help and suggestions at various stages. A seminar series at the Institute of Classical Studies, London (published as *History as Text* [London: Duckworth, 1989]), enabled me to clarify some ideas as they began to take shape. Many friends and colleagues have allowed me to see their own work in advance of publication, among them Peter Brown and Andrew and Anne-Marie Palmer. A series of lectures given at the Collège de France in 1987 at the invitation of Gilbert Dagron allowed me to develop further some of the ideas in the final chapter. Margaretha Debrunner Hall helped to remove many blemishes at the final stage, and Lucas Siorvanes and Richard Williams gave invaluable assistance with the illustrations. I thank André Deutsch, Ltd., for permission to reproduce the lines from Stevie Smith's poem "A Dream of Comparison" in chapter 5, and the late Professor K. T. Erim for allowing me to use the photograph from Aphrodisias. For all this I am grateful, but most of all I am grateful to the Classics Department at Berkeley for the invitation that first set my thoughts in this direction. The faults are many, the subject far too big, but they are mine, and I am indeed grateful in writing, delivering, and revising these lectures to have had so exhilarating an experience.

King's College London
5 April 1990

Abbreviations

ANRW	*Aufstieg und Niedergang der römischen Welt. Geschichte und Kultur Roms im Spiegel der neueren Forschung.* Ed. H. Temporini and W. Haase. 3 secs., and in individual vols. Berlin: Walter de Gruyter, 1973–.
BMGS	*Byzantine and Modern Greek Studies*
DOP	*Dumbarton Oaks Papers*
EHR	*English Historical Review*
GRBS	*Greek, Roman, and Byzantine Studies*
HSCP	*Harvard Studies in Classical Philology*
JHS	*Journal of Hellenic Studies*
JÖB	*Jahrbuch der österreichischen Byzantinistik*
JRS	*Journal of Roman Studies*
JThS	*Journal of Theological Studies*
SCH	*Studies in Church History*

Introduction

In the beginning was the Word . . .

It is no longer a novelty to hold that societies have characteristic discourses or "plots," or that the development and control of a given discourse may provide a key to social power, or even that an inquiry into the dissemination of knowledge by oral or written means ought to be high on the agenda for historians. A religion that succeeded (if slowly) in establishing itself as the prevailing religious system of the wider society to which it was at first only marginal, and laid a quite exceptional emphasis throughout this process on the verbal articulation of the faith, must cry out for analysis in these terms.

There is an enormous and ever-growing bibliography on the "rise" of Christianity. Its progress from marginal cult to world religion has, it would seem, been studied from every angle—theological, sociological, historical. Naturally, a great deal of attention has already been paid to early Christian literature of all kinds, and to its manner of expression, whether rhetorical, linguistic, or conceptual. One of the central themes studied has been the relation of Christianity to a supposed Greco-Roman background, and specifically to Greek terminology and literary forms. It will be seen that I start from the position that this attempt to separate the Greek "elements" in early Christianity is fundamentally misleading. Although it is not the subject of this book, scholars have also been concerned to relate Christian texts and modes of expression to Jewish ones. Current research into the history of Judaism in the imperial period suggests that the older notion of separability is as difficult to sustain here as it is in relation to Greek culture.

At the moment there is indeed a particular emphasis in works by theologians and students of the New Testament on the application of literary analysis to Christian texts. But on the whole, histories of the development of Christianity in the Roman Empire written by historians and from the historical point of view have focused more on its social and institutional dimensions than on its modes of expression. There are two reasons for this: first, it is part of the wider indifference among historians to the use of literature (as distinct from "literary sources") as evidence,[1] and second, it stems from the well-established practice of leaving Christian texts aside except where they seem to provide factual evidence.

But most of us now are more conscious of the sheer power of discourse, even in societies like the Roman Empire where communication was as a rule extremely poor. The very fact that Christianity was able to spread and become established as it did in such unpromising conditions asks for analysis in these terms. It is clear that Michel Foucault, who has been more than anyone responsible for this changed awareness of the importance of discourse in history, was thinking a great deal at the end of his life about the question of how Christianity was able to develop what we can call in his terms a totalizing discourse.[2] Foucault's interest was directed in the first place toward the sphere of morals and especially toward the history of the individual; but there

1. F. Moretti, *Signs Taken for Wonders: Essays in the Sociology of Literary Forms,* trans. S. Fischer, D. Forgacs, and D. Miller (London: Verso, 1988), 18, refers to "the adamantine lack of interest that historians 'proper' have always displayed towards literary (and more generally, artistic) historiography."
2. See M. Foucault, *Le souci de soi* (Paris: Gallimard, 1984).

are many other points of view from which Christian discourse needs to be investigated if we are to understand its general evolution in the early period. While these lectures were being revised there appeared the first volume of Michael Mann's *Sources of Social Power: A History of Power from the Beginning to A.D. 1760* (Cambridge: Cambridge University Press, 1986), which uses a more political approach to the analysis of early Christianity while still stressing the importance of discourse. One might quarrel with some of the positions taken (the author is a sociologist, not a Roman historian), but it is nevertheless striking to find the degree of emphasis laid here on the "systematic moral life plan" and "transcendent ideological power in human history" offered by early Christianity in relation to its growth in the context of the Roman Empire. What is different, then, in these approaches from the familiar strategy in which Christian ideology plays a secondary role in relation to economic and institutional factors is the stress laid on articulation and ideology as dynamic factors in themselves.

Quite apart from these considerations, the post-structuralist analysis being applied to New Testament texts cries out to be carried over into other early Christian literature, in particular theological writings. Why not ask what kind of texts these are, or how they seek to represent Christian truth, and in what ways they can be related to the general culture of the Roman Empire? At the same time, when even history itself has been feeling the effects of the heightened awareness of rhetoric, it ought to be obvious that the older style of empiricist analysis of early Christianity is due for revision. At the very least, we might expect to see a greater stress on its rhetorical strategies and—in view of recent work on orality and the significance of writing—on the role of communication, written and oral, in its spread. It has barely been noticed as yet what an extraordinarily suitable field early Christianity provides for this kind of inquiry.

That the nature of early Christianity was in fact multiform, especially in the earlier stages, is less an argument against seeing its eventual success in the Roman Empire in terms of the sociology of knowledge than part of the answer to the question of how it succeeded. For the study of Christian discourse in the Roman world is the study of reception, and this is a two-way process—not merely how Christian discourse made its impact on society at large, but how it was itself transformed and shaped in the endeavor. Christian discourse would have been different without the environment of the Roman world; and that environment itself was subject to geographical and diachronic variance. What we study is a dynamic process in which both sides are changing.[3]

It is not my aim here to try yet again to explain the rise of Christianity. A call has been made for a greater use of archeological evidence in studying ancient religion.[4] But no one explanation can be adequate. A whole battery of concurrent or converging explanations is needed, which will only in part be related to the nature of Christianity and the particular characteristics of Christian communities. It is equally necessary to consider the changing nature of the Roman Empire itself. We should not forget that, just as one would expect in so traditional a social structure, Christianity was extremely slow to achieve a dominant position. Some modern books give the impression that the conversion of Constantine brought an immediate transformation of society, but the truth was far otherwise.[5] So these lectures take a broad chronological sweep. I have chosen to begin effectively with the second century (though the reader will naturally

3. This is more readily recognized in relation to Christian art than to Christian writing: see, e.g., "early Christian art is never a naive, storytelling art," in T. F. Mathews, "The Early Armenian Iconographic Program of the Ējmiacin Gospel (Erevan), Matenadaran MS. 2374, *olim* 229," in *East of Byzantium: Syria and Armenia in the Formative Period,* ed. N. G. Garsoian, T. F. Mathews, and R. W. Thomson (Washington, D.C.: Dumbarton Oaks, 1982), 200.

4. G. Fowden, "Between Pagans and Christians," *JRS* 78 (1988): 173–82.

5. For a skeptical view, see R. MacMullen, "What Difference Did Christianity Make?" *Historia* 35 (1986): 322–43.

find many references to the first-century New Testament texts) so as to avoid the technical and highly disputed issues of Christian origins and the domain of New Testament scholarship proper. But I am also concerned with the place of Christianization in the transition to "late antiquity," and I wish to make a further connection between the Christianization of the Roman Empire and the nature of representation in the early Byzantine world; the final chapter deals therefore with the bridge between the two: the Eastern Empire in the sixth century.

Finding suitable terminology is difficult. Rather than a single Christian discourse, there was rather a series of overlapping discourses always in a state of adaptation and adjustment, and always ready to absorb in a highly opportunistic manner whatever might be useful from secular rhetoric and vocabulary. Nevertheless, in totality they did in the long term come to dominate social discourse as a whole in both East and West; I hope then that it may be legitimate for convenience to use the singular term "discourse" without being accused of distortion. I mean by it all the rhetorical strategies and manners of expression that I take to be particularly characteristic of Christian writing. It certainly does less than justice to the subject as a whole to concentrate on written texts, or on texts that would have been read only by an educated audience (though chapters 2, 3, and 5 emphasize the communicative power of such Christian forms as the apocryphal narratives and the homilies delivered week after week in the churches). But we can only dimly reconstitute the power of the spoken word, even when we know that it was great, and the critic must start somewhere.

Many early Christian writers were already preoccupied with the question of the nature of Christian discourse, as they debated the relation of Christian to classical rhetoric, or the problem of reaching the uneducated in their preaching, or the nature of Christian knowledge, and especially the problem of how Christian truth could be represented in words at all. Yet few of them doubted that it was essential to make the attempt. And this evolution of an organized system of thought and expression, at once flexible and all-inclusive, did mark Christianity off from pagan cults.[6] Moreover, Christianity had a special relation to textuality. As Geoffrey Harpham has recently argued, it was centered on texts and took its metaphors from them: "the Christian God is modelled on language."[7]

This is not a theological book. I write from the standpoint of a historian, although I have deliberately used the techniques of sociology of knowledge and literary theory. My concerns are twofold: to show that a large part of Christianity's effectiveness in the Roman Empire lay in its capacity to create its own intellectual and imaginative universe, and to show how its own literary devices and techniques in turn related to changing contemporary circumstances.

A series of lectures on such a theme can do no more than suggest some general directions. The selection of material is necessarily partial and impressionistic, and any reader will find many gaps. In particular, the footnotes provide a running commentary that is no doubt more illustrative of my own interests and reading than it is comprehensive; I hope, however, that they will serve to locate the main argument in a wider context and suggest further lines of inquiry. As far as the main text is concerned, my aim has been less to present a detailed justification of any one part of the argument than to make a series of suggestions; together these attempt to present a coherent, if partial, view of the whole.

One particularly important element in the formation of Christian discourse is almost entirely omitted here, namely the his-

6. W. Burkert, *Ancient Mystery Cults* (Cambridge, Mass.: Harvard University Press, 1987), 66–88, argues against attempts to find comparable pagan "theologies."

7. G. G. Harpham, *The Ascetic Imperative in Culture and Criticism* (Chicago: University of Chicago Press, 1987), 17.

tory of the Bible and its reception. Christians of whatever background in the early centuries formed their discourse on and around the Scriptures, so that what they wrote could often turn into a counterpoint of biblical types and biblical phraseology. Nevertheless, I have chosen to concern myself primarily not with the relations of Christians to their own texts, but with Christian discourse in the context of the discourses of society at large.

Again, the absorption into social discourse at large of scriptural models and language is an integral part of the process I am trying to trace, although it has not yet, I think, been analyzed from that point of view. But because that would take far more space than I have available, I have preferred to select certain other themes relating to Christian discourse in the broader sense. Thus, in contrast to the common emphasis on the distinctiveness of Christian writers, it is basic to my approach that they be seen as reflecting and responding to the same influences that were making themselves felt on pagan discourse. They were both less and more distinctive than they themselves supposed. Indeed, the prominence of the notion of the *difference* between Christian and pagan expression in the work of the Christian writers themselves is to be read as a rhetorical device and a symptom of adjustment rather than as a description of a real situation. It was a theme that, as we shall see again and again, allowed them to exploit that difference even while ostensibly defending themselves against pagan criticism. As for the occasional pagan complaints about the uncouthness of Christian literature, having begun with exaggeration, they go on to testify to the growing strength of the very phenomenon that they deplore. Christian and pagan writers alike indulged in a species of metadialogue serving the purposes of both sides.

Similarly, it is tempting to read the gradual progress of Christian discourse to center stage as representing a taking over of elite culture by popular, whether in terms of encroaching "irrationality" or an eventual "democratization" of culture. Running through the book, therefore, the reader will find the suggestion that these terms, as usually used, are unhelpful or ill defined. It is true of Christianity (and one of its major strengths) that it was inclusive in a way in which pagan culture always remained elitist; the most sensitive Christian thinkers were acutely aware of this advantage and paid a great deal of attention to its exploitation by the effective presentation of the faith at all intellectual and social levels, and by the widest possible means. But that is quite different from suggesting, as is often done, that the general adoption of Christianity implied the defeat of the intellect and the triumph of popular religion.[8] Any halfway adequate explanation of the phenomenon must do as much justice to the appeal of Christianity to the most highly educated, and to its most sophisticated theological formulations, as to any supposedly popular piety or superstition.

In these lectures I have therefore given theological discourse—writing about God—a central place in the context of explanations of the spread of Christianity. If it is significant (as I believe it is) that Christianity developed a systematic world-view, it must also be important to understand how its more technical aspects were formulated. Since the Christian faith and the Christian world-view were expressed in language, as well as through moral example and ritual action, the definitions and formulas of theology proper can hardly be marginal to their impact. Theological writings—the technical treatises of Christianity—will thus be given as much weight and attention here as other historical documents, for they represent stages in the formulation of Christian knowledge. In order then to understand the evolution of a Christian world-view, we must look not only to stories, as in the Gospels or the apocryphal *Acts* or, later, the

8. A.-M. Palmer, *Prudentius on the Martyrs* (Oxford: Clarendon Press, 1989), 32–56, rightly refuses to separate Christian and pagan taste, but then speaks of a "naiveté commune."

Lives of saints, or, for instance, to the moral and interpretative content of sermons, but also to the philosophical and rhetorical argument of theological treatises. The question then arises how this world-view was constituted—whether the discussion should be confined to mainstream or "orthodox" works. It is an important part of my argument that the very multiplicity of Christian discourse, what one might call its elasticity, while of course from the Church's point of view needing to be restrained and delimited, in fact constituted an enormous advantage in practical terms, especially in the early stages. No account of Christian development can work if it fails to take this sufficiently into account. I therefore draw equally on the apocryphal and "popular" stories, which, it can be argued, were of as much importance in formulating the Christian synthesis as the canonical texts.

Very little ground can be covered in six lectures, and I have limited myself mainly to the Greek tradition; there is much less than there should be, for instance, on the contribution of the Eastern churches and their literatures, even though there is a growing tendency among specialists to bring the Greek and the Eastern traditions together instead of emphasizing their differences.[9] A great deal more could be done, too, to explore the connection between Christian discourse and the language of contemporary philosophy, for although it may seem that there is already a vast literature on the subject, it has in most cases focused on content rather than on mode of expression. Whereas the idea of the interpenetration of Christian texts by Greek philosophical ideas and language is commonplace, what that re-

---

9. See II. J. W. Drijvers, *East of Antioch* (London: Variorum, 1984); and S. H. Griffith, "Ephraem, the Deacon of Edessa, and the Church of the Empire," in *Diakonia: Studies in Honor of Robert T. Meyer,* ed. T. Halton and J. P. Williman (Washington, D.C.: Catholic University of America Press, 1986), 22–52, esp. 52.

lation contributed to the development of a specifically Christian discourse is, I think, yet to be told. Probably the most serious lack, however, is the absence of a Jewish dimension, which in this compass I have not felt able to supply. A proper account of the rise of Christianity will from now on have to include a far better understanding of the actual pervasiveness of Judaism in the empire after the Diaspora than we have had to make do with up to now. Between the death of Jesus and the surviving records of his life and sayings lay the destruction of the Jewish Temple: "in the Gospels we meet, not the world of Jesus, but the very different, more tense, world of his disciples."[10] Already the infant faith had left the Palestinian *chora* behind for the cosmopolitan world where Diaspora Jews and Jewish sympathizers mingled with Greek and Roman pagans.[11] The interpenetration was such that even after several centuries some texts remain hard to classify. At risk of some distortion, then, I keep my focus on features that I have taken to be typically Christian ones.

Peter Brown's book *The Body and Society: Men, Women, and Sexual Renunciation in Early Christianity* (New York: Columbia University Press, 1988) came out at a late stage in the preparation of these lectures for publication. Whereas both in general terms and in view of the prominence of asceticism as a theme in Christian texts it inevitably covers some of the same ground, it does so from a different perspective altogether. Brown's emphasis is not on textuality; although he several times raises the question of the relation of the texts he uses to "real life," his own inquiry remains within their parameters.

Nevertheless, even while these lectures were being written and thought about, I have on many occasions found my views

10. P. Brown, *The Body and Society: Men, Women, and Sexual Renunciation in Early Christianity* (New York: Columbia University Press, 1988), 41.
11. On Jesus and Judaism, see E. P. Sanders, *Jesus and Judaism* (Philadelphia: Fortress Press, 1985); and cf. his *Paul, the Law, and the Jewish People* (Philadelphia: Fortress Press, 1983).

confirmed in general terms by work being done in other periods or by scholars in different disciplines. In particular, literary studies and a literary approach to the texts now seem to constitute a strong current in contemporary theological writing. Not histories of Christian literature in the traditional sense, but analyses—deconstructions, in fact—of the texts *qua* texts, and the consciousness of the social power of such discourses. But such approaches, familiar to New Testament scholars, have only rarely been extended toward other sorts of Christian literature. Some moves have been made in this direction by anthropologists, especially in the analysis of individual doctrines, but they have not on the whole been concerned with the specifics of discourse as such; in addition, they have more often been concerned with practice than with the actual formulation of belief. One would also have thought that there would have been a greater body of work directed toward early Christianity in the field of sociology of knowledge, where Mann's book is still unusual. His identification of ideology as a source of social power and his positioning of ideology not as secondary but as integral to the multiple, varied, and overlapping networks of power that constitute society[12] points unequivocally in the direction of regarding Christianity in the Roman Empire as an important source of power relations. I am concerned to show that this tendency did not simply follow the acquisition of economic or political power by the church, or its association with the state, but was present in the very roots of Christianity. Paul, who had never seen Jesus and whose writings are earlier than the first of the Gospels, established the precedent that Christianity was to

---

12. See Mann's own comment on the unevenness of the scholarly literature concerning the development of Christianity, which tends in his words to be either "inspirational" or "doctrinal," i e either committed or marginalized and technologized; see M. Mann, *Sources of Social Power: A History of Power from the Beginning to A.D. 1760,* vol. 1 (Cambridge: Cambridge University Press, 1986), 303; also chap. 1.

be a matter of articulation and interpretation. Its subsequent history was as much about words and their interpretation as it was about belief or practice.

The subject lends itself with peculiar appropriateness to a methodology based on hermeneutics, and I have learned much from this direction; it is an approach that also leads to the questioning of historical method and the nature of history, and to the problem of how truth can be known and expressed. Now that these are central issues for all kinds of historians,[13] we come back yet again to Christianity as a major arena of hermeneutics and a fit subject for our time.[14]

All kinds of questions cluster around the "rise of Christianity." J. B. Bury could still think of the conversion of Constantine as demonstrating the power of contingency in history: "it is hardly likely that unassisted by the stimulus which privileged position and power of persecuting gave to proselytising the Church would in less than 150 or 200 years have embraced such a majority of the population that it could have imposed upon the state its recognition as the exclusive religion."[15] This view is still held in the name of history, usually by rationalists like Bury himself, as is the complementary one, more overtly ideological and based on an idealized and nostalgic view of the Christianity of the Gospels, that Constantine's conversion in fact irrevocably corrupted the faith.[16] Such views obscure the fact that we have

13. See my collection *History as Text* (London: Duckworth, 1989).

14. These considerations are also often close to the hearts of feminist theologians who must rescue the text of Christianity if they are to save themselves; see in particular E. Schussler Fiorenza, *In Memory of Her: A Feminist Theological Reconstruction of Christian Origins* (New York: Crossroads, 1983).

15. See J. B. Bury, "Cleopatra's Nose," *RPA Annual for 1916*, 16–23; reprinted in *Selected Essays of J. B. Bury*, ed. H. Temperley (Cambridge: Cambridge University Press, 1930), 60–69. This famous essay was preceded in the previous year and followed in the next by others forecasting the eventual demise of Christianity in the light of human progress.

16. For this view, see, e.g., A. Kee, *Constantine Versus Christ: The Triumph of Ideology* (London: SCM Press, 1982).

in the spread of Christianity a problem of the first dimension in the social history of the empire, in the course of which Constantine marks a convenient but not an all-important landmark. Literacy, communication, the spread of ideas, the use of reading and writing, the organization of social groups, the establishment of restrictions on belief, the institutionalization of practice and belief together—these are only some of the other issues involved. The spread of Christianity follows the general history of the empire. As it came to prevail it provided plots according to which the majority of the inhabitants of the empire, and after that of Byzantium and the medieval West, lived out their lives. For any kind of cultural historian it is a subject of the first order.

Finally, a problem with the word "rhetoric," for I do not (obviously) use it in its technical sense, but rather in the current, far looser sense it seems to have acquired, by which it can mean something like "characteristic means or ways of expression"; these modes may be either oral or written, or indeed may pertain to the visual or to any other means of communication. It will be seen that the theme of visual art becomes increasingly central as these lectures progress, for I see the subject of Christian representation as involving both the visual and the verbal. More than that, I would argue that despite traditional (and controversial) Christian opposition to figural representation, a Christian figural art was the inevitable product of the ways of seeing embedded in Christian language. It follows that the Iconoclastic movement of the early Byzantine period has its roots in the problem of Christian representation witnessed from the very beginnings of Christianity and not merely in contemporary circumstances or recent theological disputes. The increased attention paid to religious images and the debates about their significance that become such a feature of Byzantine life from the sixth century onward constitute a crisis of representation whose roots lie in the very nature of Christian discourse. Even after the defeat of Iconoclasm, the Byzantines would retain a particularly acute consciousness of the relation between the Christian word and the Christian image.[17] A larger book than this could use more extensive illustration to bring out the interconnection between verbal and visual discourses; even so, those interested in Christian art will not fail to see the connection.

At present we are in danger of seeing rhetorics behind every tree. But it is still useful and important to ask how Christians, the quintessential outsiders as they appeared to men like Nero, Pliny, Tacitus, and Suetonius, talked and wrote themselves into a position where they spoke and wrote the rhetoric of empire. For it is perfectly certain that had they not been able to do this, Constantine or no Constantine, Christianity would never have become a world religion. This, simply, is the subject I had in mind in these lectures.

17. I have developed these ideas to some extent in a lecture given at the Collège de France in 1987 and hope to write on them again elsewhere, but they fall outside the scope of the present book.

CHAPTER ONE

How Many Rhetorics?

The Legacy of Separation

Christians in the Roman Empire placed a premium on words. Cicero, Quintilian, Fronto, Ausonius—all emphasize the need for the orator to nurture his voice as a musician cares for his instrument; it is his first qualification to be an orator. But in the formulation of Gregory of Nyssa, "the human voice was fashioned for one reason alone—to be the threshold through which the sentiments of the heart, inspired by the Holy Spirit, might be translated clearly into the Word itself."[1] That is, the trained voice of the orator was to be put at the service of the Word of God. Even when Christian writers and preachers questioned the very possibility of expressing their faith in words, as Gregory himself also did,[2] they were doing so in a context in which the language of Christian faith was seen as being of paramount importance. Augustine, writing on the relation of education and inspiration, and of human speech and the Word, was returning to a Pauline theme: "When we cannot choose words

1. *Comm. on Song of Songs* 7.933M, p. 235, ll. 3–5 (Langerbeck ed.), on Cant. 4.4; cited in an interesting article by A. Rousselle, "Parole et inspiration: le travail de la voix dans le monde romain," *History and Philosophy of the Life Sciences,* sec. 2, Pubblicazioni della Stazione zoologica di Napoli 5.2 (Naples, 1983), 129–57.
2. See R. Mortley, *From Word to Silence,* vol. 2: *The Way of Negation, Christian and Greek,* Theophaneia 31 (Bonn: Habelt, 1986), 171 ff.; see also below, chapter 5.

in order to pray properly, the Spirit himself expresses our plea in a way that could never be put into words, and God who knows everything in our hearts knows perfectly well what he means" (Rom. 26–27).

In choosing to consider Christian rhetoric in its broadest sense—as the modes of expression within which early Christianity was articulated and the power of that expression to persuade—I am conscious of reacting to late-twentieth-century concerns. Earlier lectures in this series too, including some of the most influential, reflect the contemporary intellectual situation. E. R. Dodds's title *The Greeks and the Irrational,* for instance, might not seem so appropriate today, when we are much less sure about what constitutes rationality and irrationality, but in its time it opened the eyes and answered to the needs of a whole generation.[3] To take only one other example, Moses Finley's *The Ancient Economy* provided both a distillation of his own thought over some years and a model within which subsequent ancient historians have had to work; the reevaluation of the economy of late antiquity that is now under way constantly finds itself working with Finley's framework.[4] The subjects chosen have had a tendency to emerge from the relation of lecturer, audience, and prevailing trends in contemporary scholarship. Insofar as the Sather Professor is first asked to deliver a series of lectures and then to write them down into the format of a book, subject, text, and reception stand in as close a

3. E. R. Dodds, *The Greeks and the Irrational* (Berkeley and Los Angeles: University of California Press, 1951). For the origins and development of Dodds's lifelong interest in what he called the "irrational," see his autobiography, *Missing Persons* (Oxford: Oxford University Press, 1977); on his experiences as a Sather Professor, see ibid., 180–84.

4. M. I. Finley, *The Ancient Economy* (Berkeley and Los Angeles: University of California Press, 1973; 2d ed., with supplementary notes, Harmondsworth, Eng.: Penguin Books, 1985). See the revisionism of P. Garnsey, K. Hopkins, and C. R. Whittaker, eds., *Trade in the Ancient Economy* (London: Chatto & Windus, 1983); and esp. A. Giardina, ed., *Società romana e impero tardoantico,* vol. 3: *Le Merci, gli insediamenti* (Rome: Laterza, 1986).

relation to one another as does the Christian rhetoric I shall be discussing to its own historical context in the Roman Empire.

There are several good reasons for returning to religion as a theme, and for placing the focus on the development of Christianity in the Roman Empire. After two centuries, Gibbon's conception of the Roman Empire as inexorably doomed to decline and fall[5] is still very much with us, though not many, perhaps, would go so far as to write the following: "A darkness of irrationality thickened over the declining centuries of the Roman empire, superstition blacked out the clearer lights of religion, wizards masqueraded as philosophers, and the fears of the masses took hold on those who passed for educated and enlightened."[6] Nevertheless, the powerful consciousness of enfolding gloom pervades so many unlikely books on apparently neutral subjects[7] that it can still plausibly be said to belong to the general consciousness. Of course, the horizons of Anglo-Saxon scholarship have expanded since Gibbon, with consequently increased need for fresh historical explanations: What *were* the most important factors in "the making of late antiquity" or "the trans-

5. On which see P. Gay, *The Enlightenment: An Interpretation,* vol. 1 (London: Weidenfeld & Nicolson, 1967), 112 ff., 207 ff.

6. R. MacMullen, "Constantine and the Miraculous," *GRBS* 9 (1968): 92.

7. See, e.g. (to take examples near home), G. Williams, *Change and Decline: Roman Literature in the Early Empire* (Berkeley and Los Angeles: University of California Press, 1978), 292 ff.; C. Habicht, *Pausanias's Guide to Ancient Greece* (Berkeley and Los Angeles: University of California Press, 1985), 118 ff.; C. Fornara, *The Nature of History in Ancient Greece and Rome* (Berkeley and Los Angeles: University of California Press, 1983), 190: "we observe the intellectual debasement of even the 'elite' of the empire. . . . The tastes of the reading public progressively turned soft, self-indulgent and superficial." E. R. Dodds's classic *Pagan and Christian in an Age of Anxiety* (Cambridge: Cambridge University Press, 1965) is written against a background of a presumed descent to irrationality (cf. 132–33: "paganism had lost faith both in science and in itself"). R. MacMullen's *Corruption and the Decline of Rome* (New Haven: Yale University Press, 1988) appeared as this book was being completed. On the broader notion, see R. Starn, "Meaning-Levels in the Theme of Historical Decline," *History and Theory* 14 (1975): 1–31.

Figure 1. The epitome of classical decline. Th. Couture, *Les Romains de la décadence* (detail). (Paris, Musée d'Orsay)

formation of the Roman world"?[8] How and when are we to draw the line between Rome (representing the classical world) and Byzantium (representing a Christian theocracy)?[9] But something on which nearly all interested scholars would probably agree is that the transition to Christianity must be placed somewhere near the heart of this change.

At the same time, we are witnessing an increasing tendency among historians to turn to anthropology as a methodological guide for understanding ancient society, which also brings with

8. P. Brown, *The Making of Late Antiquity* (Cambridge, Mass.: Harvard University Press, 1978); L. White, Jr., *The Transformation of the Roman World: Gibbon's Problem After Two Centuries* (Berkeley and Los Angeles: University of California Press, 1966); J. Herrin, *The Formation of Christendom* (Oxford: Basil Blackwell, 1987); Giardina, *Società romana e impero tardoantico.*

9. On this perennial theme, see A. Kazhdan and A. Cutler, "Continuity and Discontinuity in Byzantine History," *Byzantion* 52 (1982): 429–78.

it a new focus of interest on religion.[10] And if we are to study cultural history, then naturally we must turn to religion.[11] It is only surprising, in these circumstances, that despite the deluge of recent writing on early Christianity, there is still relatively little attempt to see it in this way.[12]

We are also in the midst of an intense interest in discourse, the expression of ideas. Christianity was not just ritual. It placed an extraordinary premium on verbal formulation; speech constituted one of its basic metaphors, and it framed itself around written texts. Quite soon this very emphasis on the verbal formulation of the faith led to a self-imposed restriction—an attempt, eventually on the whole successful, to impose an authority of discourse. And eventually—though only after much struggle and with many variations—this approved discourse came to be the dominant one in the state. The story of the development of Christian discourse constitutes part of political history.

This is all quite remarkable. It makes Christianity in the Roman Empire an obvious case for the application of the interest currently shown by many scholars in different fields in the phenomenon of shifts of thought, or changes in historical paradigms.[13] Did Christianity in the Roman Empire replace one major paradigm with another? If so, what part did Christian

10. See the introductory chapter to S. R. F. Price, *Rituals and Power: The Roman Imperial Cult in Asia Minor* (Cambridge: Cambridge University Press, 1984).

11. See in particular C. Geertz, "Religion as a Cultural System," in *Anthropological Approaches to the Study of Religion,* ed. M. Banton (New York: Praeger, 1966), 1–45; C. Geertz, *The Interpretation of Cultures* (London: Hutchinson, 1975); P. L. Berger and T. Luckmann, *The Social Construction of Reality* (Harmondsworth, Eng.: Penguin Books, 1967).

12. Though see Mann, *Sources of Social Power,* vol. 1.

13. In the first place, see T. S. Kuhn, *The Structure of Scientific Revolutions* (Chicago: University of Chicago Press, 1962; 2d, enlarged ed., 1970); for the relation of Michel Foucault's epistemes (*The Order of Things,* trans. A. Sheridan-Smith [New York: Random House, 1970]; *The Archaeology of*

rhetoric, the techniques of persuasion, play in the process? The questions have changed, and the answers will no longer be found in the old places, whether in the traditional formulation of Christianity's "relation to" or "conflict with" classical culture[14] or in the much-studied yet limited field of Christian-pagan polemic;[15] we shall need instead to look to the broader techniques of Christian discourse and its reception in the social conditions of the empire.

What we might call the "rhetoric" of early Christianity is not, then, rhetoric in the technical sense; rather, the word is used in its wider sense, denoting the manner and circumstances that promote persuasion. Early Christian rhetoric was not always, I shall argue, the specialized discourse its own practitioners often claimed it to be. Consequently, its reception was easier and wider ranging than modern historians allow, and its effects correspondingly more telling. The seemingly alternative rhetorics, the classical or pagan and the Christian, were more nearly one than their respective practitioners, interested in scoring off each other, would have us believe.

Building on the tendency to accept the Gibbonian view of inexorable decline, and with it to lay the blame on Christianity,

---

Knowledge, trans. A. Sheridan-Smith [New York: Harper & Row, 1972]) to Kuhn's paradigms, see H. L. Dreyfus and P. Rabinow, *Michel Foucault: Beyond Structuralism and Hermeneutics* (Chicago: University of Chicago Press, 1982), 44–78, esp. 58–59; see J. G. Merquior, *Foucault* (London: Fontana, 1985), 70, on "epistemic earthquakes."

14. See, e.g., H. Chadwick, *Early Christian Thought and the Classical Tradition* (Oxford: Oxford University Press, 1966); W. R. Schoedel and R. L. Wilken, eds., *Early Christian Literature and the Classical Intellectual Tradition: In Honorem R. Grant* (Berkeley and Los Angeles: University of California Press, 1979); A. Momigliano, ed., *The Conflict Between Paganism and Christianity in the Later Roman Empire* (Oxford: Basil Blackwell, 1963); M. L. W. Laistner, *Christianity and Pagan Culture in the Later Roman Empire* (Ithaca, N.Y.: Cornell University Press, 1951).

15. For a recent work, see R. L. Wilken, *The Christians as the Romans Saw Them* (New Haven: Yale University Press, 1984).

modern scholarship has too often worked within a set of simple binary oppositions: Christian versus pagan.[16] The effect of such a procedure is often paradoxically to reverse the Gibbonian view; if it does not stem from a Christian triumphalism it is very likely actually to lead to it. But if ever there was a case of the construction of reality through text,[17] such a case is provided by early Christianity. Out of the framework of Judaism, and living as they did in the Roman Empire and in the context of Greek philosophy, pagan practice, and contemporary social ideas, Christians built themselves a new world. They did so partly through practice—the evolution of a mode of living and a communal discipline that carefully distinguished them from their Jewish and pagan neighbors[18]—and partly through a discourse that was itself constantly brought under control and disciplined.[19]

The second century, in particular, was a battleground for the struggle of Christians to control their own discourse and define their faith. Indeed, the continuance of that struggle, which has characterized Christianity throughout its history, is demonstration enough of the crucial importance of text in historical growth and the acquisition of power. The history of Christianity could literally depend on one word, as happened at the first ecumenical council at Nicaea in A.D. 325.[20] While that and the later councils, both the remaining six officially styled and recognized

16. Accepted most recently in R. Lane Fox's stimulating book *Pagans and Christians in the Mediterranean World from the Second Century A.D. to the Conversion of Constantine* (Harmondsworth, Eng.: Viking Press, 1986).

17. Cf., e.g., D. Lowenthal, *The Past Is a Foreign Country* (Cambridge: Cambridge University Press, 1985); E. Hobsbawm and T. Ranger, eds., *The Invention of Tradition* (Cambridge: Cambridge University Press, 1983).

18. See esp. W. Meeks, *The First Urban Christians: The Social World of the Apostle Paul* (New Haven: Yale University Press, 1983).

19. For some aspects of this process see E. Pagels, *The Gnostic Gospels* (New York: Random House, 1979); and E. Pagels, *Adam, Eve, and the Serpent* (London: Weidenfeld & Nicolson, 1988).

20. The term *homoousios* (consubstantial), allegedly and tellingly introduced into the discussions by the Emperor Constantine himself.

as "ecumenical"[21] and the many others, either regional and partial in character or also claiming ecumenical status, arose to a large extent from the political needs of the post-Constantinian era,[22] they were also the outward and public manifestations of a process that had been going on within Christianity from the beginning.

The question I wish to address here concerns the relation of Christian discourse to its context in the Roman Empire. We cannot separate it entirely from consideration of the process of Christianization, of which the standard view is that Christian teaching and writing—the doctrinal and moral content of Christianity—made little if any impression on contemporary pagans, who knew little of it and cared less.[23] Other reasons must then be found to explain conversion to Christianity—the supposed decline of late Hellenistic paganism, social compensation, the fame of miracle cures, psychological need,[24] increased superstition,[25] self-interest (in particular after Constantine), or what have you. But to deny the importance of Christian ideas altogether seems paradoxical. Even the upper-class pagan critics of Christianity in the first and second centuries knew that it had content as well as a code of practice.[26] Somehow pagans and

21. Those in A.D. 381 (Constantinople), 431 (Ephesus), 451 (Chalcedon), 553 (Constantinople), 680–81 (Constantinople), and 787 (Nicaea).

22. See Herrin, *Formation of Christendom*, s.v. councils in index; on creeds as a necessary product of the need for unity under Constantine, see H. V. Campenhausen, "Das Bekenntnis Eusebs von Caesarea," *Zeitschrift für die Neutestamentliche Wissenschaft und die Kunde der alteren Kirche* 67 (1976): 123–39.

23. See R. MacMullen, *Christianizing the Roman Empire, A.D. 100–400* (New Haven: Yale University Press, 1984), 20–21, for a sharp statement.

24. Dodds, *Pagan and Christian*, 132 ff.

25. R. MacMullen, *Paganism in the Roman Empire* (New Haven: Yale University Press, 1981), 72: "It is rationalism, as we would call it, that now must defend itself; and it is easily put to rout by Constantine."

26. Tacitus *Ann.* 15.44; Suet. *Nero* 16.2 (superstition); Lucian *Peregr.* 11 (cult); Celsus, ap. Origen, *c. Cels.* 6.34. Galen treated Christianity as a philosophical system; see Wilken, *Christians as the Romans Saw Them*, 72 ff.

Jews heard about Christian teaching as well as Christian community behavior, even if that was not necessarily what first drew them to convert. It is these early years that are of course the most difficult to understand. In the fourth century, it is easy to chart the rapid emergence under imperial support of a complex and powerful Christian discourse in an increasingly secularized form suitable for the growing power of the church in society at large; the complement to this development was the technologizing of religious language.[27] But these developments, which are rightly seen as underscoring the importance of the decision of Constantine and his successors to support the church, could only have happened in the context of a long earlier evolution in the articulation of Christianity.

The next two chapters will focus on two features of Christian discourse in the period before Constantine, each of which helped it to develop in its own right and to plant its roots more firmly in the contemporary culture of the empire. The first is its essentially figural character, a feature well known and much discussed in the context of Christian literature and Christian exegesis, but much less so in terms of the relation of Christian and pagan discourse.[28] The second is the role of Christian myth as story, against the background of other literary developments in the early empire. Again, narrative, or story, is already attracting considerable attention among New Testament scholars and theologians; I shall argue that historians, too, may learn something from a wider consideration of other Christian narratives against their cultural background.[29] I shall not consider here the standard problems of the actual origins of Christianity or the traditional concerns of New Testament scholarship; rather, I wish to stress the continuity of development of the Christian text (in the broad sense) from the early period, especially from the end of

27. See chapters 4 and 5. 28. See chapter 3. 29. See chapter 3.

the first century A.D.,[30] to the time when there can plausibly be said to be a Christian empire, if not yet a wholly Christian one.[31] I do not regard this change as having been brought about by Constantine. The book will end, rather, with the end of classical antiquity in the late sixth or seventh century. There was nothing inevitable about the process of Christianization; nevertheless, my contention will be that Christian discourse per se was one factor that made such a process possible.

Newness or Decline

Sometimes contemporary fiction has something for the historian too: in Anthony Burgess's novel on Christian origins, *The Kingdom of the Wicked,* an old man (Dionysius, of course) comes up to Paul after his speech to the Areopagus in Athens and says, "Interesting. And it has the charm of the exotic. Are there books on the subject?" It is Paul's reply that is suggestive: "Not yet, alas. It is too new to have settled itself into books."[32] This is just the point. A few New Testament critics, taking "new" in its most literal sense, have made extravagant claims: "a new speech from the depths"; "the miraculous unedited newness of the word."[33] Yet this "new" Christianity was able to develop a "pedagogic action" for the reproduction of its own ideas, a means to ensure its place as a rival to and then inheritor of the old elite culture.[34] An answer to the question of how this

30. This period was chosen as a starting point for similar reasons by MacMullen, *Christianizing the Roman Empire;* and Lane Fox, *Pagans and Christians.*

31. See chapter 6.

32. Anthony Burgess, *The Kingdom of the Wicked* (New York: Arbor House, 1985), 218.

33. A. Wilder, *Early Christian Rhetoric: The Language of the Gospel* (London: SCM Press, 1964), 24–25.

34. For the concept, see P. Bourdieu and J.-C. Passéron, *Reproduction in Education, Society, and Culture,* trans. R. Nice (London: Sage, 1977), vi.

pedagogic action was achieved in rhetorical terms might well be found by looking along the same lines as those observed by anthropologists studying political rhetoric in other traditional societies. I shall argue, therefore, that Christian discourse too made its way in the wider world less by revolutionary novelty than by the procedure of working through the familiar, by appealing from the known to the unknown.[35] That was certainly the case in the fourth century, when the social and political conditions, at least in the cities, began to be genuinely supportive of Christian advancement in ways not open before. But how different was the situation in the early centuries? We have less direct evidence about the transmission of Christian ideas in the second and third centuries, and much of what we think we know depends on partial testimony. But it would be surprising if Christians really distanced themselves from pagans as much as they sometimes claimed.

If an emphasis on Christian discourse as an active agent has not up to now been common in discussions of Christianity in the Roman Empire, particularly those in English, it is partly because of the demarcation between academic constituencies. Ancient historians have customarily been wary of committed writing on early Christianity, of the "hidden agenda"; ironically, however, it has often been the practice to write in academic books about the period of the Christianization of the Roman Empire from an opposite but equally committed point of view. Whether viewed from the rationalist or the overtly Marxist perspective, the advance of Christianity is seen as bad in itself, and Christian rhetoric as a patent justification of that advance.[36] It is surprisingly hard to escape from the pervasive association of Christianity

35. See M. Bloch, ed., *Political Language and Oratory in Traditional Society* (London: Academic Press, 1975); and chapter 4 below.
36. With the well-known views of Gibbon on the subject, compare H. Lloyd-Jones, *The Justice of Zeus*, 2d ed. (Berkeley and Los Angeles: University of California Press, 1983), 184: the efforts of would-be pagan persecutors "had

with ideas of "decline," "authoritarianism," and "irrationality," which tend to be expressed in words such as "gloom" or "twilight."[37] From a deep-seated habit of privileging the classical, Christianity is relegated to the realm of the irrational, that which we do not ourselves care to accept.[38]

But Christianity in the Roman Empire is also often dismissed by being deemed to represent the ideological superstructure and therefore, though important, to be essentially secondary. It is by now respectable, if relatively new, for Marxist/socialist historians of other periods to allow a primary place to religion in the process of historical change;[39] however, this change of emphasis has yet to make its impact significantly felt in relation to the Roman Empire. Clearly, this book is not written from the materialist point of view. It is not concerned with the economic or

---

infinitely little success in comparison with what Christianity perpetrated while it had the power to enforce doctrines not yet liberalized out of recognition by dilution from alien sources and involving interferences with nature far more startling than any postulated by the Greek religion"; T. D. Barnes, *Constantine and Eusebius* (Cambridge, Mass.: Harvard University Press, 1981), 220, on Constantine's "morbid and unwholesome" legislation on sexual matters, said to have disregarded "the natural appetites of men and women in favour of an abstract ideal of purity, deduced from Christian tenets of asceticism"; G. E. M. de Ste. Croix, *The Class Struggle in the Ancient Greek World* (London: Duckworth, 1981), 439: "Why did early Christianity so signally fail to produce any important change for the better in Greco-Roman society?"

37. See note 6 above; cf. Fornara, *Nature of History*, 192, on the "degeneration" of history in the later (i.e., Christian) empire: "it is a saddening story, especially when taken in conjunction with the numerous other signs of social collapse, anarchy, despotic rule and the fading away of intellectual liberty"; E. Auerbach, *Mimesis: The Representation of Reality in Western Literature*, trans. W. R. Trask (Princeton: Princeton University Press, 1953), 53: "From the end of the imperial age something sultry and oppressive appears, a darkening of the atmosphere of life."

38. For an introduction to the problem, in philosophy and as perceived by anthropologists, see B. R. Wilson, ed., *Rationality* (New York: Harper & Row, 1970); and J. Overing, ed., *Reason and Morality*, Association of Social Anthropologists Monographs 24 (London: Tavistock, 1985).

39. See, e.g., the introduction to J. Obelkovitch, L. Roper, and R. Samuel, eds., *Disciplines of Faith: Studies in Religion, Politics, and Patriarchy* (London: Routledge & Kegan Paul, 1987).

institutional structure of the church as such, and does not consider Christianization in relation to the development of an institution or set of institutions. It is not, therefore, either a study of the economic and political dimension of Christian faith or of its "structural role" in Roman imperial society,[40] though naturally these aspects are interconnected. Rather, it looks at a particular element in the establishment of Christian belief, and at the relation between Christian modes of expression and those prevailing in the general cultural context. There is much more to the advance of a faith like Christianity than its social and institutional structures may reveal, just as there is more to the understanding of the rise of celibacy as a Christian practice than can be seen from the development of organized monasticism.[41] However much can be learned about Christianization from a study of its social and economic practices and of the implications of its growth on contemporary social organization, we must account for the fact that it did in fact establish itself in the hearts and minds of people.[42]

Antony's exchange with his pagan critics goes to the heart of the matter:

"Since of course you pin your faith on demonstrative proofs and this is an art in which you are masters, and you want us also not to worship God without demonstrative arguments, do you first tell me this. How does precise knowledge of

40. For the latter approach, see Herrin, *Formation of Christendom*, 7. Herrin does make Christianity the major agent in the change from the ancient to the medieval world (see esp. 143, following closely the views of Gibbon and A. H. M. Jones: "as Gibbon revealed [*sic*], the faith could be identified as a fundamental cause of the decline of the Roman Empire"), but evades the question of how or why that faith became established before Constantine.

41. Ibid., 8, 64–65.

42. See P. Ariès and G. Duby, eds., *A History of Private Life*, vol. 1; *From Pagan Rome to Byzantium*, ed. P. Veyne, trans. A. Goldhammer (Cambridge, Mass.: Harvard University Press, 1987), 5–234 ("The Roman Empire," P. Veyne), 235–312 ("Late Antiquity," P. Brown); also P. Veyne, "La famille et l'amour sous le haut empire romain," *Annales E.S.C.* 33 (1978): 35–63.

things come about, especially knowledge about God? Is it by verbal proof, or by an act of faith? And which comes first, an active faith or verbal proof?" When they replied that the act of faith takes precedence and that this constitutes accurate knowledge, Antony said, "Well said! Faith arises from the disposition of the soul, while dialectic comes from the skill of those who devise it. Accordingly, those who are equipped with an active faith have no need of verbal argument, and probably find it even superfluous. For what we apprehend by faith, that you attempt to construct by arguments; and often you cannot even express what we perceive. The conclusion is that an active faith is better and stronger than your sophistic arguments."[43]

There is of course an element of disingenuousness in this familiar argument, for rhetoric—the strategies of discourse—was itself one of the many technologies by which early Christianity implanted "habits of the heart" more powerful than institutions and more lasting than social welfare.[44]

Subjectivity lurks in every part of our topic. While historians are readily criticized if they show sympathy for Christianity, New Testament scholars will not only admit but actually demand personal engagement with the subject, or even voice actual suspicion of "the historical method."[45] But perhaps now, when one effect of the present awareness of the importance of

43. *V. Ant.* 77 (trans. Meyer).
44. The term is taken from R. Bellah et al., *Habits of the Heart* (Berkeley and Los Angeles: University of California Press, 1985).
45. Cf. C. Murray, "History and Faith," in Cameron, ed., *History as Text,* 165–80; G. N. Stanton, "Interpreting the New Testament Today," Inaugural Lecture, King's College London, 1978, 7 ff.; J. M. Robinson and H. Koester, *Trajectories Through Early Christianity* (Philadelphia: Fortress Press, 1971), 269: "We have tried to avoid the pitfalls of 'disinterested research,' for we have sensed the danger of merely playing in the sandbox of irrelevant scholarship." On the problem of interpretation generally, see P. Ricoeur, *History and Truth,* trans. Charles A. Kelbley (Evanston, Ill.: Northwestern University Press, 1965); P. Ricoeur, *The Conflict of Interpretations: Essays in Hermeneutics,* ed. Don Hide (Evanston, Ill.: Northwestern University Press, 1974).

texts is to break down the barriers between different kinds of academic writing,[46] we have more chance than previously to avoid either extreme.

Christianity and Communication

But if the subject of Christianity still invites an undertext, so does that of rhetoric. "Mere rhetoric"—the phrase speaks for itself.[47] Admittedly, the new fashion for rhetoric should have reversed the situation, but in the context of Roman imperial literature rhetoric has yet to find a sympathetic modern champion. And rhetoric and Christianity together are apt to evoke a pained recoil.[48]

What can such a collocation teach us? It is worth quoting Ernest Gellner's dictum on traditional, that is agrarian, societies: "To try to impose on all levels of society a universalized clerisy and a homogenized culture with centrally imposed norms, fortified by writing, would be an idle dream. Even if such a programme is contained in some theological doctrines, it cannot be, and is not, implemented. It simply cannot be done."[49] Perhaps not, yet it happened in the Roman empire. Emphasize as we may the plurality of early Christianity (the very word imposes a

46. For examples of "historical" books written by professional English scholars (and combining fictional and documentary material), see E. Said's *Orientalism* (London: Routledge & Kegan Paul, 1978) and E. Showalter's *The Female Malady: Women, Madness, and English Culture, 1830–1980* (New York: Pantheon Books, 1985).

47. Applied to Greek and Roman historians by Fornara, *Nature of History*, 200.

48. Jasper Griffin cites the story of the Harvard aesthete Charles Eliot Norton who on reaching heaven was struck with utter dismay and exclaimed, "Oh, so overdone! So Renaissance!" (*Oxford Book of Snobs* [Oxford: Oxford University Press, 1982], 86). On hostility to rhetoric (in the narrow sense), see G. Williams, *Change and Decline*, 266–67, 306–7, and passim. The social history of rhetoric in the Roman Empire has yet to be written.

49. E. Gellner, *Nations and Nationalism* (Oxford: Basil Blackwell, 1983), 17 (from a chapter entitled "Culture in Agrarian Society").

false sense of unity) and the resistance of pagan attitudes,[50] the very imposition which Gellner declares to be impossible did eventually take place, and that is what must be explained, in cultural as well as structural and economic terms.

We should not minimize the extent of the change that did in fact take place in this traditional society. To get an idea of its scale, it is useful to refer to Gellner's list of the hallmarks of cultural reproduction—control of communication—in a traditional society, and to apply them to the example of the early, or "high," empire. The Roman Empire of the first two centuries A.D. was indeed characterized by all of the following: a strong horizontal demarcation line between the educated elite and the rest of society; an elite maintained and controlled by elaborate regulating mechanisms; control of military and civil power by the same group; and finally, a mass population cut off and mostly illiterate, with the gap reinforced by the high level of traditional literary culture practiced by the elite. By the fourth century A.D., however, the situation has significantly changed: the civil and the military are now separated; an increase in the number of government posts has opened up the elite and confused the old demarcation lines; the traditional culture is challenged by an alternative, Christian one; and an alternative, institutionalized elite has come into being in the persons of Christian bishops. It can be seen that in such a context Christian ideas and Christian discourse have been able to penetrate various levels of society and to generate a universalizing impetus. In Gellner's view, there is only one way for a traditional society like that of the early empire to open itself to such a penetration, and that is through economic transformation. Yet what most needs to be explained in our context is not how Christianity could advance after the economic and political changes of the third and early fourth centuries and the advent of imperial support, but why it was

50. Herrin, *Formation of Christendom*, 54–55.

that when those changes took place it was already in a situation from which such advance was possible—in other words, in what ways cultural control had already been broken down in the early empire.

Some recent works have addressed this question by suggesting that the values and life-style of the elite were themselves already in a state of change by the second century A.D., if not indeed before that,[51] and by connecting that change with the establishment of a new political order. Christian ideas and practices are seen as corresponding in many ways with those of the rest of society, rather than being in conflict with them. Such a model has obvious advantages for explaining some of the ways in which Christianity continued to take root even when from time to time its adherents were punished by the state. But I am concerned here with just one aspect of this relationship: that of discourse, the way Christians articulated their faith. This too, while multiple in origin, had a powerful impulse toward totalization (all the more apparent as it continued to wrestle with its own refractory material)[52] and was far from being simply the product and justification of increasing autocracy.[53] Christian discourse, as an active force in Christianization, was integral to Christianity.

Like the good Jewish teacher he was, Jesus taught in words, especially in parable.[54] Within the first decades after his death came that sophisticated instrument, Pauline rhetoric,[55] and only after it came the Gospels—rewritings, or recreations, of the text

51. See esp. Veyne, "La famille et l'amour"; P. Brown, *Making of Late Antiquity;* Foucault, *Le souci de soi;* and below, chapter 2.

52. See chapter 5.

53. Though for this aspect see de Ste. Croix, *Class Struggle,* 394 ff.; and chapter 4 below.

54. On the Jewish background of the teaching of Jesus, see G. Vermes, *Jesus the Jew* (London: Fontana, 1976; 2d ed., 1983); and G. Vermes, *Jesus and the World of Judaism* (London: SCM Press, 1983).

55. See W. Wuellner, "Greek Rhetoric and Pauline Argumentation," in Schoedel and Wilken, eds., *Early Christian Literature,* 177–88.

of the life of Jesus.[56] At no point that we can now recapture was there a "first Christianity" distinct from its verbal expression. Nor, despite the gentile mission, was there clearly or uniformly for many years to come a Christianity easily separable from Judaism. That distinction often remained hard to draw, and the boundary was more fluid than we like to imagine. But the articulation of faith was of paramount importance. Early Christianity was not purely a matter of ritual or ethical behavior, or of miracle cures done by a wonder-worker and his successors;[57] it was always a matter of teaching, of interpretation, and of definition. As Christ "was" the Word, so Christianity *was* its discourse or discourses. It is the relation of those discourses to their wider cultural context in the Roman Empire that needs to be explored again.

A favored tactic has been to see Christian writing as a matter of "popular culture," and to regard the long-term story as one of an eventual defeat of elite pagan culture by an alternative that was in its origins essentially lower-class. This type of explanation comes in two versions—in one it fits the model of increased superstition and decreased "rationality" to which I have already referred, while in the other, based on a more favorable, indeed a triumphalist, attitude toward Christian literature,[58] it belongs within an overall conception of Christianity as new, distinctive, and somehow more vital than the "sterile" pagan culture it is seen as having supplanted.

56. See, e.g., R. M. Grant, *The Earliest Lives of Jesus* (London: SPCK, 1961); G. N. Stanton, *Jesus of Nazareth in New Testament Preaching* (Cambridge: Cambridge University Press, 1974); E. L. Schuler, *A Genre for the Gospels: The Biographical Character of Matthew* (Philadelphia: Fortress Press, 1983).

57. There is a large literature on the relation of the figure of Jesus to pagan wonder-workers or "divine men"; see D. Georgi, "The Records of Jesus in the Light of Ancient Accounts of Revered Men," *Society of Biblical Literature, Proceedings of the 108th Annual Meeting* (Philadelphia, 1972), 2:527–42.

58. See, e.g., M. Dibelius, *A Fresh Approach to the New Testament and Early Christian Literature* (New York: Scribner's, 1936).

Both these versions find their attraction in the fact that they seem to be supported by contemporary texts, both pagan and Christian. It was not just that pagan critics jeered at the low social background of early converts; the most sophisticated Christian writers of the late fourth century could still profess to feel embarrassed before their pagan contemporaries: "the language of fishermen" (*sermo piscatorius*) was not on the face of it suitable for educated men.[59] On the other hand, the universal appeal of Christianity could be turned to useful effect: "It is possible for the person who lives according to our teaching to philosophize even without learning, whether barbarian or Greek, or slave; whether an old man, a child or a woman."[60]

There was much mileage for Christians in the claim (following St. Paul's precedent) that they possessed the "true philosophy," in contrast to the wisdom of the world.[61] But in this claim there also lay a deep ambiguity, seen nowhere more clearly than in the writings of Paul himself. "And I, brethren," he claims, "when I came to you, came not with excellency of speech or wisdom, declaring unto you the testimony of God."[62] The sayings are familiar: "Hath not God made foolish the wisdom of this world.?"[63] But the same Paul himself deploys supreme rhetorical and intellectual skill.[64] The hermit Antony, in whose *Life* so much is made of the rejection of the world, resorted to verbal

59. On this see E. Auerbach, *Literary Language and Its Public in Late Antiquity and in the Middle Ages,* trans. R. Manheim (New York: Pantheon Books, 1965), 22 ff. Origen's answer to pagan criticism of the "plain style" of the Scriptures may be found in *c. Cels.* 6.2.

60. Clement *Misc.* 4.6.58.3, alluding to Rom. 3:28.

61. Cf. I Cor. 1:17–2:16; 3.18–20, in particular 3.19: "The wisdom of this world is foolishness with God."

62. I Cor. 2:1.

63. I Cor. 1:20.

64. See, e.g., E. A. Judge, "Paul's Boasting in Relation to Contemporary Professional Practice," *Australian Biblical Review* 16 (1968): 37–50; and C. Forbes, "Comparison, Self-Praise, and Irony: Paul's Boasting and the Conventions of Hellenistic Rhetoric," *New Testament Studies* 32 (1986): 1–30.

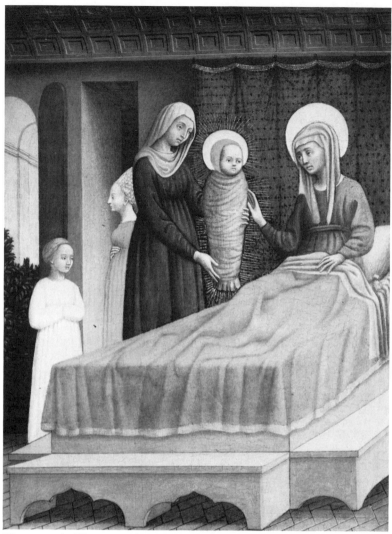

Figure 2. A. Vivarini, *The Birth of St. Augustine*. Venice, fifteenth century. (Courtauld Institute Galleries, London)

argument as well as personal example. Augustine, more conscious even than Paul of the essential ambiguities and contradictions in the very concept of Christian rhetoric,[65] similarly deploys
every technique of the art of eloquence, even while concluding
that the conditions for truth must lie elsewhere.[66] The art of
rhetoric is essential, as Augustine explains, even though it will
not in itself suffice.[67] He was well aware of the contradictions
implicit in the manner of the Pauline Epistles, and goes on to
discuss the very point, analyzing II Cor. 11:16–30 as a speci-
men of true rhetorical skill and as a defense of Christian eloquence against pagan criticism. When Paul says, "Though I be
rude in speech, yet not in knowledge," Augustine admits that
"he seems to be speaking as if granting so much to his detractors," but recognizes the point that Paul is trying to make: for
even his detractors admitted that in fact his letters were "weighty
and powerful."[68] At the same time, there was no one more conscious than Augustine of the need to reach all sections of the
populace or of the appropriate methods by which this could be
done. The concern for audience is amazingly modern: at times
the preacher would feel total dissatisfaction with his own performance, but he should not despair, Augustine says, for the actual effect might be quite different.[69] In the presence of such sophistication and such a high degree of self-consciousness, it is
perhaps wiser not to rely too much on the apparently artless
statements of Christians looking to turn an apparent weakness
into an advantage.[70]

    65. Cf. the opening chapters of *De doctr. christ.* 4, concerned with the at-
tempt to define Christian eloquence and putting secular rhetoric in a secondary
place; they could only have been written by a supreme practitioner of the art.
    66. See below, chapter 5.
    67. *De doctr. christ.* 4.2.3.
    68. Ibid., 7.15; cf. II Cor. 11:6, 10:10.
    69. *De rud. catech.* 2.3.
    70. Cf. Athenagoras *Ep. to Diognetus* 15–16: "Among us you may find
uneducated persons, workmen, and old women, who if by word are unable to

But whereas both sides knew that the capacity of Christian discourse to address itself to all sections of the public was a hall-mark and could be a strength, it is all too easy to overlook the difficulties involved in assigning early Christianity to the realm of popular culture. While for later periods—early modern Europe, say—the vast increase in documentation allows historians to write meaningfully about levels of culture,[71] this is hardly the case for the Roman Empire, where the cultural mix of the provincial towns in which both Christian apocryphal writings and various forms of ancient fiction developed is still barely charted.[72] "Popular culture," a problematic concept at the best of times, cannot be a genuinely helpful one unless much more evidence is available. It must even be doubted whether anything can now safely be labeled "popular culture" in our period; it is certain that many discussions of religion have been seriously distorted by the unthinking application of modernizing assumptions from our own culture.[73]

There are a number of other reasons against accepting the view of early Christianity as a "popular" movement. It is no longer generally argued, for instance, that the majority of early

---

present the benefit which comes from our doctrines, by deed demonstrate the benefit which comes through persuasion."

71. Though the concept is not without its problems: see, e.g., P. Burke, "What Is the History of Popular Culture?" *History Today* (December 1983): 40: "Both 'popular' and 'culture' are problematic terms. Firstly, who are 'the people'? Are they the poor? the powerless? the uneducated? These are negative terms again. And in any case, since all children are brought up by adults, what does 'uneducated' mean? Do different subordinate groups—male and female, young and old, urban and rural—share the same culture and in every society? Secondly, what is culture?" Burke goes on: "It is also hard to say what is not 'popular,' for popular culture is not exclusive like high culture. It is open to all. . . . Can we even exclude the social and political elite?"

72. See chapter 5.

73. For a warning against the common assumption that "religious" developments considered by moderns to be "irrational" must stem from popular culture, see A. Momigliano, "Popular Religious Beliefs and the Late Roman Historians," *SCH* 8 (1971): 1–18.

converts came from the lower classes.[74] Closer analysis of the available material shows that even from the earliest stages, as can be seen from the Acts of the Apostles, converts included—indeed, depended on—people of substance who proceeded to lend their patronage to the missionaries and to fellow converts. Scholars are working hard to try to define early Christian groups more closely—not only their own social stratification, but also the degree of their interrelation with or separation from Jewish communities and the diffusion of their ideas in gentile circles.[75] Whether it can plausibly be argued, in view of the comparatively late date of the Gospels and the enormous problems surrounding their interpretation, that early Christianity moved during the first century from an original social radicalism to a more respectable movement advocating the acceptance of existing social norms (Theissen's "love patriarchalism") is a difficult question to which the answers given will probably reflect the prior positions of their proponents.[76] But even if it can be so argued, it is clear even in the very imperfect state of our knowledge that from immediately after the death of Jesus, if not in his own lifetime, Christian groups included people from a wide social spectrum. The myth of early Christianity as the resort of the poor and underprivileged is precisely that, and a very convenient one it has been.

It is a myth that rests, moreover, on the fallacy of an original

74. For discussion and bibliography, see Meeks, *First Urban Christians*, 51 ff., following in particular E. A. Judge, A. Malherbe, and G. Theissen.

75. See, e.g., besides Meeks (ibid.), many articles by G. Theissen, esp. in the convenient collection *The Social Setting of Pauline Christianity*, ed. J. H. Schutz (Philadelphia: Fortress Press, 1982); and J. Gager, *Kingdom and Community: The Social World of Early Christianity* (Englewood Cliffs, N.J.: Prentice-Hall, 1975).

76. For the natural desire of, for instance, liberation and feminist theologians to read the texts in this way, see C. Murray, "History and Faith"; and for some characteristically penetrating observations, see G. E. M. de Ste. Croix, "Early Christian Attitudes to Property and Slavery," *SCH* 12 (1975): 1–38.

Christianity uncontaminated by external influences; but its hold-
ers then have to explain how this "new" faith could make the
leap to center stage. Thus, we have been told, "the naiveté of the
early Christian speech came in the course of time to wed itself to
the cultures of the world."[77] But while much of current New
Testament scholarship is directed at the internal (that is, theological) articulation of the texts,[78] there is also a perceptible
trend toward a mode of interpretation that balances the external
and internal factors operative in the literary texts. It is thus less
a question of the degree of "influence" of Greco-Roman or Jewish literary or philosophical elements on early Christian writing
than of their integral relationship. The culture of the Roman
Empire—Jewish, Greek, Roman—should not be read as the
"background" to the New Testament, as it still is in so many
textbooks; rather, the Christian writings are themselves from
the very start "rooted in the attempt to attract and convince persons of the Hellenistic world, be they already Christians, Jews or
pagans."[79] It seems obvious, indeed, not only that the early writings of the New Testament are permeated by literary elements
that they have in common with other sorts of writing, but also
that they are subtle and complex productions in their own right
—considerations that together rule out the notion of the first
Christian writings as naive spontaneous outpourings and make

77. Wilder, *Early Christian Rhetoric*, 125.

78. Brief accounts of the history of New Testament criticism abound; see,
e.g., C. Murray, "History and Faith"; Stanton, *Jesus of Nazareth*; Vermes,
Jesus the Jew.

79. E. Schussler Fiorenza, "Miracles, Mission, and Apologetics: An Introduction," in *Aspects of Religious Propaganda in Judaism and Early Christianity*, ed. E. Schussler Fiorenza (Notre Dame, Ind.: Notre Dame University
Press, 1976), 1–25, at 2. (The use of the term "Hellenistic" rather than "Roman" to designate the contemporary context for early Christianity is largely a
matter of convention, much dependent on whether the writer is a theologian
or an ancient historian by training.) A similar conviction about the insepa-
rability of Christian from other (usually styled "Greco-Roman") writings lies
behind such recent works as C. W. Votaw, *The Gospels and Contemporary
Biographies in the Greco-Roman World* (Philadelphia: Fortress Press, 1970).

it impossible to be satisfied with categorizing them as "popular literature."[80] This is not quite the same as saying, with Fiorenza and others, that the apologetic aim needs always to be emphasized, even though that is part of my point.[81] Rather, the argument is twofold: first, on closer inspection, Christian literature is not simple at all, however much it suited some Christians to claim that it was; and second, it is in principle almost always wrong to look for an original and unique "Christian" expression, since (especially in view of the emphasis placed on proselytizing and conversion) Christian groups were open and Christian discourse was a product of its multiple and complex environment like any other.[82] Both these features together made the later "leap" possible.

I propose to start at the other end by looking at some features that, whatever their source, do seem characteristic of Christian discourse, and to explore them in relation to their context in the development of the empire. As long as it was possible to marginalize Christian discourse, it was easy to maintain that it played little part in conversion and that practical, or indeed even disreputable, motives were more important. But that view fails to answer the question of how people heard about Christianity in

80. For an example of a far more sophisticated approach, see F. Kermode, *The Genesis of Secrecy: On the Interpretation of Narrative*, The Charles Eliot Norton Lectures, 1977–78 (Cambridge, Mass.: Harvard University Press, 1979), with N. Perrin, *What Is Redaction Criticism?* (Philadelphia: Fortress Press, 1967), 7 ff., discussing W. Wrede, *Das Messiasgeheimnis in der Evangelium* (Göttingen, 1901). For "rhetorical criticism," see P. Trible, *God and the Rhetoric of Sexuality* (Philadelphia: Fortress Press, 1978); the "simplicity" of II Cor. 1:12 (cf. also, e.g., Origen *c. Cels.* 6.2) would repay deconstruction. Particular themes in this kind of approach have so far been those of parable (e.g., S. McFague, *Speaking in Parables: A Study of Metaphor and Theology* [Philadelphia: Fortress Press, 1975]; and chapter 5 below) and story or narrative (see chapter 3).

81. And perhaps does need restating, in view of the common position that Christian writing reached only an audience of insiders.

82. Lucian scoffs at the Christian openness to strangers, a theme indeed stressed in Christian propaganda: *Peregr.* 13; cf. Clement *Paid.* 9.87.

the first place, or to take account of the process of conversion itself, in which preaching and teaching must have had some role;[83] the evidence from Egypt shows Christians there as having been unusually literate and interested in books at a time when literacy generally was extremely restricted, with little or no impetus to extend it.[84] Naturally Christian writers themselves, in particular those writing during or after the persecutions, would present an at times highly colored view of their communities as a beleaguered minority ever in danger of being thrown to the lions, or contrast the care taken by Christian catechists in admitting students for instruction with the public discourse of philosophers, open to all indiscriminately.[85] There was good debating material here, just as in Clement's presentation of the Christian message as a "new song," the Word of God which brings to life those as good as dead.[86] But none of it obscures the fact well known to Clement himself that nothing is truly new and that the best means of persuasion is through that which is already known. In their moral and social teaching Christians came very near to pagans: Clement presupposes Christian support and ac-

83. How the faith should be taught was a matter of discussion and dispute: Clement *Misc.* 1.1.4 suggests that some thought that only oral presentation was appropriate. Once some knowledge existed, however, study was recommended; see Tert. *Contra Haer.* 12.

84. On Egypt, see C. H. Roberts, *Manuscript, Society, and Belief in Early Christian Egypt* (London: Oxford University Press for the British Academy, 1979); and C. H. Roberts and T. C. Skeat, *The Birth of the Codex* (London: Oxford University Press for the British Academy, 1983); see 67 ff. for a cautious discussion of the assumption that Christian use of the codex is to be associated with the lower-class origins of Christian communities. On literacy generally, see W. V. Harris, "Literacy and Epigraphy, I," *Zeitschrift für Papyrologie und Epigraphik* 52 (1983): 87–111 (not considering the Christian evidence); and W. V. Harris, *Ancient Literacy* (Cambridge, Mass.: Harvard University Press, 1989), esp. 319–22; but it is not just "apologists for Christianity" who see Christianity as bringing a different attitude toward written texts (see his own remarks at 220); the point lies in motivation and use.

85. Origen *c. Cels.* 3.51 (SC 136.120).

86. *Protrept.* 1.22–23, on which see R. D. Sider, *The Gospel and Its Proclamation* (Wilmington, Del.: Edwin Mellen Press, 1983), 80–81 (a useful collection).

ceptance of the prevailing political order when he likens the
Christian's feelings toward God to those of the citizen toward a
good ruler,[87] and Christians and pagans alike preached domestic
virtue and sexual continence.[88] It is just this area of ambiguity or
overlap that allows persuasion.[89]

It will be necessary to draw on a range of material far wider
than what eventually became the New Testament canon, if we
are to do justice to the spread of discourse and if we do not wish
to give a false impression of unity. In terms of the present argument, the fluidity and variety of what for convenience we can
call the new faith in the first two centuries was a strength, not a
weakness. If that situation was to change, it was with changed
conditions of reception and because their increasingly institutionalized church required an altogether more disciplined voice.
Thus in the next chapter I shall argue that certain elements in
the body of discourse loosely called Christian in the first two
centuries were in fact extremely well suited to the cultural conditions of the early empire, and that even if the nature of the
existing sources makes the reception of Christian ideas hard to
trace, these general considerations can nevertheless help us to
understand it. In chapter 3 I shall consider one element in Christian discourse—story—that establishes itself strongly in the conditions of the second and third centuries. In chapters 4 to 6 I
shall discuss a different situation: the implications for Christian
speaking and writing when Christianity came out into the open
in the fourth century and later—what were the gains and what

87. *Paid.* 9.87.
88. Cf. Plutarch *Conjug. Praec.*, on which see K. O'B. Wicker, "First Century Marriage Ethics: A Comparative Study of the Household Codes and Plutarch's Conjugal Precepts," in *No Famine in the Land,* ed. J. W. Flanagan and
A. W. Robinson (Claremont, Calif.: Scholars Press for the Institute of Antiquity and Christianity, 1975), 141–53. See also, generally, Averil Cameron,
"Early Christian Territory After Foucault," *JRS* 76 (1986): 266–71; but cf.
B. Witherington III, *Women in the Earliest Churches* (Cambridge: Cambridge
University Press, 1988), esp. 42 ff.
89. See esp. chapter 4.

the cost of access to political authority, and how did the ways in which Christians responded to the challenge of the classical past and of their own new position help them to acquire public power?

We may conclude by returning to a theme raised already, that of rationality and irrationality, polar opposites that feature constantly both in Christian discourse itself and in modern discussions of early Christianity. As will be obvious by now, I wish to reexamine the view of Christianity as essentially "irrational"; what has seemed its "irrationality" (and attracted condemnation from nonbelievers and empiricist historians alike) is in fact a feature inherent in religious language. It can moreover be argued that the successful formation of a religious discourse was one of early Christianity's greatest strengths.[90] This is precisely what both Paul and Augustine recognized. And as for the "irrationality" and "superstition" of late antiquity, we had better be a little careful about importing the ethnocentric assumption that we ourselves inhabit a world of reason. It is possible in fact to see the development of Christian discourse, and especially theological discourse, as the continuation of an impulse toward systematization of knowledge that can be seen already in the late Republic.[91] The fact that nowadays philosophers and historians alike are less certain than they once were about the objects of knowledge brings this advantage: the way is open to discard the old hierarchies of "rational" knowledge and irrationality. Instead of being forever relegated to the latter category (and for-

90. See chapter 5.
91. See E. Rawson, *Intellectual Developments in the Late Roman Republic* (London: Duckworth, 1984); A. Momigliano, "The Theological Efforts of the Roman Upper Classes in the First Century B.C.," *Classical Philology* 79 (1984): 199–211; A. Wallace-Hadrill, "Greek Knowledge, Roman Power," *Classical Philology* 83 (1988): 224–33. For theology as a science, see Proclus *On Plato's Parmenides* 5.1015.33–1016.3 Cousin, on which see H. D. Saffrey, "From Iamblichus to Proclus and Damascius," in *Classical Mediterranean Spirituality*, ed. A. H. Armstrong (London: Routledge & Kegan Paul, 1986), 250–52.

ever marginalized), Christian theological discourse can be seen as a developing system of knowledge in its own right. The process by which this happened can then be taken seriously and given its proper place in the process of Christianization and in the social and cultural changes in the empire.

As Augustine put it, Christian and pagan rhetoricians differed profoundly: the latter put their art to the defense of both the true and the false, the former only of the true.[92] It is well known that Christian writing differed from classical in that it was referential, or figural: it signified.[93] Numerous levels of representation can be identified in Christian discourse, including the "showing" that lies behind the title of my next chapter: the reference might be to a previous text, and so the question of *which* texts were to be regarded as sacred became burningly immediate; it might be to their meaning, and so the problem of interpretation is at the heart of Christian discourse; it might be to Jesus as the archetype, and so *Lives* and how to live them become a central issue. But it is not so often asked how this type of figural discourse took hold. I shall argue that the intellectual context of the early empire in fact made this symbolic or signifying mode of expression surprisingly appropriate; however limited the first audiences for Christian discourse in practical terms, it answered to the political and cultural circumstances of the new social order.

A previous series of Sather lectures also argued for the intimate connection of literature with the social and political back-

92. *De doctr. christ.* 4.2.3.
93. It accomplished this not just through allegory (on which see, e.g, R. M. Grant, *The Letter and the Spirit* [London: SPCK, 1957]; R. P. C. Hanson, *Allegory and Event* [London: SCM Press, 1959]; J. Pépin, *Mythe et allégorie* [Paris: Editions Montaigne, 1958]; R. Palmer, "Allegorical, Philological, and Philosophical Hermeneutics: Three Modes in a Complex Heritage," in *Contemporary Literary Hermeneutics and Interpretation of Classical Texts,* ed. S. Kresic [Ottawa: Ottawa University Press, 1981], 15–38), but in the assumptions it made about the relation of language to reality as well.

ground of the early Roman empire,[94] but there the literature in question was the Latin literature of the high Roman elite, and the book employs a rhetoric of decline even sharper than that of modern historians of late antiquity. By a familiar turn, moreover, it takes the attention paid to technical rhetoric in the first and second centuries, represented for us by the writings of the elder Seneca, Pliny, Tacitus's *Dialogus,* and then by the writers of the Second Sophistic, as a badge of that decline. This rhetoric—the product, it is claimed, of authoritarianism in the political order—thus served as fuel for a modern authoritarian rhetoric of condemnation.

God was not dead in the Roman Empire. Religion became, and continued to be, a main focus for discourse, and the more so as traditional political discourse closed off. Thus, if Christianity was faced with the need to create new historical horizons,[95] it was presented with this challenge at exactly the time when the nature of culture and the place of discourse in the new political order themselves had to be decided.

The second and third centuries are probably the most difficult period to interpret from the viewpoint of accounting for the spread of Christianity. Before the end of the first century, Christians were few and communities small. Pagans could afford an attitude of unselfconscious disdain. By the later second century, educated pagans were better informed about Christianity, even if no more sympathetic; and by the end of the third the church had acquired a substantial enough organization for it to respond to Constantine's invitation to take a public role in the state.[96] Since it is commonly asserted that the Christian apologists of the period wrote only for the converted and that pagans

94. See G. Williams, *Change and Decline.*
95. See A. Walker, *In Search of Our Mothers' Gardens* (San Diego/New York: HBJ/Harvest Press, 1983), 290: "If the present looks like the past, what does the future look like?"
96. Barnes, *Constantine and Eusebius,* 191–92.

were hardly touched by Christian teachings, it is obviously a problem to explain how any increase in numbers took place at all. We remain very much in the dark about the social composition of most cities. The next two chapters will not address the traditional problems of the social origins of Christians or the reasons for conversion;[97] instead they will try to argue more generally that far from being as separate and distinct as Christians liked to claim, certain of the most characteristic features of Christian discourse in fact fitted the circumstances of society at large extremely well. The remaining chapters will then trace the fortunes of that discourse in the period after the beginning of state support for the church.

Although I deliberately borrow the methods of literary criticism, only some of the texts I shall be considering have a plausible claim to be considered as "literature" in a strict sense.[98] But historians do not need deconstruction to tell them that *all* available texts go to make up a culture, not just approved "literary ones"; they also know that the rhetoric of religion may be composed of more than just its canonical works. All the same, a literary analogy may be helpful at this stage. Unlike modern literary critics, Augustine, who was after all wedded to the view that language, and especially the language of the Scriptures, signified reality, laid great weight in his theory of interpretation on authorial intent.[99] "Whoever takes another meaning out of Scripture than the writer intended, goes astray, but not through any falsehood in Scripture."[100] The reader is important too: "And, therefore, if a man fully understands that 'the end of the commandment is charity, out of a pure heart, and of a good con-

---

97. A. D. Nock, *Conversion* (Oxford: Oxford University Press, 1933), remains the classic work on conversion; cf. recently Burkert, *Ancient Mystery Cults.*
98. That is, given any conventional understanding of the term.
99. See Mortley, *The Way of Negation,* 208.
100. *De doctr. christ.* 1.37.41.

science and of faith unfeigned,' and is bent upon making all his understanding of Scripture to bear upon these three graces, he may come to the interpretation of these books with an easy mind."[101] Likewise, "the author makes his readers. . . . If he makes them well—that is, makes them see what they have never seen before, moves them into a new order of perception and experience altogether—he finds his reward in the peers he has created."[102] In just such a way did Christian literature and Christian discourse make Christians. We shall see in the next chapter some of the ways in which they did so, and whether they made them well or badly.

101. Ibid., 40.44; cf. I Tim. 1:5.
102. W. Booth, *The Rhetoric of Fiction* (Chicago: University of Chicago Press, 1961), 397–98.

CHAPTER TWO

Showing and Telling

The Power of Signs

> You with all your elegant diction do not hinder the teaching of Christ; but we, by mentioning the name of the crucified Christ drive away all the demons whom you fear as gods. Where the Sign of the Cross appears, there magic is powerless and sorcery ineffectual.[1]

To Antony in the Egyptian desert, faith, not argument, and signs, not magic arts, are the proofs of Christian truth. Christian discourse is about revelation: it appeals to hidden truths. "He that hath ears to hear, let him hear";[2] "it is given unto you to know the mysteries of the kingdom of heaven."[3] It refers, often mysteriously, to a hidden and higher reality, which, Augustine argued, it was its function to reflect, even if the writer did not himself intend or understand the true meaning of his words. It could thus carry a meaning quite distinct from what the author meant himself, yet which was guaranteed by God: "certainly the Spirit of God, who worked through the author, undoubtedly foresaw that this meaning would occur to the reader or listener. Rather, He provided that it might occur to him, since that meaning is dependent upon truth."[4] The relation of author to text is

1. *V. Ant.* 78.
2. Mark 4:9; Matt. 13:43; Luke 14:35.
3. Matt. 13:11.
4. *De doctr. christ.* 3.27.38.

one in which the author transmits a meaning that is guaranteed by reference to an independent absolute.[5]

Christian writing posed the problem of representation in an acute manner. According to the more extreme formulations, logical argument was simply irrelevant. Of course, few went quite so far, but even for those with a more realistic approach, religious truth presented itself more often in the form of signs and symbols than of rational argument. Metaphor and image constituted the characteristic literary mode of the scriptural corpus with which Christian writers of the early empire had to engage;[6] Jesus himself had spoken in parables and through scriptural allusions and typology, and the Gospels and the Pauline Epistles continued the practice. Paul lays enormous emphasis on the mystery of Christian truth and the inability of words to express it: "The kingdom of God is not in word, but in power."[7] As he puts it elsewhere, his writings are "written not with ink, but with the Spirit of the living God; not in tables of stone, but in fleshy tables of the heart."[8] The very nature of the scriptural texts laid down the manner of subsequent Christian writing; inevitably the Bible, including, as it crystallized at the end of the second century, the New Testament canon, provided the point of reference for all Christian writers and encouraged the stress on signs and symbols and typology.[9]

Yet the New Testament texts evidently seek to proclaim—to transmit the message, the kerygma; as it were, simply to make

5. See J. A. Coulter, *The Literary Microcosm: Theories of Interpretation of the Later Neoplatonists* (Leiden: E. J. Brill, 1976), chaps. 1 and 2.

6. For this quality of biblical language, see N. Frye, *The Great Code: The Bible and Literature* (London: Routledge & Kegan Paul, 1982); also chapter 5 below.

7. I Cor. 4:20.

8. II Cor. 3:3.

9. On the development of the canon from the point of view of its effect on other Christian writing, see F. Kermode, "The Canon," in *The Literary Guide to the Bible,* ed. R. Alter and F. Kermode (London: Collins, 1987), 600–610.

an announcement.[10] When Paul writes to the Corinthians, he expresses his teaching in terms of a statement of faith in Jesus as the Christ; and at Thessalonica the author of Acts makes him say, "This Jesus, whom I preach unto you, is Christ."[11] The essential preaching can be called simply "the word."[12] The statements of faith could appear in various forms—in a hymn, for instance[13]—and with differing elements,[14] but the striking feature about them for the present argument is their testimony to the centrality to early Christian teaching of the simple affirmation of faith. It was a natural extension of the conviction that religious truth must be directly presented, not through logical argument, but through proofs—signs, like the sign of the cross, or statements of faith, which the believer must simply accept. In practice, of course, it was quite impossible not to resort to logical argument, and as I have argued above, all the writers from Paul onward who argued for the primacy of faith over logic did so through the medium of rhetorical argument. The tension between the two poles, and the struggle to resolve it, can be seen in Christian writings throughout the early centuries, and this tension intensified as it became more necessary to find acceptable

10. Characteristically emphasized by R. Bultmann, *History of the Synoptic Tradition*, 2d ed. (Oxford: Basil Blackwell, 1968), and elsewhere; cf. G. Stanton, "Form Criticism Revisited," in *What About the New Testament? Essays in Honour of Christopher Evans*, ed. M. Hooker and C. Hickling (London: SCM Press, 1975), 13–27.

11. I Cor. 15:3–5; Acts 17:3. On the affirmative nature of Christian discourse in the apostolic period, see S. Laeuchli, *The Language of Faith* (London: Epworth Press, 1965).

12. Acts 17:11.

13. Phil. 2:6–11; cf. Stanton, *Jesus of Nazareth*, 99–103. On credal formulas, see H. Koester, in Robinson and Koester, *Trajectories Through Early Christianity*, 207–11. The origins of the (later) formal creeds themselves are somewhat controversial; see A. M. Ritter, "Glaubenbekenntnis(se), V (Alte Kirche)," in *Theologische Realenzyklopädie*, ed. G. Krause and G. Müller (Berlin: Walter de Gruyter, 1977–), vol. 13 (1984), 399–412.

14. O. Cullmann, *The Earliest Christian Confessions* (London: Lutterworth Press, 1949).

doctrinal formulations. But it is the figural and demonstrative side of Christian discourse that will concern us first: its resort to signs, of which its characteristic use of metaphor is a part, and its performative and declaratory quality. How do either of these fit the context of the empire, or do they? First it will be necessary to examine the figurality of Christian discourse in more detail; but then I wish to construct a hypothesis to bring the characteristic Christian literary forms, and especially the development of an oral mode in the form of regular preaching, into closer relation with the prevailing culture.

There were various ways in which the figural quality could manifest itself. One was certainly metaphor. Ignatius of Antioch, whose letters to young Christian communities were written while under guard or en route to Rome where he was to undergo martyrdom, takes up the manner of Paul: "Put away, therefore, the bad leaven which is old and stale, and be converted into the new leaven which is Jesus Christ. Be salted in Him, lest any of you lose your savor, for by your savor will you be judged."[15] But there is also the explicit or implicit contrast between the surface meaning and the hidden meaning: "Beg only that I may have inward and outward strength, not only in word but in will, that I may be a Christian not merely in name but in fact. For, if I am one in fact, then I may be called one and be faithful long after I have vanished from the world. Nothing merely visible is good, for our God, Jesus Christ, is manifest the more now that he is hidden in God."[16] Seeing in visions is another manifestation of this tendency. The second-century writing known as the *Shepherd of Hermas* operates with many layers of visions, each with a meaning in need of interpretation. Revered and beautiful ladies appear to the author with revelations. An angel, a beautiful young man, explains that the first of

15. *Ep.* 2.10 (trans. Walsh).
16. *Ep.* 4.3 (trans. Walsh).

these ladies represents the church; she reveals the meaning of Hermas's vision of the building of a large tower constructed on water, built by male angels and supported by seven female figures—Faith, Continence, Simplicity, Knowledge, Innocence, Reverence, and Love.[17] Another young man explains the meaning of the visions of the church in the changing form of a woman; revelation is central to Christian faith, and dependent on it:

> "Why do you ask for instant revelations in your prayer? Be careful lest you injure your flesh by heavy requests. The present revelations are all you need. Can you see greater revelations than those you have seen?" In answer, I said to him, "Sir, I am only asking for a revelation complete in every detail about the three forms of the elderly lady." For answer, he said to me: "How long are you going to be without perception? It is your doubts that make you so and the failure to have your heart directed to the Lord."[18]

Accounts of martyrdom lent themselves perfectly to this mode; the martyr and his death became at once the enactment and the symbol of Christian perfection. "Upon Polycarp's entrance into the arena there came a voice from heaven, 'Be brave, Polycarp, and act like a man.'" Polycarp, martyred at Smyrna in the mid–second century, prays before the pyre is lit: "I bless Thee, because I may have a part, along with the martyrs, in the chalice of Thy Christ, 'unto resurrection in the eternal life,' resurrection both of soul and body in the incorruptibility of the Holy Spirit. May I be received today as a rich and acceptable sacrifice."[19] Polycarp's death is given a meaning and made a part of the whole mystery of Christian dispensation, in which things are no longer as they seem on the surface. Irenaeus, bishop of Lyon

17. *Shepherd*, Visions 1–8. No doubt significantly, Continence alone is said to "look like a man."

18. Ibid., 8.7–9.

19. *Martyrdom* 9, 14 (trans. Glimm).

Figure 3. The Good Shepherd. Catacomb of St. Callistus. Third century A.D. (Photograph: Scala)

shortly after the persecution there in A.D. 177 under Marcus Aurelius, devoted many pages to refuting erroneous interpretations of the often mysterious words of Scripture; it was a matter of understanding it right. The Father, he concluded, "is indeed invisible," but has been revealed in various forms through the Word: "not in one finger or character, did He appear to those seeing Him, but according to the reasons and effects aimed at in His dispensations, as it is written in Daniel." But "it was not by means of visions alone which were seen, and words which were proclaimed, but also in actual works that He was beheld by the prophets, in order that through them He might prefigure and show forth future events beforehand." [20]

How deep-seated the figurality of Christian discourse came to be can also be seen from what may seem a paradoxical example: the early-fourth-century *Life of Constantine* by Eusebius, a work overcriticized on historical grounds and understudied as a literary text. [21] The example is paradoxical not merely in that this may seem an unusual kind of Christian literature from which to draw general conclusions, but also because Eusebius himself has commonly been cited as an opponent of Christian images in visual art and was presented as such by the Iconoclast side in the eighth century during the Iconoclastic controversy. [22] Yet his literary presentation of Constantine is figural to a high degree. He

20. *Against Heresies*, 4.20.11–12.

21. The vast bibliography (for which see esp. F. Winkelmann, "Zur Geschichte des Authentizitätsproblems der *Vita Constantini*," *Klio* 40 [1962]: 187–243) focuses largely on historical issues and the question of authorship; see Barnes, *Constantine and Eusebius*, 265 ff., regarding Eusebian authorship as settled. The *Vita Constantini* is not usually included in discussions of Christian lives, despite its obvious relation to the biography of Origen in *HE* 6, for which compare P. Cox, *Biography in Late Antiquity* (Berkeley and Los Angeles: University of California Press, 1983). Harpham, *Ascetic Imperative*, chap. 1, offers an interesting discussion in these terms of the slightly later *Life of Antony* (see below, chapter 5).

22. See S. Gero, "The True Image of Christ: Eusebius's Letter to Constantia Reconsidered," *JThS*, n.s. 32 (1981): 460–70.

is highly conscious of the novelty of writing about an emperor who was a Christian, and indeed the reversal of events from persecution to imperial favor in his own writing career was startling.[23] But despite its clear debts to secular panegyric, he writes of Constantine in this, his last, work very much according to his own tradition of interpretation, in which the emperor assumes a role in the divine dispensation akin to Moses, if not to Christ himself. Eusebius presents his work, in a daring analogy, as a "proclamation" of Constantine, and the emperor himself as a "bold proclaimer" of the Christian faith.[24] His exposition, he implies, will not be an argument so much as a demonstration, a showing; in fact, it will be a "word-picture."[25] A true likeness, however, would need to be vindicated by proofs of verisimilitude, and sure enough, Eusebius uses the language of signs. The most prominent sign in the work is the sign of the cross, the "saving sign"; according to the *Life,* Constantine himself was granted a vision of the cross,[26] and his reign is said to be successful because of the proofs sent by God that his life is to be interpreted through signs.[27] Eusebius even calls the emperor himself "a pattern."[28] By analogy, and by a strikingly bold transference, his court will be the earthly counterpart of heaven and the gathering of the bishops at his table after the Council of Nicaea an image of Christ's heavenly kingdom.[29]

The *Life of Constantine* unites in an interesting, if at times

---

23. For the effect of this reversal on the stages of composition of the *Church History,* see T. D. Barnes, "The Editions of Eusebius's *Ecclesiastical History,*" *GRBS* 21 (1980): 191–201.

24. *VC* 4.75, 1.10.

25. *VC* 1.10; his use of the language of visual art is striking, but cf. also Greg. Nyss. *Life of Moses* 3, 15: "trace in outline . . . the perfect life." For antecedents, see Plut. *Alex.* 1 (comparison of biography to portraiture). I owe this reference to Prof. R. Mortley; Dr. P. Cartledge also points out the parallelism of treatment in Plutarch's *Agesilaos.*

26. *VC* 1.28–29.   27. *VC* 1.4.   28. *VC* 1.3; cf. 4.74.

29. *VC* 3.15.

uneasy, way the traditions of imperial rhetoric and those of Christian writing. Leaving aside the many historical arguments leveled against its authenticity, unity, and reliability, its awkwardnesses of structure have led to the view that it represents a mixture of genres and was written at different periods.[30] Whether or not that is the case, it is also a work that displays both the characteristics and the problems of Christian discourse. An elaborately rhetorical preface utilizing familiar modesty motifs combined with equally traditional claims to originality is juxtaposed in the first book with consistent use of Old Testament parallels and imagery; the latter is thoroughgoing in its repeated likening of Constantine to Moses, leading his people from the captivity of persecution as Moses led the Israelites out of Egypt.[31] Eusebius thus locates the emperor within the context of Old Testament typology as one who can through his actions demonstrate the fullness of God's plan for the world. But he makes concessions to imperial rhetoric: when he makes specific reference to the Old Testament text, he does so within a self-conscious context of mystification and euphemism.[32] Yet the references to the Scriptures are vital to his argument; they serve to validate the narrative of the *Life*, just as in the *Tricennalian*

30. See G. Pasquali, "Die Composition der *Vita Constantini* des Eusebius," *Hermes* 45 (1910): 369–86; and T. D. Barnes, "Panegyric, History, and Hagiography in Eusebius's *Life of Constantine*," in *The Making of Orthodoxy: Essays in Honour of Henry Chadwick*, ed. R. Williams (Cambridge: Cambridge University Press, 1989), 94–123. I am grateful to the author for allowing me to see this essay in advance of publication.

31. Eusebius had already employed the analogy in the *Ecclesiastical History* of the engulfment of Maxentius's army at the Battle of the Milvian Bridge (*HE* 9.9.5–6); cf. esp. *VC* 1.12. Eusebius inherited the emphasis on Moses from earlier Christian writers, including Origen, and used it himself in the *Praeparatio Evangelica*. On the technique of Old Testament typology, see J. Daniélou, *From Shadows to Reality*, trans. Dom Wulstan Hibberd (London: Burns & Oates, 1960).

32. Cf. *VC* 1.12, "an ancient story" known to most and regarded as myth; cf. 20, 38.

Oration his emphasis on the influence of the Logos supports the rule of Constantine and demonstrates that it can indeed be seen as a signifier of God's will. Whatever the immediate reception of the *Life,* which in the absence of direct evidence remains a considerable mystery, it is clear that Eusebius was deliberately trying to combine typically Christian elements with the technical requirement of high style demanded of imperial panegyric. It is all the more striking in view of his evident stylistic aspirations[33] that he nevertheless draws so extensively and conspicuously on the existing Christian repertoire of sign and image and employs a writing style so full of visual metaphor and imagery drawn from visual art.

We can perhaps understand better what Eusebius was doing if we look at the *Life* in relation to a work of a related though somewhat different kind, the *Life of Moses* written by Gregory of Nyssa later in the fourth century.[34] This account, too, begins with an elaborately rhetorical preface reminiscent in its classical imagery of the *Life of Constantine* and the *Tricennalian Oration,* but it goes on, after the narrative of the life of Moses, to interpret the events in it in allegorical and typological terms. Moses is used as a figure of Christian spirituality, that is, of Gregory's understanding of Christian truth; indeed, the work has often been regarded as the culmination of Gregory's mystical thought.[35] It is characteristic of Christian writing in general, however, that he should have chosen to express himself in just such a way, through the presentation and interpretation of a figure conceived as a "pattern" or image of spiritual virtue. Else-

33. See esp. the prefaces to both *VC* and *LC.*
34. *Life of Moses,* ed. J. Daniélou, Sources chrétiennes 1 bis (Paris: Cerf, 1955); for a useful translation with notes, see *Gregory of Nyssa: The Life of Moses,* trans. and ed. A. J. Malherbe and E. Ferguson (New York: Paulist Press, 1978). The work seems to belong to the 390s.
35. See Malherbe and Ferguson, trans. and eds., *Life of Moses,* 9–10, with further bibliography.

where, Gregory conceives the Christian self in terms of painter, paint, and image: [36] the self-conscious Christian creates his own self, and does so through the medium of texts, which in turn assume the function of models.

There were many reasons, quite apart from the existing background of pagan *Lives,* why Christians should have felt drawn to a form of spiritual biography; [37] working out the implications of a biographical mythology, they perceived the world in terms of the human body and soul. [38] In a concrete sense, then, written *Lives* provided the guidelines for the construction of a Christian life, and the ascetic model to which we shall soon come provided the guidelines for the construction of a specifically Christian self. But it is important to realize also that their way of interpreting the lives they wrote about was part of the wider realm of Christian discourse and illustrates its figural character particularly well. Written *Lives* were mimetic; real ascetic discipline in turn imitated the written *Lives.* [39] Like visual art, early Christian discourse presented its audience with a series of images. The proclamation of the message was achieved by a technique of presenting the audience with a series of images through which it was thought possible to perceive an objective and higher truth. That the images carried a meaning, whether hidden or not, was not in doubt: "now we see through a glass darkly, but then face to face; now I know in part, but then shall I know even as also I am known." [40]

Consciousness of the referential quality of Christian language carried several powerful advantages for the Christian preacher and writer. He could claim that true wisdom lay in the Christian message, even if it needed elucidation ("we speak the wisdom of

36. See Harpham, *Ascetic Imperative,* 24–25.
37. See chapter 5.
38. P. Brown, *Body and Society,* 108–9.
39. Harpham, *Ascetic Imperative,* 13–14.
40. I Cor. 13:12.

God in a mystery, even the hidden wisdom, which God ordained before the world to our glory");[41] not only that—the correct interpretation of that message would become a matter of authority. Finally, since a potential higher reference was now claimed a fortiori for all language and all rhetoric, not just the specifically Christian, it would be open for him to achieve a totalizing interpretation in which secular discourse could be subsumed and brought within the universal Christian interpretative field. The figural quality of Christian expression, and the theory of reference on which it rested, were major enabling factors in its development toward a totalizing discourse.

Metaphor is at the heart of Christian language. "We are members of his body, of his flesh, and of his bones. . . . This is a great mystery, but I speak concerning Christ and the church."[42] Later theologians asked themselves how religious truth could be expressed in language. For Gregory of Nyssa, the best theologian is one who "assembles more of Truth's shadow."[43] His contemporary, Gregory of Nazianzus, debates the same issue in philosophical terms, with the standard answer that God is describ-

41. I Cor. 2:7. On the concept of Christian wisdom, see J. Mahoney, "The Ways of Wisdom," Inaugural Lecture, King's College London, 1987. On the "hiddenness" of Christianity, Matt. 13:35 is a key text ("I will open my mouth in parables; I will utter things which have been kept secret from the foundation of the world"; cf. Ps. 78:2), on which see R. Girard, *Des choses cachées depuis la fondation du monde* (Paris: B. Grasset, 1978). Clement of Alexandria is important for this theme; see Mortley, *Way of Negation*, 36 ff., on the tension expressed by Clement and others between the ideas of mystery and revelation; also A. Böhlig, *Mysterion und Wahrheit* (Leiden: Otto Michel, 1968); Burkert, *Ancient Mystery Cults*, intro. (comparison with pagan mysteries); Chadwick, *Early Christian Thought*, 35 ff.

42. Eph. 5:30, 32. On metaphor and paradox as intrinsic to religious language, see below, chapter 5; cf. Frye, *Great Code*, 53–77; also Aug. *De doctr. christ.* 4.7.15: "I see, then, that I must say something about the eloquence of the prophets also, where many things are concealed under a metaphorical style, which the more completely they seem buried under figures of speech, give the greater pleasure when brought to light."

43. See further F. M. Young, "The God of the Greeks and the Nature of Religious Language," in Schoedel and Wilken, eds., *Early Christian Literature*, 45–74.

able only by analogy, that is, through metaphor. The issue is an
ongoing one,[44] even if the parameters have moved somewhat.
This question of the status of language in early Christianity was
seen by some contemporaries, often those most influenced by
Platonism, as a major issue; but although a few came to deny
even that analogy was possible,[45] the more widespread idea that
images represented truth showed an obstinate persistence, and
its application in visual art was finally vindicated against opposition by the defeat of Byzantine Iconoclasm in the ninth century.[46] It was a small step from pervasive metaphor in Christian
language to the symbolic repertoire of early Christian art—the
Good Shepherd, the vine, and so on. For Christian language,
like Christian art, was trying to express mysteries that were essentially inexpressible except through symbol. As no one knew
better than Augustine, the Scriptures came in "fleshly wrappings" that needed to be carefully opened and unfolded. It is essential to make clear the "hidden meaning, the existence of
which is the reason why they are called also mysteries," so that
Christians might learn "how ideas are to be preferred to words,
just as the soul is preferred to the body."[47] Similarly, the continued struggles over doctrinal definitions throughout the first
centuries of Christianity, while on one level contests for institu-

44. See, e.g., I. T. Ramsey, *Religious Language* (London: SCM Press,
1957); A. Macintyre, "Is Understanding Religion Compatible with Believing?" in *Faith and the Philosophers*, ed. J. Hick (London: Macmillan, 1964),
115–33; J. Macquarie, *God-Talk* (London: SCM Press, 1967); P. Ricoeur,
The Rule of Metaphor, trans. R. Czerny, with K. McLaughlin and J. Costello
(Toronto: University of Toronto Press, 1977); L. S. Mudge, ed., *Essays on Biblical Interpretation* (Philadelphia: Fortress Press, 1980), esp. 73 ff. and Mudge's
preliminary essay, 1–40; S. McFague, *Metaphorical Theology: Models of
God in Religious Language* (Philadelphia: Fortress Press, 1982).

45. Mortley argues for a "decline of confidence in reason and language" in
late antiquity, in both Christian and Neoplatonist thought; his most extreme
examples are Damascius among the Neoplatonists and ps.-Dionysius among
Christian writers.

46. See chapter 6.

47. *De rudibus catechizandis* 9.13.

tional supremacy, are evidence of the remarkable efforts made
to overcome this central problem and of the importance attached by the church to finding a solution. However difficult,
the attempt to find satisfactory verbal statements of the faith
was never abandoned. Indeed, it is more than ever obvious in
the intensity of the early Byzantine debate about images: whether
in individual theological writings or in the debates of the official
and unofficial councils held on this issue, all parties accepted
unquestioningly that such statements were in principle possible.

But metaphor, or image, was not the only technique employed. Miracle, too, functioned in early Christian literature as
a device—a trope—to allow the articulation of the relation between the human and divine worlds.[48] Miracle, the suspension
of normal laws of nature, is to be seen less as an example of "irrationality" or credulity than as an instance of the symbolic interface of human and divine: it functions as a rhetorical device to
express what is otherwise inexpressible. In much the same way,
parable (currently a major topic of study from the rhetorical
standpoint)[49] surprises by suspending normal expectation. It
operates by telling—not through argument, but by revelation,
through hidden meanings. The texts rely on these devices; indeed, they lay some stress on their importance and on the difficulty of understanding them, as when Jesus says to his disciples,
"unto you it is given to know the mystery of the kingdom of
God, but unto them that are without, all these things are done in

48. P. J. Achtemeier, "Jesus and the Disciples as Miracle-Workers in the
Apocryphal New Testament," in Fiorenza, ed., *Aspects of Religious Propaganda,* 149–86; for the later period, see L. Cracco Ruggini, "Il miracolo nella
cultura del tardo impero: concetto e funzione," in *Hagiographie, cultures, et
sociétés, IVe–XIIe siècles* (Paris: Etudes Augustiniennes, 1981), 161–204.
49. See, e.g., D. O. Via, Jr., *The Parables* (Philadelphia: Fortress Press,
1967); McFague, *Speaking in Parables;* D. Patte, ed., *Semiology and Parables*
(Pittsburgh: Pickwick Press, 1976); A. N. Wilder, *Jesus' Parables and the War
of Myths: Essays on Imagination in the Scriptures* (London: SPCK, 1982).

parables."⁵⁰ It is this feature, in particular, of early Christian discourse that deserves much more attention than it has so far received except from specialists, for it raises exactly those issues of language and representation that are now for us again problematic.⁵¹

The *Life of Constantine,* it is true, does not resort to parable (although in a sense it tells a story), but it does rely heavily on signs, especially the signs that demonstrate God's favor to Constantine. The emperor, Eusebius says, was inspired by the way God had sent him "many manifestations and tokens,"⁵² of which we should read the famous vision sent before the battle against Maxentius in A.D. 312⁵³ merely as the most spectacular. Despite the enormous amount of scholarly writing devoted to this account, the language in which it is described is not often singled out for comment;⁵⁴ yet Eusebius specifically calls the vision a "sign," and the statue allegedly put up by Constantine in Rome to commemorate the victory bore, according to Eusebius, an inscription with the same word.⁵⁵ The inscription does not survive, and despite his claim to have heard of the vision from the lips of the emperor himself, the circumstances of Eusebius's

50. Mark 4:11, on which see Wilder, *Early Christian Rhetoric,* 90–91; cf. Isa. 6:9; Mark 8:18; see too Matt. 11:15: "He that hath ears to hear, let him hear."

51. These discussions about religious language cannot, of course, be detached from the wider context of literary and philosophical issues; for the role of paradox and the idea of rhetoric as a suspension of logic, see P. de Man, *Blindness and Insight* (New York: Oxford University Press, 1971); P. de Man, *Allegories of Reading* (New Haven: Yale University Press, 1979); discussion in relation to history in D. La Capra, *History and Criticism* (Ithaca, N.Y.: Cornell University Press, 1985), 15–44, esp. 39–40.

52. *VC* 1.57.

53. *VC* 1.28 ff.

54. Among the most notable works are N. Baynes, *Constantine the Great and the Christian Church* (London: British Academy, 1930; repr. 1972); H. Grégoire, "La vision de Constantin 'liquidée,'" *Byzantion* 14 (1939): 341–51.

55. *VC* 1.40; cf. *HE* 9.9.10–11.

Figure 4. Head, colossal statue of Constantine the Great. Early fourth century A.D. (Rome, Palazzo dei Conservatori)

knowing about the statue and the inscription remain obscure.
Yet it is significant for us that the latter appealed for its elucidation to a visual image, the representation in one form or another
of a cross.[56] Constantine himself returned to the theme in the
letter addressed to the provincials after his last victory over Li-
cinius in A.D. 324.[57] Elsewhere in the *Life,* the signs are both
verbal and visual. Over the palace in Constantinople, we are
told, was a picture representing "the sacred signs," above a symbolic representation of the Devil as a serpent.[58] Eusebius explains the picture for us: it is an allegory inspired by God in the
mind of the emperor, to be understood by reference to Isaiah
27:1, "In that day the Lord with his sore and great and strong
sword shall punish leviathan the piercing serpent, even leviathan
that crooked serpent; and he shall slay the dragon that is in the
sea." Of this scene Constantine's picture is said to be a "true
and faithful representation." It is an interesting comment on the
standard view that Eusebius was hostile to the principle of
Christian art[59] that the *Life of Constantine* should be revealed
as a text wholly articulated through a network of signs, within
which the visual has an important place, as can be seen also
from the allusions to the iconography of Constantine's coins in
the concluding pages, where Eusebius not only describes the images but also (controversially) interprets them.[60]

As is well known, Eusebius devotes a good deal of space in
the *Life* to the description of Constantine's churches in the Holy

56. For the cross as a theme in the *VC* and elsewhere, see R. H. Storch,
"The Trophy and the Cross: Pagan and Christian Symbolism in the Fourth
and Fifth Centuries," *Byzantion* 40 (1970): 105–18.

57. *VC* 2.55.

58. *VC* 3.3.

59. This view is challenged by C. Murray, "Art in the Early Church,"
JThS, n.s. 28 (1977): 303–45. The issue turns in part on the authenticity of
the letter to the Empress Constantia adduced in the context of eighth-century
Iconoclast polemic; see Gero, "True Image of Christ."

60. *VC* 4.15, 73.

Land,[61] and also to his mausoleum in Constantinople. Eusebius had himself earlier delivered a panegyrical speech on the church at Tyre, which he incorporated in his *Church History,* and he was one of the orators who spoke in praise of the new church of the Holy Sepulcher at Jerusalem when it was dedicated in A.D. 335.[62] Imperial building and rhetorical *ekphraseis,* or formal descriptions of works of art, were both traditional subjects for an orator.[63] All the same, there is surely more involved here than that; these themes in the *Life of Constantine* belong in an overall context of attention to signs. From now onward, appeals to visual evidence and discussion of visual art become extremely prominent in Christian writing,[64] and they usually focus on its meaning—that is, on the relation between the sign and the signified. For the first time, perhaps, in the *Life of Constantine,* we can see this typically Christian language of signs being consistently applied to a public, imperial subject.

It is used there in a number of different ways. But once we see how deeply it is engrained in the whole texture of the work, it becomes quite clear what role the descriptions of pictures, coins, and buildings are required to play in the overall scheme.

Fourth-century writers like Eusebius had inherited a highly

61. *VC* 3.25 ff., 4.58–59. On Constantine's churches, see G. Dagron, *Naissance d'une capitale: Constantinople et ses institutions de 330 à 451* (Paris: Presses universitaires de France, 1974), 388 ff.; C. A. Mango, *Le développement urbain de Constantinople* (Paris: Boccard, 1985), 35. I am indebted to Cyril Mango for exposition of Eusebius's description.

62. On Tyre, see *HE* 10.4; on Jerusalem, *VC* 4.46. For the identification of *Tric. Or.* 11–18 with part or all of that speech, see H. A. Drake, *In Praise of Constantine* (Berkeley and Los Angeles: University of California Press, 1976), 30–45.

63. See, e.g., D. Geanokoplos, "Church Building and 'Caesaropapism,' A.D. 312–565," *GRBS* 7 (1966): 167–86; and on the theme in the *VC,* S. MacCormack, "Latin Prose Panegyrics: Tradition and Discontinuity in the Later Roman Empire," *Revue des études augustiniennes* 22 (1976): 29–77.

64. See the useful collection of extracts in C. A. Mango, *The Art of the Byzantine Empire, 312–1453* (Englewood Cliffs, N.J.: Prentice-Hall, 1972).

developed technique and practice of allegorical interpretation from a series of earlier writers.[65] It is usual to see the disputes that took place between allegorizers and literalists as competitions between "schools" over interpretation. The Scriptures, once it had been agreed that they must be retained by Christians, had to be explained: how was this to be achieved? It was a struggle over the correct understanding of the sacred texts, and one conducted in traditional terms drawn from earlier discussions of how to interpret prophecy or poetic inspiration. The technique of allegory, crude and implausible though it often seemed in Christian hands, was a way of getting around the charges of irrationality and incompatibility.

But it was also a rhetorical device. Figural imagery was embedded in the language of the Bible, and its exploitation by commentators made possible an acceptable presentation of Christian ideas to outsiders as well as of the Old Testament to Christians themselves. The "stumbling block" of the Christian myth[66] had to be rendered presentable, its relation to Jewish Scripture smoothed out and an accommodation shown to be possible between Christian faith and classical learning. Appeal to the language of signs, the argument that God made himself known through a veil that could only be penetrated by the science of hermeneutics,[67] was a way of neutralizing the difficulty. At the same time, certain key texts (notably the Song of Songs) and fig-

65. Philo, Clement, and Origen stand out; see Mortley, *Way of Negation,* 39 ff.; Coulter, *Literary Microcosm,* 25 ff., with further bibliography and discussion of allegory in relation to Plato and the Neoplatonist commentators, esp. Proclus.

66. I Cor. 1:23. For the biblical roots of Christian typology, see Daniélou, *From Shadows to Reality,* 11.

67. The image was also used of myth in Neoplatonist criticism; see J. Bouffartigue, "Représentations et évaluations du texte poétique dans le Commentaire sur la République de Proclos," in *Le texte et ses représentations,* ed. P. Hoffmann, J. Lallot, and A. le Boulluec, Etudes de littérature ancienne 3 (Paris: PENS, 1987), 130–31.

ures (notably Moses) assumed the role of traditional themes in the repertoire of Christian interpreters, and were not without a wider influence.

Allegory and signs go together. Augustine devotes two books of the *De doctrina christiana* to divine signs, while grappling with the problem of the roots of Christian learning. His own solution to the problem of the relation of Christian to classical learning (and he is thinking chiefly of rhetoric) relies heavily on the concept of divine revelation through signs. Language itself, a complex of signs, is for him the means of access to divine truth. Thus, while one may take the best from pagan knowledge and pagan writing, access to the true knowledge, which alone can bring a complete and right synthesis, can be gained only through direct awareness, through God's signs. The world, therefore, is known by revelation, and whereas that revelation need not (indeed, as I shall argue later, cannot) exclude pagan knowledge altogether, its ultimate source is the true teacher, Christ: it is a matter of demonstration, not of reason alone.[68] By Augustine's day, a huge volume of sophisticated argument had been developed on the theme of the relation between classical culture and Christian knowledge, and, on the Christian side, on the best ways of bridging the gap. Origen's pupil Gregory Thaumaturgus describes how the study of classical rhetoric should lead naturally to that of the Scriptures, as to a higher truth: the Christian could rightfully embrace "every doctrine, barbarian or Greek

68. This is the argument of the *De magistro*. See further, e.g., R. A. Markus, "St. Augustine on Signs," and B. D. Jackson, "The Theory of Signs in St. Augustine's *De doctrina christiana*," in *Augustine*, ed. R. A. Markus (New York: Anchor Books, 1972), 61–91 and 92–147, respectively; K. Burke, *The Rhetoric of Religion* (Berkeley and Los Angeles: University of California Press, 1962), chap. 2 (on the *Confessions*); K. Burke, *Language as Symbolic Action* (Berkeley and Los Angeles: University of California Press, 1966), 359–79. I was much influenced by a paper on the subject given by Prof. Louis H. Mackey at a symposium entitled "Augustine and the Classical Tradition" organized by Prof. Sabine MacCormack at the University of Texas at Austin, November 1981.

. . . things spiritual and secular, divine and human." [69] All is to lead to the knowledge of God. But many Christians, including Augustine in certain moods and for certain purposes, adopted a more critical view toward classical culture. Indeed, Gregory of Nazianzus tells us how some "spit on it as treacherous and dangerous, and separating us from God." [70]

Typically, Augustine faced the problem head-on and decided that Christian knowledge was indeed different: it came only from God and could be apprehended only through inspiration, that is, through signs. He begins the first book of the *De doctrina christiana,* on the understanding of Scripture, with a general assertion that all doctrine is taught by signs, and demonstrates it by a bold appeal to the "irrationality" of the Christian message: "The foolishness of God is wiser than men, and the weakness of God is stronger than men"; and "He saw fit to appear to those whose eye is weak and impure," and even to fleshly eyes, for "after that in the wisdom of God the world by wisdom knew not God, it pleased God by the foolishness of preaching to save them that believe." [71] Christian discourse could be represented as irrational, even absurd, but this very irrationality could be turned into a strength.

Two opposing tendencies can therefore be seen to be at work: on the one hand, demystification, the continuing attempt to define and explain the Christian paradox in familiar words, both for the purpose of establishing correct doctrine and to bring Christian discourse out into the world of classical rhetoric; on the other hand, its very opposite—increased emphasis on, indeed exploitation of, the very element of mystery that Augustine here stresses. The tensions between these two impulses will be

69. *PG* 10.1096A–B. On Gregory, see R. Van Dam, "Hagiography and History: The Life of Gregory Thaumaturgus," *Classical Antiquity* 1 (1982): 272–308.

70. *PG* 36.508B.

71. I Cor. 1:25; *De doctr. christ.* 1.11.11, 12.11; I Cor. 1:21.

the subject of later chapters. Meanwhile, we can note that Augustine, advocate, against some contemporary trends, of the efficacy of language, a former rhetor himself and supremely conscious of the power of words, was deeply aware of the tension, and at times emphasized it to rhetorical effect.[72] For the danger of demystification was precisely, as he saw, that the mystery that constituted the strength of the faith might itself be lost.[73]

We have already had reason to draw on the most characteristic of Christian metaphors, that of the body: "for as the body is one and hath many members, and all the parts of that one body, being many, are one body: so also is Christ."[74] The theme of the Incarnation of Christ imposed the language of the body, and with it bodily symbolism, on Christian writing. All the central elements in orthodox Christianity—the Incarnation, the Resurrection, the Trinity, the Virgin Birth,[75] and the Eucharist—focus on the body as symbolic of higher truth. As we have seen, the deep-seated bridal imagery of the Bible also contributed greatly to such an emphasis in Christian discourse. This body symbolism later became a powerful component in a Christian theology

72. See Mortley, *Way of Negation,* 192 ff.
73. See R. Girard, *Violence and the Sacred,* trans. P. Gregory (Baltimore: Johns Hopkins University Press, 1977), 24.
74. I Cor. 12:12 (and 12–31 generally). From a mounting literature, see M. Douglas, *Natural Symbols* (London: Barrie & Rockcliff, Cresset Press, 1970); N. O. Brown, *Love's Body* (New York: Random House, 1966), 126–40, 201 ff.; J. A. Baker, "The Myth of the Church: A Case Study in the Use of Scripture for Christian Doctrine," in Hooker and Hickling, eds., *What About the New Testament?* 165–77; J. Gager, "Body-Symbols and Social Reality: Resurrection, Incarnation, and Asceticism in Early Christianity," *Religion* 12 (1982): 345–64. On biblical imagery, see Frye, *Great Code,* 139–68.
75. See chapter 5 below; and Averil Cameron, "Virginity as Metaphor." There is much of interest on the implications of the theme of the Eucharist for medieval concentration on the body and flesh of Christ in C. Bynum, *Holy Feast and Holy Fast: The Religious Significance of Food for Medieval Women* (Berkeley and Los Angeles: University of California Press, 1987).

of monarchy.[76] But it did not in this period lead to the morbid preoccupation with the body of Christ found in later centuries. In contrast, it led to an emphasis on the subjection of the human body by celibacy and asceticism far more extreme than that of philosophical *askesis*.[77] But it also made it possible for Christians to link their own emphasis on the individual[78] with their conception of God. Moreover, since human society was presented as naturally ordained according to hierarchical principles, in a context in which the same ordering, with Christ as the head, was seen as analogous to the human body,[79] it provided the potential for a totally integrated rhetoric of God, community, and individual. The psychological and ideological advantages of this integration would be hard to overestimate.

There was of course an underside to this language of the body, which finds expression in the loving detail with which the pains and tortures of the martyrs are recounted—the rack, the breaking of limbs on the wheel, the gouging out of eyes, the reenactment in fact of the breaking of the body of Christ. The experience of persecution thus opened up a whole new avenue for the rhetoric of the body.[80] Asceticism, both before and after the ending of actual persecution, continued this magnifying focus on the physical body. It was accompanied by a mushrooming in the

76. For its later development, see E. Kantorowicz, *The King's Two Bodies* (Princeton: Princeton University Press, 1957).

77. "Christian asceticism in the third and fourth centuries tended to move from salutary self-discipline to extremes of self-torment which only increased preoccupation with the body" (G. Clark, *Iamblichus: On the Pythagorean Life* [Liverpool: Liverpool University Press, 1989], xiii).

78. See L. Dumont, *Essays on Individualism*, trans. L. Dumont and P. Hockings (Chicago: University of Chicago Press, 1986).

79. In particular I Cor. 12:12–31, with Rom. 13:1; Eph. 5:22–33; Col. 3.18–23; see Wicker, "First Century Marriage Ethics." On the Eucharist as integrative in this period, see Bynum, *Holy Feast*, 31 ff.

80. Naturally, Christians were exposed to all the increasingly brutal punishments in use in the empire, for which accounts of martyrdoms and tortures provide much of our information; see the striking evidence collected in

recording of greater and greater feats of physical endurance; the body became less a symbol of integration than an obstacle to be overcome. After Constantine, extreme asceticism filled the void left by the denial of martyrdom.[81] Eusebius well conveys the heights to which the imagination could turn this attention to the physical body when he describes the death of his mentor Pamphilus, tortured and killed with eleven others during the Great Persecution.[82] To heighten the pathos, he does not recount Pamphilus's death directly; instead, having related what happened to one of his companions, he merely says in subdued tones that Pamphilus and the rest suffered in the same way. The splendor of the martyrdom of Pamphilus is shown through the sufferings of his companions, and especially by the story of the young man Porphyry, who comes forward from the crowd protesting against the proceedings, declares himself a Christian, and is cruelly tortured: his flesh is scraped to the very bone, not like a human being, but like "stones or wood, or any other lifeless object." He is then burned in a slow fire, and as he died, Eusebius says, one could see him, "his countenance bright and cheerful . . . , with a courageous and exulting mind advancing on his way to death. Truly filled with the divine Spirit, [he was] covered only with his philosophical garb thrown round him like a cloak," and he kept silent until the very end, when he uttered only the name of Christ. The nakedness and laceration of Porphyry's body, which seem at first to deny his humanity, are transformed into the focus of his triumph. The martyr accounts

---

F. Millar, "Condemnation to Hard Labour in the Roman Empire, from the Julio-Claudians to Constantine," *Papers of the British School at Rome* 52 (1984): 124–47; R. MacMullen, "Judicial Savagery in the Roman Empire," *Chiron* 16 (1986): 147–66.

81. See M. Alexandre, "Les nouveaux martyrs," in *The Biographical Works of Gregory of Nyssa*, ed. A. Spira (Philadelphia: Philadelphia Patristic Foundation, 1984), 33–70, for the repeated association of virginity with martyrdom. But P. Brown, *Body and Society*, 208, rightly stresses that asceticism did not wait for Constantine or Antony to become established.

82. *HE* 8.12.

serve thus to confirm the position that the body had already held—if in a different way—as a central focus of Christian discourse. It was a focus that was in no way to diminish when martyrdom ceased. Nor was it only suffering that counted. As the abbot Pambo died, we are told, it was of his bodily existence that he thought, how he had managed his body: he could boast that he had never touched bread unless he had produced it with the work of his hands.[83] But others could do much better. One old monk had lived for fifty years without bread and with little water; another ate only every third day; another even rooted out the few blades of green that had sprouted in his cell.[84] A saying of Daniel summed it up: "As the body is cherished, so does the soul wax lean; and when the body hath grown lean, then does the soul wax fat."[85]

These incidents and sayings form the ascetic literature of the fourth and fifth centuries and later belong to a particular and well-defined tradition of their own.[86] Yet the language of the physical body had always been prominent in Christian writing. It was built into the Pauline rhetoric of resurrection:

> All flesh is not the same flesh; but there is one kind of flesh of men, another flesh of beasts, another of fishes, and another of birds. . . . So also is the resurrection of the dead. It is sown in corruption; it is raised in incorruption. It is sown in dishonour; it is raised in glory; it is sown in weakness; it is raised in power. It is sown a natural body; it is raised a spiritual body. There is a natural body and there is a spiritual body.[87]

Already in the second and third centuries we can see the theme of the human body centrally displayed. The issue of sexual rela-

83. *Vit. Patr.* 5; a convenient translation may be found in H. Waddell, *The Desert Fathers* (London: Fontana, 1962), 80.
84. Waddell, *Desert Fathers,* 110–12.
85. Ibid., 112.
86. See the excellent chapter in P. Brown, *Body and Society,* 213–40.
87. See I Cor. 15:39–44.

tions assumed major importance as a theme of controversy,[88] and here too, while this development had part of its origins in the social conditions and beliefs of Christian groups in the first century, the very imagery of the Bible, in particular its recourse to bridal and marriage images, dictated the topic as a center of attention for Christian discourse. But further, the central Christian mystery of the Incarnation focused on the relation of body and spirit, and in particular on the problem of gestation and parturition both human and divine.

A major area in which Christian preoccupations with language and with the body can both be seen is indeed that of female sexuality. The general language of asceticism and its particular manifestations in relation to the topic of female virginity lent themselves peculiarly well to Christian writing. It was natural, in view of the attention paid from an early stage to Eve and Mary in expounding the Christian dispensation of salvation,[89] that later Christian writing on marital and sexual matters should have focused on women. Their physical behavior and appearance had been early regulated,[90] and the strong recommendation to virginity in much later Christian writing is often combined— as by Jerome, for example—with strictures on female dress, makeup, and general appearance; rhetorically speaking, these themes form two poles of the same concern. In social and practical terms, it is not very surprising if Christians were more con-

88. See Clement *Misc.* 3, which argues for marriage against Gnostic views, both ascetic and liberal; also chapter 5 below. For Paul on marriage, see I Cor. 7.

89. Especially by Irenaeus; see Daniélou, *From Shadows to Reality,* 43 ff. See also Pagels, *Adam, Eve, and the Serpent.*

90. E.g., already in I Cor. 7, 11; and Tertullian, *De cultu feminarum* and *De velandis virginibus.* Cyprian and Ambrose also wrote on the subject; see H. Bloch, "Medieval Misogyny: Woman as Riot," *Representations* 20 (Fall 1987): 1–24. A helpful and sensible discussion of the New Testament texts can be found in B. Witherington III's *Women in the Ministry of Jesus* (Cambridge: Cambridge University Press, 1984) and *Women in the Earliest Churches* (Cambridge: Cambridge University Press, 1988).

cerned to control women's moral behavior than men's.[91] But it is more than that: the rhetorical construction of woman itself served as a mode of theological expression. When we find so many of the fourth-century Christian writers—Ambrose, John Chrysostom, Gregory of Nyssa, Augustine, Jerome— addressing themselves to the theme of virginity, the phenomenon has a rhetorical and figural as well as a theological or moral dimension. But we shall see further below how in its very paradoxical nature it could also stand for the essential "irrational" or metaphorical element in religious language, which was in danger of being lost as Christianity became increasingly institutionalized.

But how does this figural discourse relate to the context of the Roman Empire, especially in the late first to third centuries? Was it an alien growth, a scandal to the gentiles, a new language against a background of faded myth, "an epochal revolution in the gamut and power of language, including new imagery, a liberation of human speech and a new grasp on reality?"[92] Or was it something less dramatic, but more easily understood?

The Death of Rhetoric

How convenient, we may think, that Pliny's *Panegyricus*, that monster of bad taste in modern eyes, belongs so neatly to the year A.D. 100, and that Tacitus's *Dialogus de Oratoribus*, so nearly contemporary, effectively mourns the demise of classical

91. Thus the canons of the Synod of Elvira, A.D. 305, which are very much concerned with marital and sexual matters, concentrate largely on the behavior of women.

92. Wilder, *Jesus' Parables*, 113, written as still commonly against the supposition of contemporary religious and social crisis: "the ideology of the Greek polis had long been in trouble and, as today [*sic*], the masses craved for some new crystallization of meaning and community."

oratory.[93] Not so very much later, Tacitus's *Annals* marked the culmination, and for several generations the end, of Roman senatorial history. Suetonius, the younger contemporary of Pliny and Tacitus, and Pliny's protégé, established the biographical form that would for long be the preferred alternative.[94] All these writers were exponents of the rhetoric of decline. Tacitus makes one of his speakers complain that there is nothing left to write about under the Principate, and looks back himself to the days when history was really history, when it was still possible to write of battles and conquered kings instead of closet politics.[95] These complaints, like those of Juvenal and Martial, paint a gloomier picture than is justified. After all, the Senate was still surprisingly active, and some people at least were able, like Pliny and Tacitus themselves, to tread the narrow path between flattery and undue frankness and so proceed without serious difficulty to the top of the career ladder. Our elite sources give us a highly colored and hostile impression, which has duly been enshrined in many modern works.[96]

Nevertheless, it was during this time that an educational system narrowly based on rhetorical exercises became the norm for

93. For the date of the *Dialogus,* usually put sometime after A.D. 100, see C. E. Murgia, "The Date of Tacitus' *Dialogus,*" *HSCP* 84 (1980): 99–125; C. E. Murgia, "Pliny's Letters and the *Dialogus,*" *HSCP* 89 (1985): 171–206 (arguing for A.D. 97).

94. See A. Wallace-Hadrill, *Suetonius: The Scholar and His Caesars* (London: Duckworth, 1983).

95. *Ann.* 4.32.

96. E.g., A. Leeman, *Orationis Ratio,* vol. 1 (Amsterdam: A. M. Hakkert, 1963) (see 13, which cites with approval what the author calls the "deeply-rooted aversion of modern man from rhetoric"); G. Kennedy, *The Art of Rhetoric in the Roman World, 300 B.C.–A.D. 300* (Princeton: Princeton University Press, 1972); A. Spira, "The Impact of Christianity on Ancient Rhetoric," paper delivered at the Ninth International Congress of Patristic Studies, Oxford, 1983; A. Spira, "Volkstümlichkeit und Kunst in der griechischen Väterpredigt des 4. Jahrhunderts," *JÖB* 35 (1985): 55–73; the last two (with justification) present Christian oratory as the new force and heir to the classical past (I am grateful to Professor Spira for letting me read his unpublished Oxford Congress paper).

the upper classes, and it remained so as long as the empire lasted, with the exceptions only of the more specialized areas of philosophy and law. Tacitus links his view of the decline of oratory to the new rhetorical education, which he contrasts with an idealized Republican model of practical and moral training for statesmen. Such an interpretation lent itself extremely well to his general political analysis. Since, in the familiar words of Cassius Dio, after Actium government went on behind closed doors,[97] there was no longer any place for political oratory in the grand and established manner; Roman orators in search of wealth and reputation were all too likely, in Tacitus's view, to turn to the "corrupt eloquence" of the prosecutions for treason and, using the skills they had acquired from the practice of declamation, to turn on their peers. The *Dialogus* is itself a highly rhetorical composition; cast in the form of a philosophical dialogue, it offers a conspectus of opinions expressed in such a way as to show off their differences to maximum advantage. Because the *Dialogus de Oratoribus* is itself a display of rhetoric, it is doubly rash to identify any of the speakers too quickly with Tacitus himself.[98] The work ends on a characteristically ambiguous note. The day is over, but the possibility of further discussion remains. In a sense, Messalla, the protagonist of the idea of oratorical decline, might be said to have the last word when he suggests that he has an answer for Maternus's concluding plea for a recognition that times have changed and that the great political oratory of the Republic had after all been born of political strife.[99] Yet the dialogue actually ends without a resolution, as Aper and Maternus embrace, jokingly accusing each other of being antiquarian and scholastic, respectively. By the concluding remarks,

97. Dio, *Hist.* 53.19.3–4.
98. For the question of authorial intention in works cast in dialogue form, see M. Beard, "Cicero and Divination: The Formation of a Latin Discourse," *JRS* 76 (1986): 33–46.
99. *Dial.* 42; cf. 40.2–4. Parts of the speeches of both Secundus and Maternus are in fact lost.

Tacitus gently reminds the reader that, after all, individuals do and will continue to differ; the rhetoric of decline is only one possibility.

Tacitus and Pliny, of course, belong to the very limited circle of the Roman senatorial elite; curiously, perhaps, these two are also our earliest Roman witnesses to Christianity. Predictably, the prejudices of their education and social class made them impervious to Christian ideas. We must assume that senators like them were almost completely insulated from contact with the Christian community in Rome that was the recipient of Paul's Epistle to the Romans almost on the eve of Nero's attack.

Yet the place and function of rhetoric in the public life of the empire had changed. Between the reign of Augustus and the end of the second century every city in the Greek East that still had any vestige of democracy shed it on coming under the umbrella of Rome.[100] In Rome, where political office now came largely through imperial patronage, individual members of the upper class no longer had to appeal to the people for support.[101] Nevertheless, the imperial system had its requirements, among them an urgent need in so far-flung an empire for the public affirmation and display of the system itself.[102] Emperors were rarely seen in the provinces, and the people, citizens or not, had no political voice; yet peace brought greater prosperity and relative ease of travel, as we can see indeed from the missionary journeys of the first generation of Christians among the mixed Greek-

100. See the excellent discussion by de Ste. Croix, *Class Struggle,* 518 ff.
101. On patronage, see R. Saller, *Personal Patronage Under the Early Empire* (Cambridge: Cambridge University Press, 1982); A. Wallace-Hadrill, ed., *Patronage in Ancient Society* (London: Routledge & Kegan Paul, 1989); K. Hopkins, *Death and Renewal* (Cambridge: Cambridge University Press, 1983), chap. 3. On the place of oratory in competition for office during the Republic, see F. Millar, "Politics, Persuasion, and the People Before the Social War (150–90 B.C.)," *JRS* 76 (1986): 1–11.
102. Price, *Rituals and Power,* has shown how the temples, priests, and rituals of the imperial cult could also serve this end.

Figure 5. Provincial splendour: Aphrodisias, Tetrapylon. Second century A.D. (Photograph: Aphrodisias Excavations, M. Ali Dögenci)

speaking communities of the coastal cities. Anyone who has traveled in North Africa or Turkey will know the extent to which, by the end of the second century, any city of note had adopted an increasingly Roman appearance, sometimes owing to Roman, or even imperial, initiative, but more often the work of the local wealthy elite who rushed to imitate their Roman patrons and rulers. And with the grandiose Romanized architecture went Romanized styles of government. In Rome itself the people no longer counted (how could they, when the empire was so huge?), and the provincial cities, too, were now run by and in the interests of their wealthy citizens, who vied with one another in the lavishness of their spending.[103] We are still far from understanding the articulation of social relations in the average provincial city of the early empire, but it is clear enough that this spending provided a physical setting not only for the festivals characteristic of the Greek East during this period[104] but also for public rhetoric. The buildings demanded a *praxis,* the civic pride its own articulation, the proud identification with Rome a verbal as well as artistic expression. We can see, from the elaborate reliefs of its Sebasteion (temple of the imperial cult), how far the notables of the small city of Aphrodisias in southwest Turkey were prepared to go, and from the epigraphic evidence for Hadrian's new Greek league, the Panhellenion, how willingly leading provincials accepted imperial patronage.[105] It was enough that the league existed, just as the very existence of the Aphrodisias Sebasteion (and presumably many others like it elsewhere) demonstrated the sense of a set of links at multiple levels between the local community and the center of power.

The buildings, and the cities generally, required and got an appropriate discourse. Yet given our own cultural stress on content over form, on originality over technique, modern scholars have viewed the literary output of this milieu with disapproval if not actual hostility.[106] From the literary point of view, the productions of the period are seen not only as sterile and empty but also as both explicitly and implicitly derivative.

Roman imperial culture, especially in the cities of the Greek East, in the second century, a crucial time for the incipient

103. See esp. P. Veyne, *Le pain et le cirque* (Paris: Seuil, 1976).

104. See A. J. Spawforth and S. Walker, "The World of the Panhellenion" (parts 1 and 2), *JRS* 75 (1985): 78–104 and 76 (1986): 88–105.

105. See R. R. R. Smith, "The Imperial Reliefs from the Sebasteion at Aphrodisias," *JRS* 77 (1987): 88–138; and R. R. R. Smith, "Simulacra gentium: The *Ethne* from the Sebasteion at Aphrodisias," *JRS* 78 (1988): 50–77.

106. See, e.g., J. J. Murphy, *A Synoptic History of Classical Rhetoric* (New York: Random House, 1972), 177 ff., for a typically dismissive approach;

Christian faith, had become in political terms a spectator culture. Men looked on at the civic rituals of their own towns, in which rhetorical displays occupied a large role, and viewed the emperor, if at all, from far away. If they entered imperial political life, it would be a matter of affirmation rather than of conflict.[107] Showing, performance, and affirmation became as important as argument.

It was precisely in these Greek cities that Christian communities first became established. I have emphasized in the earlier part of this chapter not only the figural aspect of Christian language but also the declaratory. While some of the Christian writings of the second century ("apologetic") were designed explicitly to persuade, and to explain and justify Christian belief and practice, the quality of proclamation was also of fundamental importance. It is best seen in the case of Christian preaching, the hidden iceberg of Christian discourse; Christians not only sought to teach but, through regular repetition and by continually drawing on and reinterpreting an increasingly familiar body of texts, also constantly reaffirmed the essence of the faith and the constituents of membership of the Christian community. The regular homily, like the episcopal letter, might use the arguments of apologetic, but it also confirmed the structure of the Christian groups and continually reminded the faithful of the essentials of the system to which they now belonged. Preaching therefore became for most Christians the medium through which they heard and were regularly reminded of the interpretation of the Scriptures, the relation of the Old Testament to the life of Jesus, and of both to the overall divine providence. While many preachers themselves saw their role as that of teacher, that func-

---

G. Kennedy, *Greek Rhetoric Under Christian Emperors* (Princeton: Princeton University Press, 1983), 50, while warning against this modernizing view, seems to accept the premises on which it is based ("the world was growing old and tired . . .").

107. On civic life in the second century as based on a "model of parity" see P. Brown, *Making of Late Antiquity,* 27–53.

tion was carried out as much by the regular repetition and affirmation of familiar themes as by actual argument. It may be objected that the content of that system was by no means as yet agreed upon—and indeed, the struggles for agreement on major issues of definition were to intensify rather than diminish. But consciousness of such a system was what the preachers tried to convey.

Signs, metaphors, and symbols were among the most useful tools, both for their own suggestiveness and for their referential capacity. Yet it still seems necessary to explain how this highly self-conscious and systematized conception of religion, conveyed not only through ritual but also through the regular repetition of familiar themes and familiar words, relates to the pagan context, in which on the whole it seems to have been notably lacking.[108]

Of the various attempts so far made to place Christian rhetoric in relation to this classical—that is, pagan—background, two in particular stand out. The first, in which Christian writing is seen as representative of a new and in some sense more spiritual climate of opinion, locates rhetoric in a relation of contrast, even while recognizing its debts in matters of form to existing genres. Thus, for instance, Reardon places his discussion of Christian literature in a section called "le nouveau," in contrast to "l'ancien." [109] The development of Christian discourse is thus put in a historical context, but given an explanation in terms of perceived general religious change, for which it is at the same time the evidence. The second approach presents the question in terms of association, either tracing the appropriation of classical

108. For the Jewish background of preaching and teaching in the synagogue, see the remarks of A. Momigliano, "Religion in Athens, Rome, and Jerusalem in the First Century B.C.," *Annali della Scuola Normale di Pisa*, 3d ser., 14 (1984): 873–92.

109. B. Reardon, *Courants littéraires des IIe et IIIe siècles après J.-C.* (Paris: Belles Lettres, 1971), 275–308.

rhetorical elements by Christian writers[110] or seeing Christian rhetoric as restoring the vitality that Maternus in Tacitus's *Dialogus* associated only with the Republic.[111]

But while we must indeed both read Christian writing against its own historical context and be fully aware of the extensive common ground in technical matters between Christian and pagan writers, the view of Christian oratory as revitalizing classical rhetoric is in danger of placing too much premium on the impact of a relatively small number of outstanding Christian writers, and of reading them against too narrow a classical background. Whether or not we can agree with Maternus that oratory was in decline, it is undeniable that Tacitus's dialogue considers only political oratory as practised by the elite in Rome itself. As in Tacitus's historical work, the subject matter is rigorously limited to the traditionally senatorial, and thus to judicial or forensic oratory; despite the author's own complaints about the difficulty of writing in that mode in the early second century,[112] the abundant outpouring of epideictic in both Greek and Latin in the context of the civic life of the early empire is passed over in silence.

Almost too conveniently, the lament for the decline of oratory that appears at the end of the first century not only in Tacitus's *Dialogus* but also in a whole range of contemporary Latin writers coincides exactly with the composition in A.D. 100 of Pliny's *Panegyricus* in praise of the Emperor Trajan, in which I do not believe any modern critic has yet found anything to commend.

110. See, e.g., the useful discussion by R. D. Sider, *Ancient Rhetoric and the Age of Tertullian* (London: Oxford University Press, 1971); cf. the different perspective of Chadwick, *Early Christian Thought.*

111. For a not dissimilar view, but one from a more theoretical standpoint, see G. A. Kustas, *Studies in Byzantine Rhetoric* (Thessalóniki: Patriarchal Institute for Patristic Studies, 1973), 40–41. On Tertullian, see also Kennedy, *Art of Rhetoric*, 610: "a force unheard in Latin rhetorical literature since the *Philippics* of Cicero."

112. *Ann.* 4.32: "nobis in arto et inglorius labor."

Yet Pliny's speech is merely an overgrown and metropolitan example of what could be heard in provincial cities on every public occasion. Since relatively few examples survive, it is hard to get a real sense of the extent to which these showpieces of oratory— praising a city on an anniversary, commemorating a festival— were regular concomitants of urban life. A single speech was rarely enough: audiences used to sitting through a number of speeches on the same theme would soon develop a fine judgment on performance. Because we are not practised ourselves in hearing or reading epideictic oratory, we are likely to bring the wrong expectations and ask the wrong questions: To what extent is it propaganda? Is it evidence for imperial policy? Our eyes glide over the repeated words, the overfamiliar tropes, the allusions that seem so cliché-ridden. *Pietas, gravitas, tranquillitas*—to us they may seem hackneyed, but to a contemporary they would probably seem reassuring and impressive. Like ritual, rhetoric involves performance, and in epideictic oratory performance is all.[113] In a more comprehensive view of rhetoric, it can be seen that it was not merely Christian oratory that brought a new vigor into discourse. Neither the orators and writers of the Second Sophistic nor their audiences would have recognized themselves in the modern conviction of their "sterility" and emptiness; far from being marginalized into "mere rhetoric," their oratory was an integral part of civilized life with a definite and public role to play.

That role can be seen as an affirmation of the social order. The orators did not advocate upsets to the political or social system; rather, they confirmed its structure and reminded their audiences of its articulation and of their place within it. The vocabulary and tropes were familiar because by using this technique the orators were more likely to impress and reassure, while the

113. See L. W. Rosenfeld, "The Practical Celebration of Epideictic," in *Rhetoric in Transition,* ed. E. E. White (New York: Praeger, 1980), 131.

whole was perpetuated and supported by an educational regime designed to equip men to write and speak in exactly this manner. The Second Sophistic and the heyday of epideictic also focused attention even more than formerly both on words and on oral delivery. Now, when the Second Sophistic is at its height, we begin to see popular acclamation as a regular feature of public life both at Rome and in the provincial cities.[114] Even the senators began to shout their assent instead of debating issues by the third century. But before that, crowds in the theater and before provincial governors acclaimed or attacked the famous and chanted their approval or dissent. From this point to the end of the empire, and long into Byzantium, verbal acclamation was to remain a major part of public occasions. It was soon put to use in the struggle between pagan and Christian groups, and Paul had already encountered it at Ephesus, when the cry "Great is Artemis of the Ephesians" roused and unified the people until they all shouted it in unison. Changes were taking place in the role of orality in the society of the early empire, in the context of which Christian discourse must be understood.[115]

Thus the people found a role again, and a relation with public events and public figures. And oratory, oral presentation, kept

114. For a brief outline of the development of acclamation in the empire, see C. M. Roueché, "Acclamations in the Roman Empire," *JRS* 74 (1984): 181–88.
115. Acts 19:23–34. On the general issues see, e.g., W. Ong, *Orality and Literacy: The Technologizing of the Word* (London: Methuen, 1982); B. Stock, *The Implications of Literacy: Written Language and Models of Interpretation in the Eleventh and Twelfth Centuries* (Princeton: Princeton University Press, 1983); *New Literary History* 16, no. 1 (Fall 1984), special issue entitled "Oral and Written Traditions in the Middle Ages." J. Goody, *The Logic of Writing and the Organization of Society* (Cambridge: Cambridge University Press, 1986), places an overstrong emphasis on literacy alone as the key factor in the creation of a power discourse, at least so far as early Christianity is concerned. Not simply a heightened awareness of books, but also the practice of regular oral teaching (which is much harder for us to recapture), served to diffuse its ideas.

its central position even while Maternus claimed that it was dead. As for the Christians, they had learned the practice of preaching the faith from the Jews (who also, we should not forget, inhabited the urban centers of this Roman world), and themselves engaged in preaching against the background of public oratorical displays, rapt audiences, spoken discourse, and popular acclamation. Christian sermons, it may be argued, had a different message, but their form, expression, and delivery linked them as much with the rhetorical practice of the wider society as with Jewish custom. Even the highly figural nature of Christian discourse, its extensive reliance on metaphor and symbol, can be read in this way. For the epideictic oratory of the empire, especially the panegyric literature of which there was so much, relied heavily for its effectiveness on a repertoire of symbolic evocation.[116] The repeated allusions to stock examples (historical figures, "good" and "bad" emperors, kingly figures like Cyrus and Alexander), stock virtues, and stock themes form the technical armory of evocation. Epideictic oratory does not use the language of signs to refer to a higher certainty, but it does use the language of symbol to achieve its performative effect.

The Place of Christian Discourse

The context for the development of an ostensive Christian discourse was thus more favorable than the proponents of the rhetoric of decline would care to admit. Not only did Christian preachers find conditions in which oratory was valued and admired, but they also deliberately addressed themselves to a much wider audience than the pagan sophists. Moreover, the Christians themselves claimed one great advantage over their rivals:

116. For the concept of evocation see D. Sperber, *Rethinking Symbolism* (Cambridge: Cambridge University Press, 1975), 85 ff.

their rhetoric, they believed, constituted a pathway, through signs, to truth.[117]

The relation of Christian discourse to classical discourse is not to be seen in terms of linear progression from the one to the other. Nor is it a simple one. It remained convenient to be able to decry classical rhetoric even while drawing heavily on it. When Tertullian asks what Athens has to do with Jerusalem, or when Jerome, two centuries later, presents himself as a Ciceronian, not a Christian, they do so with the uneasy feeling that in their own case the resolution has been far from complete. At times it was useful to emphasize the difference, to stress the "simplicity" of Christian literature over the conceit and trickery of rhetoric, or to insist on the irrational, the leap of faith, contrasted with the implied rationality of worldly learning. Such self-conscious exploitation of the tensions in which Christian writing existed was taken to extremes by Tertullian, a writer deeply imbued with traditional rhetoric yet one who seems to glory in paradox for its own sake.[118] The tensions in his work indicate both the closeness of Christian to pagan writing and its struggle to disengage itself from it.

I have emphasized the performative, declaratory aspect of Christian rhetoric, to which its reliance on the figural was an important contributor, and tried to indicate the receptivity of audiences increasingly accustomed to the similarly performative but more ritualistic epideictic. In a certain sense, Maternus was right: for a time, at least, the old style of deliberative political oratory was indeed dead, and when it received a revival, it was largely in the context of Christian political strife in the fourth

117. Grant, *Letter and Spirit*, 120 ff. provides a useful discussion of the terminology employed.
118. Chadwick, *Early Christian Thought*, chap. 1; but see R. H. Ayers, *Language, Logic, and Reason in the Church Fathers* (Hildesheim: Georg Olms Verlag, 1979).

century.[119] But oratory in the wider sense was far from dead; on the contrary, it already enjoyed a new vigor in the conditions of the second-century cities and was aided then and later by the school training that continued to be the norm. This was the reality of the situation in the cities where Christianity grew. Many of the Christian writers of the period were themselves converts from the educated class, well trained in classical rhetoric. Thus they had both an advantage and a problem: they needed to use classical rhetoric and indeed could not help but do so, yet they also wished to separate themselves from it. The use and theory of signs, in which they both drew on and differentiated themselves from earlier philosophical and literary theory, was one way of achieving this end.

The relation was not by any means static, however. As Christianity was slowly evolving its own body of theoretical knowledge during the early empire, rhetoric, not philosophy, was coming to provide a pagan counterpart. The development of Christianity coincided exactly with the technologizing of rhetorical education, which was in fact virtually the only form of education available. From the first century on, a growing body of rhetorical theory came into existence, which, together with practical exercises, formed the main educational fare. With this rival body of knowledge, which was also in most cases the source of their own conceptual training, Christians had no choice but to engage. The problem was that the theory and practice of rhetoric not only informed the attitudes and tastes of every educated person; they also provided the only frame within which the truly paradoxical nature of the faith could be put into words at all.

The Christian discourse of the early period ranged from gospel narratives through preaching to a highly rhetorical level of apologetic. Without arguing that any of it reached wide audiences at this stage, I have tried to suggest certain ways in which

119. See chapter 4.

its characteristic features were appropriate in their historical context. In doing so I have not attempted to discuss another feature that may be equally important, namely the appeal to the emotions, greatly aided though it must have been by the evocative nature of Christian language. The subsequent history of Christian rhetoric in the Roman Empire can be seen, however, in terms of a tension between two impulses, each essential to the formation of a genuinely powerful and totalizing discourse.

The first, to be discussed mainly in chapter 4, is the steady urge, which obviously gains momentum with imperial support for Christianity in the fourth century, toward absorption of all the forms of classical rhetoric and their appropriation within a Christian system. Classical rhetoric constituted both a technique—a form of specialized knowledge[120]—and a means of institutional power. The appropriation is represented at its height by the great Christian writers and speakers of the later fourth century—in Greek, Gregory of Nazianzus and John Chrysostom; in Latin, Ambrose. Other figures, especially Augustine and Jerome, represent both the possibilities and the exceptional difficulty of this process.

Appropriation had certain corollaries, which can be seen in the second of the tendencies I have mentioned: namely, that it carried the risk of smoothing out or even eliminating altogether the essentially paradoxical element at the heart of the faith. This is partly a matter of feeling, the heart as well as the head; but it is also in this case a function of the specific problems of representation posed by Christianity. Thus, while the fourth-century Christian orators produced compositions worthy of the greatest of their classical models,[121] a parallel development can be observed, sometimes even led by the same people, toward empha-

120. Cf. La Capra, *History and Criticism*, 42.
121. See Kennedy, *Greek Rhetoric*, 50: "Gregory of Nazianzus and Synesius of Cyrene are the greatest Greek orators since Demosthenes and have not since been surpassed."

sizing the paradoxical side of Christian discourse, which in some cases led to the questioning of the very possibilities of language as a vehicle for religious truth. From the fourth century onward the newly emergent state-supported church was engaged in a prolonged struggle, through a long series of general councils, to find ways of defining its faith in linguistic terms. The whole question of the capacity of language to represent truth therefore became one of the most profound issues of the day, and we can see in the writings of many contemporaries how crucial it was that it be solved. I shall return in chapter 5 to the paradoxical, or in a sense, the "irrational," side of Christian rhetoric. Finally, we must broaden the inquiry to consider the question of images and Christian representation in general.

For when all is said and done, Christianity implies belief; it claims a relation to truth. There was indeed a contradiction to be resolved. In an episode from a short story by Milan Kundera, set in Czechoslovakia before 1989, a rather naive young man finds himself, to his surprise, going completely against the party line and believing in God. He is summoned by the local committee: "Please tell how you, a young man, can believe in God!"

The young man replies, "I can't help it. I don't want to believe in Him. Really I don't."

The teacher laughs. "But there's a contradiction in that."[122]

122. M. Kundera, "Edward and God," in *Laughable Loves*, trans. S. Rappaport (Harmondsworth, Eng.: Pelican Books, 1985), 217–18.

CHAPTER THREE

Stories People Want

Just tell a story. Make sure it's a good story. It doesn't even have to be a true story, but stories are what people want.

Would not an old woman who sings a story to lull a little child to sleep have been ashamed to whisper tales such as these?

Origen c. Cels. 6.34

Christianity was a religion with a story. Indeed, it possessed several different kinds of stories. But two were pre-eminent: *Lives,* biographies of divine or holy personages; and *Acts,* records of their doings, and often of their deaths. Narrative is at their very heart; for whatever view one takes of the evolution of the Gospels, the remembered events and sayings from the life of Jesus were in fact strung together in a narrative sequence and ever afterward provided both a literary and a moral pattern. Neither the *Passions* of martyrs nor, later, the *Lives* of saints could escape this model, and I shall have more to say on the latter in a later chapter. But the Acts of the Apostles also provided an example of Christian narrative, and one that was eagerly followed up at the very time when story was enjoying a prominence unusual in the ancient world. This is what I want to explore in this chapter, for the existence of Christian stories within this narrative context cannot be without significance for the diffusion of Christianity as a whole.

The Christian stories were stories with meanings—let us call them myths. They were mostly evangelistic. But they were also just stories. I shall not attempt here to discuss the narrativity of the Gospels themselves. Rather, what I shall do is ask how the late-second- and third-century stories later labeled "apocryphal acts" relate to the reception of narrative in the period which was so crucial for the diffusion and reception of Christian discourse. For we must remember that even while the sense of a New Testament canon was coming into being, the concept of what counted as a Christian writing was far different and more elastic than it was to become later, and infinitely more so than it is for us, brought up as we have been on the canonical New Testament. Even after the acceptance of the canon, and, therefore, their exclusion from it, the popularity and influence of the apocryphal narratives was so enormous and so widespread at all levels that they must rank high among the contributors to the early Christian world-view. The formation of the New Testament canon in the late second century may have succeeded in defining a set of authoritative texts, but it had no dampening effect at all on the proliferation of the subapostolic "acts" and other such writings.

An association of some kind has commonly been assumed between the apocryphal acts—stories supposedly of apostolic times and centered on characters such as Peter and Paul—and the ancient novel, subject of much current controversy.[1] They

1. See, notably, E. von Dobschütz, "Der Roman in der altchristlichen Literatur," *Deutsche Rundschau* 111 (1902): 87–116; R. Söder, *Die apokryphen Apostelgeschichten und die romanhafte Literatur der Antike* (Stuttgart: Kohlhammer, 1932; repr. 1969); H. Dörrie, "Die griechischen Romane und das Christentum," *Philologus* 93 (1938): 273–76; also B. E. Perry, *The Ancient Romances* (Berkeley and Los Angeles: University of California Press, 1967); R. Merkelbach, *Roman und Mysterium in der Antike* (Munich: C. H. Beck, 1962); Reardon, *Courants littéraires;* G. Anderson, *Ancient Fiction: The Novel in the Graeco-Roman World* (London: Croom Helm, 1984). A useful brief guide to the large literature can be found in T. Hägg, *The Novel in Antiquity* (Berkeley and Los Angeles: University of California Press, 1983) (with 154 ff. on the Christian texts); a good brief discussion is also contained in E. A. Clark, *The Life of Melania the Younger: Introduction, Translation, and Commentary* (New York: Edwin Mellen Press, 1984), 158 ff.

share many features in common—damsels in distress, the quest theme, the miraculous escape, and so on. A great deal of attention has thus been given to origins and supposed influences, to the idea of romance as a kind of semipopular literature, and to the location of this literature within the social and religious climate of the period, conceived in terms of insecurity, the supposed breakdown of "stable traditions and fixed values,"[2] and the need of individuals for social identity.[3] Their status as narratives, however, remains relatively unexplored. Yet two other tendencies in recent scholarship indicate that it might be fruitful to look at the Christian acts in their pagan context precisely as narratives. After all, the Christian story is itself a biography. In New Testament scholarship, which has moved beyond the attempt to reconstruct from the canonical Gospels a historical record of the life of Christ, an enormous literature has been building up on their literary status, and especially the relation they might have to contemporary Greco-Roman biographical literature.[4] Further, the broader interest now being taken in narrative from both the literary-critical and the historical points of

2. Hägg, *Novel in Antiquity,* 89, discussing Perry and Reardon.
3. Cf. the similar explanation offered by Reardon for Christian literature generally.
4. Excellent guides are now available, e.g., D. Tiede, "Religious Propaganda and Gospel Literature of the Early Christian Mission," in *ANRW* II.25.2, ed. H. Temporini and W. Haase (Berlin: Walter de Gruyter, 1984), 1705–29; D. Dormeyer and H. Frankemolle, "Evangelium als literarische Gattung und als theologischer Begriff. Tendenzen und Angaben der Evangelienforschung im 20. Jahrhundert, mit einer Untersuchung des Markus Evangeliums in seinem Verhältnis zur antiken Biographie," in ibid., 1543–1704. For the relation of the Gospels to "divine man" literature (aretalogy) see, e.g., M. Hadas and M. Smith, *Heroes and Gods: Spiritual Biographies in Antiquity* (New York: Harper & Row, 1965); M. Smith, "Prolegomena to a Discussion of Aretalogies, Divine Men, the Gospels, and Jesus," *Journal of Biblical Literature* 90 (1971): 181–84; H. C. Kee, "Aretalogy and Gospel," *Journal of Biblical Literature* 92 (1973): 402–22; J. Z. Smith, "Good News Is No News: Aretalogy and Gospel," in *Christianity, Judaism, and other Greco-Roman Cults. Part 1: New Testament,* ed. J. Neusner (Leiden: E. J. Brill, 1975), 21–38.

view has begun to find its way into theological studies in general.[5] Both these tendencies suggest a consideration of the narrative quality of later Christian writing in similar terms.

The question of truth and fiction immediately arises. In a recent treatment, it is claimed that biography is "always a human story, and always (in intention) a true story. Perhaps these two marks of biography make it the form of story most nearly suited to Christian faith."[6] One could argue the case in exactly opposite terms: that one should ask rather why orthodox Christianity chose to express itself in (mainly biographical) narrative, and what advantages it thereby gained; in particular, whether it was not the very construction of the narratives that gave the appearance of truth.[7] There were in practice a number of different techniques by which Christian literature claimed to represent a higher truth, including, as we have seen, allegory and symbol, by which it was possible to accommodate not merely disparate elements but actual contradictions.[8] Another method, we now see, was the deployment of narrative form to inculcate and confirm belief. If in some of its aspects Christian literature related to

5. For a good introduction, see W. J. T. Mitchell, ed., *On Narrative* (Chicago: University of Chicago Press, 1980); R. T. Scholes and R. Kellogg, *The Nature of Narrative* (Oxford: Oxford University Press, 1966; repr. 1976). In relation to history, see H. White, "The Question of Narrative in Contemporary Theory," *History and Theory* 23 (1984): 1–33. In theology, see, e.g., J. D. Crossan, *The Dark Interval: Towards a Theology of Story* (Niles, Ill.: Argus Communications, 1975); J. D. Crossan, *Four Other Gospels* (Minneapolis: Winston Press, 1985), 187 (on narrative gospels and discourse gospels); in general, see S. W. Sykes, "The Role of Story in the Christian Religion: An Hypothesis," *Journal of Literature and Theology* 1 (1987): 19–26; in relation to ascetic literature, see Harpham, *Ascetic Imperative*, 67 ff.

6. J. W. McClendon, Jr., *Biography as Theology* (Nashville: Abingdon Press, 1974), 189; see also chapter 4 below.

7. For truth as a function of narrative shape, see M. J. Wheeldon, "'True Stories': The Reception of Historiography in Antiquity," in Cameron, ed., *History as Text*, 36–63.

8. For the motif of misunderstanding as a technique of gospel narrative, see J. Smith, "Good News Is No News," 36; on the tension in story between secrecy (the need for interpretation) and sequence (narrative), see F. Kermode, "Secrets and Narrative Sequence," in Mitchell, ed., *On Narrative*, 79–97.

the prevailing mode of epideictic by its emphasis on performance, repetition, and proclamation, in others, and perhaps
more fundamentally, it built up its own symbolic universe by ex-
ploiting the kind of stories that people liked to hear, and which
in their turn provided a mechanism by which society at large
and the real lives of individuals might be regulated.[9] The better
these stories were constructed, the better they functioned as
structure-maintaining narratives and the more their audiences
were disposed to accept them as true.

In the early period, the stories in question are not yet the lives
of saints, nor yet in general the passions of martyrs, but the Gospels and their successors, the apocryphal acts of the apostles,
and the stories of the life of Mary, which we encounter from the
second century onward—at much the same time, it should be
said, as biography seems to have replaced traditional classical
history in popularity (at least in Latin) and when lives of philosophers, sages, and political figures of past history competed
for attention with the stories in the ancient novel.[10] It is not surprising, perhaps, that psychological or sociological explanations
have readily suggested themselves for this phenomenon.[11] Increasing individualism may be part of the explanation;[12] nevertheless, I wish here to consider it in more closely literary terms.

9. See Berger and Luckmann, *Social Construction of Reality*, 115 ff.
    10. For a general introduction to biography, see Cox, *Biography in Late
Antiquity*, 3–65; C. H. Talbert, "Biographies of Philosophers and Rulers as
Instruments in Religious Propaganda in Mediterranean Antiquity," *ANRW*
II.16.2, ed. H. Temporini and W. Haase (Berlin: Walter de Gruyter, 1978),
1619–51. On the literature of the second century and later as a sign of cultural
"decline," see Habicht, *Pausanias*, 126–27, 129.
    11. See also, on "the invocation of pervasive moods and of public misfor-
tunes" as a mode of historical explanation (especially in cultural or religious
matters), P. Brown, *Making of Late Antiquity*, chap. 1; P. Brown, "Approaches
to the Religious Crisis of the Third Century A.D.," *EHR* 83 (1968): 542–58
(reprinted in his *Religion and Society in the Age of St. Augustine* [London:
Faber, 1972], 74–93), in reaction to Dodds, *Pagan and Christian*.
    12. See Averil Cameron, "Redrawing the Map: Early Christian Territory
After Foucault," *JRS* 76 (1986): 266–71.

One feature of the apocryphal *Acts* that is particularly striking in view of the attention given to language in more theoretical
Christian writing is the degree of self-consciousness they too
display toward speech, preaching, and indeed language. The action in the late-second-century *Acts of Peter*[13] is centered on a
seemingly artless narrative. Yet the spoken word is interposed
with striking frequency, sometimes conversationally, but more
often in the form of direct or indirect preaching. A typical passage combines both kinds: "Now on the Lord's day, as Peter dis-
coursed unto the brethren, and exhorted them unto the faith of
Christ, there being present many of the senate and many knights,
and rich women and matrons, and being confirmed in the faith,
one woman that was there, exceeding rich, which was surnamed
Chryse, because every vessel of hers was of gold . . . said unto
Peter . . ."[14] In Rome, the four "concubines of Agrippa the pre-
fect" were "smitten in their souls," "hearing the word concerning chastity and all the oracles of the Lord."[15] Peter delivers long
speeches before he is crucified and when he hangs from the
cross. His words are far from artless: "It is right to mount upon
the cross of Christ, who is the word stretched out, the one and
only, of whom the Spirit saith: 'For what else is the Christ, but
the word, the sound of God?' So that the word is the upright
beam whereon I am crucified. And the sound is that which
crosseth it, the nature of man. And the nail which holdeth the
cross-tree unto the upright in the midst thereof is the conversion
and repentance of man."[16] The story has already undergone sev-

13. On the date, see Stevan L. Davies, *The Revolt of the Widows: The Social World of the Apocryphal Acts* (London: Feffer & Simons, 1980), 6–7. On
the Acts generally, see F. Bovon et al., eds., *Les Actes apocryphes des apôtres*
(Geneva: Labor & Fides, 1981), with useful bibliographical indications at
289 ff.
14. *Acts of Peter,* in *The Apocryphal New Testament,* ed. and trans. M. R.
James (Oxford: Oxford University Press, 1924), 330.
15. Ibid., 332.
16. Ibid., 335.

eral stages of interpretation. And it is the word which converts. In the *Acts of Paul,* Thecla "sat at a near-by window and listened night and day to the word of the virgin life as it was spoken by Paul." She saw many flocking to Paul, and longed herself "to stand in Paul's presence and hear the word of Christ; for she had not yet seen Paul in person but only heard his word." Her mother tells Thecla's fiancé that her daughter at the window "devotes herself to a strange man who teaches deceptive and subtle words"; in a striking phrase, she says she is "like a spider at the window, bound by his words." [17] In the *Acts of Andrew,* the narrative is orchestrated by the contrast between the speech that changes lives and the "dullness and unbelief and simplicity" of those who will not hear, as also between the noisy support of the crowd and the silence of the proconsul at Andrew's martyrdom. [18] Andrew, too, delivers a passionate oration from the cross, while the proconsul "stood there speechless." [19]

The contrast is not confined to the *Acts.* In the so-called *ps.- Clementines,* part narrative, part theological tracts, formal disputation between Christian and pagan spokesmen and the contrast between Greek learning and the true message are main elements. The cities of the empire are said to be inhabited by men "full of false doctrine," men who "profess to be grammarians and sophists," while Christians like Barnabas speak not with "mere rhetorical finery," but "simply and without circumlocution." Welcomed by the "simple people," who, the author says, "willingly assented to such sincere words, and welcomed his simple manner of speech," Barnabas is subjected to the clever arguments of so-called "scholars and philosophers"; the writer points the contrast in a telling way: "Barnabas did not support

17. E. Hennecke, *New Testament Apocrypha,* ed. W. Schneemelcher, Eng. trans. R. M. Wilson, 2 vols. (London: Lutterworth Press, 1963–1965), 2:355 [hereafter cited as Hennecke-Schneemelcher].
18. Ibid., 420–21, 422.
19. Ibid., 422.

his assertions with plausible arguments, but brought forward, even from the circle of the bystanders, numerous witnesses of the sayings and marvels he proclaimed."[20] The entire account depends on a self-conscious articulation of the contrast between the "simplicity" claimed for Christian discourse and the sophistry of its opponents, of whom the most flamboyant—the extreme example—is Simon Magus, not a deceiver on any ordinary scale but a magician.[21] Indeed, magic accusations stand on both sides for the sharpness of the contrast.[22] Crowd reaction is also strikingly present in these writings. Barnabas's preaching, for instance, is greeted with noisy laughter; "Clement" berates the crowd for not recognizing and accepting the "heralds of God's will whose manner of discourse gives no evidence of schooling in grammar, but who communicate to you the divine commands in simple, artless words so that all hearers can follow and understand what is said."[23]

It is tempting to set aside these difficult texts of uncertain date as being outside the mainstream of Christian development.[24] They do pose problems not so far satisfactorily resolved in relation to their literary level, audience, milieu, and intention—parallel problems, in fact, to those presented by the ancient novels themselves, and remaining unanswered for the same reason, which is simply the difficulty of diagnosing with any exactness the social composition and educational level and tastes of the population of the average Greek-speaking provincial town in this period. The confusion that still reigns over the interpretation of the novels reveals all too clearly our uncertainty in this

20. Ibid., 538.
21. Ibid., 541–42.
22. Ibid., 562. See also Davies, *Revolt of the Widows*, 17 ff.; G. Poupon, "L'accusation de magie dans les Actes apocryphes," in Bovon et al., eds., *Les Actes apocryphes*, 71–93.
23. Hennecke-Schneemelcher 2:539.
24. On the date, see Hägg, *Novel in Antiquity*, 163.

area.[25] While admitting that there has been no full study of the audience of the novel, Thomas Hägg nevertheless describes it as "rootless, at a loss, restlessly searching."[26] Any answer that might be given would certainly have to confront the whole question of literacy—not merely functional literacy, but also reading and education, on which Christianity certainly had an impact. Meanwhile, various conjectures have been offered about the milieu of the Christian texts, for instance, in view of the apparent prominence of women, either that individual texts, particularly the *Acts of Paul,* were composed by women or even that all of them originated in communities of women and expressed female rebellion through the stress they laid on continence and the rejection of conventional social bonds.[27] Most critics have been struck by the prominence of virginity as a theme in these texts, and have wanted to find a general explanation for this literature in these terms.[28] But this is to get things the wrong way around: such speculation is inevitably premature until the writings have been read with more attention to the curious texts that they are. And we cannot escape the fact that these fanciful nar-

25. For an argument against a religious origin, see J. J. Winkler, "Lollianus and the Desperadoes," *JHS* 100 (1980): 155–66. The same author's *Auctor et Actor: A Narratological Reading of Apuleius's "The Golden Ass"* (Berkeley and Los Angeles: University of California Press, 1985) presents a literary interpretation of Apuleius that, even if not ultimately convincing, marks a considerable advance on earlier readings; see further below.

26. Hägg, *Novel in Antiquity,* 90, 242.

27. For the first view, see ibid., 95–96; for the second, Davies, *Revolt of the Widows;* and D. MacDonald, *The Legend and the Apostle* (Philadelphia: Fortress Press, 1983), also emphasizing the *Acts'* oral qualities, and suggesting that the Pastoral Epistles were written in answer to them. See also J. Perkins, "The Apocryphal Acts of the Apostles and Early Christian Martyrdom," *Arethusa* 18 (1985): 211–30. Tertullian, *De baptismo* 17, refused to believe that the *Acts of Paul* could be genuine, since they showed a woman preaching. On women in the *Acts,* see E. A. Clark, *Women in the Early Church* (Wilmington, Del.: Edwin Mellen Press, 1983), 77 ff.

28. See further J. Laporte, *The Role of Women in Early Christianity* (New York: Edwin Mellen Press, 1982).

ratives contributed, more than their critics would like to admit, to the total Christian world-view.

On the level of story, the apocryphal *Acts*, together with the infancy gospels and the *Protevangelium* of James (the story of Mary, the mother of Jesus),[29] constitute a world of discourse complementary to and filling the many gaps left blank in the Gospels. Officially recognized or not, it was this body of material on which later generations of preachers dwelt so often and so lovingly, and indeed we can sometimes detect the gentle exasperation that nearer-contemporaries evidently also felt when the details they would have liked—the upbringing of the Virgin, for instance—are simply omitted from the Gospel stories. Countless extant later homilies draw their material from this source. In the *Protevangelium* we find a tender portrait of Mary as a little girl, in contrast to the laconic references to her in the canonical Gospels: she walked at only six months old, and when her parents placed her on the altar to be brought up thereafter in the Temple, "she danced for joy with her feet," and her parents knew, because the child made no attempt to cling to them, that it was God's work. After this she lived in the Temple until she was twelve years old, "nurtured like a dove" and fed by an angel.[30]

As a subject of discourse, the Virgin Mary provided congenial opportunities for Christian writers. A very different rhetoric of the Virgin had developed by the fourth century, by which time

29. For the latter, see James, *Apocryphal New Testament*, 38–49; Hennecke-Schneemelcher 1:374–88. Generally, R. E. Brown et al., eds., *Mary in the New Testament* (London: Geoffrey Chapman, 1978), 243 ff.; H. Graef, *Mary: A History of Doctrine and Devotion* (London: Sheed & Ward, 1963–65; repr. 1985), 35 ff. M. Van Esbroeck, "Les textes littéraires sur l'Assomption avant le Xe siècle," in Bovon et al., eds., *Les Actes apocryphes*, 265–86, gives a detailed conspectus of the surviving texts, and thus an invaluable insight into the diffusion of one of the Marian themes.
30. Hennecke-Schneemelcher 1:374–75; cf. 493.

Figure 6. The adolescent Virgin tended by angels. G. de Crayer. Seventeenth century. (Photograph: Musées Royaux des Beaux-Arts de Belgique)

her place in Christian mythology had become a far more critical theological matter and her meaning as chief symbol of virginity more central to Christian practice;[31] but even after that, the affective narratives of the second- and third-century apocrypha are the foundation on which the elaborate rhetoric of Byzantine homilies was built, from Proclus of Constantinople in the early fifth century to George of Nicomedia in the ninth. Those that we have, though numerous, represent only the merest fraction of the homilies actually delivered through this long period; far more elaborate and technical, indeed often virtuoso, in their rhetoric than the early stories, they nevertheless still testify to the power of an imaginative world at which the New Testament itself does no more than hint, but which in practice formed the real world of Christian belief. The ninth-century writer, preaching on the presentation of Mary in the Temple after countless others had dealt with exactly the same topic, and aspiring to add a fresh nuance of his own, spends more time on the qualifications of Joachim and Anna as the parents of the Virgin and on their prayer for the child than he does on the Virgin's birth and the parents' gift of their child to the Temple—the writer's ostensible starting point. So familiar are the stories that he can take the narrative itself completely for granted and concentrate purely on his own rococo variations.

The same narrative strain can also be seen in relation to other themes traceable to the story-telling impulse of Christian groups in the Roman Empire. Particularly striking are the stories of the descent of Christ into Hell and two other themes relating to the Virgin: her lament at the cross, and her "taking up" to Heaven (in Greek terms, her *koimesis*). Of these, the story of Christ's descent into Hell after his death and his raising of Adam, the first man, and the patriarchs, prophets, and saints, appears in a

31. See Averil Cameron, "Virginity as Metaphor"; and below, chapter 5. On Mary in narrative and as image, see Harpham, *Ascetic Imperative*, 179 ff.

Figure 7. Joachim and Anna, the parents of the Virgin. Vat. ms. gr. 1613. (Photograph: Courtauld Institute of Art)

version attached to the *Acts of Pilate,* but may well be older.[32] Much-loved themes in later homiletic are already well developed here: the announcement to the dead souls by John the Baptist of the coming arrival of Christ to release them, the dialogue between Satan and Hades, the attempt to bar the gates of Hell and their bursting asunder, the arrival of Christ in glory, and the binding of Satan and the raising of the dead. The Greek homilies of the fourth to the sixth centuries on the theme, often wrongly attributed and still largely in need of modern editing, make of these components a dramatic drama with heightened and even comic dialogue.[33] Whether or how these Greek homilies are re-

32. See Hennecke-Schneemelcher 1:470–476; J. Kroll, *Gott und Hölle. Der Mythos vom Descensus-Kampf,* Studien der Bibliothek Warburg 20 (Leipzig, 1932; repr. Darmstadt: Wissenschaftliche Buchgesellschaft, 1963).
33. See G. La Piana, *Le rappresentazioni sacre nella letteratura bizantina dalle origine al secolo IX* (Grottaferrata, 1912); S. MacCormack, "Christ and

Figure 8. Christ's descent into Hades. Israhel van Meckenem, Passion Series. (Photograph: Warburg Institute)

lated to contemporary or earlier Syriac religious poetry,[34] or whether any direct connection can be traced between these and later Western cycles of mystery plays, the basis of the material on which they draw undoubtedly lies in the apocryphal narratives, a mushroom growth of religious stories expressed in narrative form.

Of the two Marian themes I have mentioned, that of her "dormition"—the taking up of her physical body to Heaven from her last home at Ephesus, where her deathbed was attended by the miraculous appearance of the apostles—was to provide one of the best-loved cycles in Byzantine art, as well as the starting point for numerous homilies in the middle and later Byzantine periods. Here we can see something of the way Christian stories could penetrate both popular and "high" literature, for it is striking to find that the most notable surviving examples, by the patriarch Germanus and St. John Damascene in the eighth century, were written by learned churchmen, whose thought-world was yet still the world of the apocrypha.[35] But even though the theme of the dormition of the Virgin did not achieve this more or less official status in art and literature until after the formal recognition of the feast on 15 August in the late sixth century,[36] the story on which it was based certainly had earlier origins, and the formative period for this diffusion and penetration of Christian narrative lay in Roman rather than Byzantine times. The Syriac texts in question seem to belong to the

---

Empire: Time and Ceremonial in Sixth-Century Byzantium and Beyond," *Byzantion* 52 (1982): 287–309; for the vivid manner, with frequent apostrophe and exclamation as well as dialogue, see C. Datema and P. Allen, *Leontii presbyteri Constantinopolitani Homiliae,* Corpus Christianorum series graeca 17 (Turnhout: Brepols, 1987), intro.

34. See, e.g., S. P. Brock, "Syriac Dialogue Poems: Marginalia to a Recent Edition," *Le Muséon* 97 (1984): 29 58.

35. See Van Esbroeck, "Textes littéraires."

36. See Averil Cameron, "The Theotokos in Sixth-Century Constantinople: A City Finds Its Symbol," *JThS,* n.s. 29 (1978): 95 and n. 4, with references.

fifth century,[37] and probably therefore coincided with the generally increased attention given to the Virgin at the time of the
Council of Ephesus in A.D. 431. Even if they go no further back
than that as fully worked out narratives, their development demonstrates the same impetus toward Christian narrative as the
earlier stories we have considered. Again it was a matter of filling
in the gaps in the Gospel stories and working out their logical implications. As the Virgin acquired a recognized near-divine status as the sinless vessel through which the Incarnation became a
possibility, so the narrative impulse demanded that the manner
of her death should also acquire a special explanation: "The ful-
fillment, under the name of Mary, of a totality made of woman
and God is finally accomplished through the avoidance of death.
The Virgin Mary experiences a fate more radiant than her son's:
she undergoes no Calvary, she has no tomb, she doesn't die and
hence has no need to rise from the dead."[38] It was the required
end of the story.

Let us consider another theme from the Marian repertoire:
Mary at the cross and after the death of Jesus. Here we can see
the continuity of Greek practice: the ritual lament (still part of
Greek funerary custom) and the emphasis in the Greek and Byzantine church on the night-long service with the mourning
around the bier symbolizing the dead Christ.[39] But the homilies
of the seventh and eighth centuries and later that include accounts of Mary and the women at the crucifixion and their
lament over the dead Christ direct their elaborate rhetoric,

37. See M. Jugie, *La mort et l'assomption de la Sainte Vierge*, Studi e testi
114 (Vatican City, 1944); A. Wenger, *L'assomption de la Très Sainte Vierge
dans la tradition byzantine du VIe au Xe siècle*, Archives de l'orient chrétien 5
(Paris, 1955).

38. J. Kristeva, "Stabat Mater," trans. L. S. Roudiez, in *The Kristeva
Reader*, ed. T. Moi (Oxford: Basil Blackwell, 1986), 168.

39. M. Alexiou, *The Ritual Lament in Greek Tradition* (Cambridge: Cambridge University Press, 1974), with considerable emphasis on the language of
the laments.

wordplay, and imaginative variation toward the same aim of overlaying, explaining, and expanding the basic narrative as we find being employed from the apocryphal narratives onward.[40] The homilists struggle to control the bareness of the Gospel record: "Now there stood by the cross of Jesus his mother and his mother's sister, Mary the wife of Cleophas and Mary Magdalene" (John 19:25). George quotes the text and continues, "Indeed, the other evangelists agree that the women who had come stood a long way away and witnessed what was done from there; but John says that the mother of Jesus and the two Marys stood beside the Cross itself. Is there a disagreement among the heralds of the truth? Certainly not!" As George explains, the apostles and the women with them did not dare to approach closer and so watched from a distance, but Mary kept close and stood firmly by, whereupon the other two women, seeing her fortitude, thought they should go and support her.[41] In another instance, he explains why it might appear to the unsuspecting that she was absent from the Last Supper: Jesus himself had given her the task of overseeing the servants and the household arrangements; thus she was present and listening even if she did not actually recline with the twelve.[42]

The rationalizations and variations of a ninth-century homilist, who was, incidentally, writing for an urban audience with high expectations, have come a long way from the stage at which these themes and stories were first formulated. Yet they do show how much effort was made to fill out and expand material presented in the New Testament. Tantalizingly laconic as the latter was in many other areas as well as in its references to the mother of Jesus, it was filled out and expanded with interlock-

40. See, e.g., George of Nicomedia *PG* 100.1457, 1489; and see H. Maguire, *Art and Eloquence in Byzantium* (Princeton: Princeton University Press, 1981), 97 ff.

41. The discrepancy remains a problem: see Graef, *Mary*, 24–25.

42. *PG* 100.1462 f.

ing and complementary narratives, of which the example of the treatment of Mary is simply one of the most striking. "Starting from this programmatic material, rather skimpy nevertheless, a compelling imaginative construct proliferated," of which the presentation of the mourning Virgin in our Byzantine homilies represents one of the later stages, where "the relationship with Mary and from Mary was to be revealed as the prototype of love relationships."[43]

The figure of Mary in the early Christian period underwent development in two main directions, both evident as early as the second century and typical of the progress of Christian discourse. First, her fundamental role in the doctrinal implications of the story of the incarnation of Christ were steadily explored and defined, from Justin and Irenaeus on;[44] second, the stories about Mary, which were so influential and widely known from at least the second century,[45] bypassed the practical questions of church order and orthodoxy by their very human and imaginative appeal and were central in the evolution of a mental world of narrative and story in which an explanation could be found for any awkwardness, however difficult. In their variation over the centuries they show the remarkable tenacity and elasticity of Christian discourse and its capacity to adapt to any social conditions.[46]

43. Kristeva, "Stabat Mater," 164; the psychological as well as the narratological utility of these stories is also evident. For the multivalence and functional utility of the idea of Mary, see M. Warner, *Alone of All Her Sex: The Myth and Cult of the Virgin Mary* (London: Weidenfeld & Nicolson, 1976).

44. See chapter 4.

45. On Mary in the possibly earlier originals of the *Gospel According to the Hebrews* and similar writings, see R. Brown et al., eds., *Mary in the New Testament*, 243–44.

46. If in the early stages it was Mary's maternal love and purity that were most emphasized, later it was often her capacity to symbolize power. In our own time, the increased reporting of Marian apparitions has been con-

In this early Christian world, although there were already strong impulses toward control of the discourse, there were also, as we can see from the case of the apocryphal *Acts,* considerable advantages in variety and multiplicity. It is clear that the *Acts* did not develop in isolation; in a happy phrase, Thomas Hägg has referred to their literary landscape as "covered by a dense, almost impenetrable vegetation."[47] It is just this obscurity that makes it so difficult to relate them to secular literature or, indeed, oral stories.

The commonest recourse of scholars faced with this problem has been to appeal to the notion of a popular literature,[48] "narratives coming from the people for the people."[49] Written for "entertainment, instruction, and edification,"[50] they are said to represent "the popular piety of the second and third century."[51] It is easy to detect in such judgments a considerable investment in presenting a certain view of the development of the early church, especially in interpretations that emphasize their role in the separation of "primitive Catholicism" from Gnosticism.[52] Nevertheless, the many scholars who stress the incorporation of

---

nected with reactionary political and social movements; see B. C. Pope, "Immaculate and Powerful: The Marian Revival in the Nineteenth Century," in *Immaculate and Powerful: The Female in Sacred Image and Social Reality,* ed. C. W. Atkinson et al. (Boston, Mass.: Beacon Press, 1985), 173–200.

47. Hägg, *Novel in Antiquity,* 162.

48. See, e.g., Söder, *Die apokryphen Apostelgeschichten,* 216, 187; see also W. Schneemelcher and K. Schäferdiek, in Hennecke-Schneemelcher 2: 167–88; Clark, *Life of Melania,* 254 nn. 85–86 ("light entertainment"). But cf. Robinson and Koester, *Trajectories,* 191–92 (more literary than earlier Christian writing); Achtemeier, "Jesus and the Disciples" ("apologetic"); and contra, H. Koester, *Introduction to the New Testament,* 2 vols. (Philadelphia: Fortress Press, 1982), 2:308 ff.

49. Söder's view, approved by Schäferdiek, in Hennecke-Schneemelcher 2:169.

50. Schneemelcher, in ibid., 273.

51. Ibid., 275.

52. See ibid., 168, 170 n. 4, 176–77; Robinson and Koester, *Trajectories,* 191–92 with n. 114.

"romance" motifs and the like are usually also importing a view of the literary level of the ancient novel that needs to be defended. Only if we knew more about the readership and circulation of the novels and the *Acts*[53] would we be in a better position to judge which of these approaches might stand further emphasis.

Some critics, indeed, have seen in the *Acts* a "literary" quality that sets them apart from other early Christian writing, and even disqualifies them from serious consideration in that context. They have been seen sometimes as belonging to the world of art rather than the world of instruction, and even as having acquired their apocryphal status for that reason.[54] Still others deny them the label "literature" altogether, on the grounds that they combine disparate kinds of material and are not literary in intent.[55]

Yet the ready use of the term "popular" rests on a multitude of preconceptions. It can convey either praise or blame, serving equally to stress the "newness" of Christian writing[56] or to dismiss it from serious consideration. It might be better to give it up for the time being in relation to this topic. But there is also the problem of the uncertain definition of "literature" itself.[57] If for the moment, however, we continue to use it in its common, if imprecise, sense—that is, as denoting consciously composed writings that, though perhaps of varying sorts, do not include documents and the like—we can isolate two features of Chris-

53. The useful discussion by Roberts and Skeat, *Birth of the Codex,* 67 ff., leaves unproven the idea that readers of both were predominantly lower class.

54. See Reardon, *Courants littéraires,* 308; for a discussion of Söder's view (*Acts* as popular, novels as sophistic), see J.-D. Kaestli, "Les principales orientations de la recherche sur les Actes apocryphes des apôtres," in F. Bovon et al., eds., *Les Actes apocryphes,* 66.

55. F. Overbeck, *Über die Anfänge der patristischen Literatur* (repr. Basel: B. Schwabe, 1954).

56. Dibelius, *Fresh Approach,* 57, 68.

57. Not always recognized in this field as a serious issue, the standard histories being largely descriptive; see, e.g., E. J. Goodspeed, *History of Early Christian Literature,* rev. R. M. Grant (Chicago: University of Chicago Press, 1966).

tian literature that deserve much fuller study than can be given here and that undoubtedly aided the establishment of the system as a whole.

The first of these features concerns the position of Christian literature in the early period in relation to literacy, orality, and educational levels in society at large. The matter is not to be settled simply by designating much of it as "popular literature" without further discussion. In fact, although it may be difficult to prove, it does seem likely that the Christian communities had an impulse toward literacy and reading that was generally lacking in pagan culture,[58] and thus that the growth of Christianity as a system brought with it a changed attitude toward texts. Christianity early became a religion of books, even if it was not for some time strictly a religion of "the book." Following Paul's example, other Christian leaders wrote pastoral letters to Christian communities—one of the earliest was Ignatius of Antioch— and these letters were evidently preserved and read.[59] Nevertheless, it is probably not the case that Christians were more literate than pagans as a result of their interest in religious writings, even though there is more Christian than pagan evidence from Egypt, which provides us with much of our material on ancient books and readers.[60] Most Christians converted not through reading books but because of personal contact or hearsay. Many of the early apologies are relatively learned productions, written by converts who had themselves been educated in secular rhetoric; they may thus be misleading, and do not give a fair impression of the average medium or the level of the arguments that were employed. Nor do the answers provided by pagan critics represent the actual discussion, which surely went on at an indi-

58. On Christian reading, see esp. Roberts and Skeat, *Birth of the Codex*, 67–68; also Roberts, *Manuscript, Society, and Belief*, 25 ff.
59. Harris, *Ancient Literacy*, 220–21. On Ignatius, see above, chapter 2.
60. Harris, *Ancient Literacy*, 319; cf. 299.

vidual level.[61] No doubt in practice most conversions happened for the same mixture of reasons and were based on the same, often erroneous suppositions that lead to such changes in individual religious or political affiliations in all societies; witness the pagan critics of Christianity like Celsus or sceptical witnesses like Lucian, who combine good observations with prejudice and misinformation.

Yet Christians not only produced an increasing amount and variety of written material, even in the early stage when followers of the religion formed only the tiniest of minorities, but also gave their written texts a special status. Even the illiterate will have been aware from the oral teaching, which was so prominent a part of early Christianity, that religious texts mattered. Fundamentally, neither they nor the classically educated converts were able to ignore the Old Testament. The very struggles over the explanation and interpretation of this material remind us of how tenaciously Christians in fact stuck to it even though it proved so recalcitrant.

This attachment to written texts was remarkable in itself, even if it did not penetrate far down the social scale; there was little or nothing in Roman culture as a whole to induce such a development, and many features in this highly traditional society in fact worked against it. The highly educated elite of the Roman Empire was trained almost exclusively in the techniques of rhetoric, and with a powerful ethos that put a premium on "classical" works of the past. Unlike the Christians, this elite had no interest in sharing its privileges with society at large, not even when the needs of imperial government might have suggested that it was in its interests to develop a larger literate class (in this sense it was not at all like the African societies recently

61. On the Christian/pagan apologetic, see Wilken, *Christians as the Romans Saw Them;* S. Benko, *Pagan Rome and the Early Christians* (London: Batsford, 1985).

studied by Jack Goody).[62] In these circumstances, Christianity brought a new leaven, possessing as it did a potential for ideological development that was glaringly lacking in the society around it.

The second feature of Christian literature to which I referred above is precisely its inclusivity. Many Christian writers were themselves highly educated and employed the style, form, and vocabulary of their own earlier training.[63] This was indeed an essential technique if they were to gain support from their pagan counterparts. Christians had to fend off pagan charges that Christianity relied on its appeal to the lowest classes of society: "in private houses also we see wool-workers, cobblers, laundry-workers, and the most illiterate and bucolic yokels, who would not dare to say anything at all in front of their elders and more intelligent masters."[64] Needless to say, such charges should be taken with a pinch of salt, and Christians were well able to deal with them. But the consciousness that Christianity and Christian discourse could and should appeal to all was never forgotten, and the Pauline claim to truth—in contrast to the "wisdom of the world"—could be turned to good effect, converting charges of uncouth lack of refinement into claims of simplicity and truth. Quite apart from any polemical value, experienced practitioners knew the value and the power of a rhetoric that could use all the techniques of classical training while combining them with a wider appeal.[65] Rhetoric was essential: "Now,

62. Goody, *Logic of Writing;* J. Goody, *The Interface Between the Written and the Oral* (Cambridge: Cambridge University Press, 1987).

63. Of the very large literature on this subject, see W. Jaeger, *Early Christianity and Greek Paideia* (Cambridge, Mass.: Harvard University Press, 1961); and Laistner, *Christianity and Pagan Culture.*

64. Origen *c. Cels.* 3.55.

65. On Augustine, see A. M. Kleinberg, "*De agone christiano:* The Preacher and His Audience," *JThS,* n.s. 38 (1987): 16–33. See also Auerbach, *Literary Language,* 33 ff.

the art of rhetoric being available for the enforcing either of truth or falsehood, who will dare to say that truth in the person of its defenders is to take its stand unarmed against falsehood?" Nevertheless, the aim of Christian teachers must be perfect intelligibility, "such clearness of speech that either he will be very dull who does not understand them, or that if what they say should not be very easily or quickly understood, the reason will lie not in their manner of expression, but in the difficulty and the subtlety of the matter they are trying to preach."[66] Sometimes the claim to simplicity was obviously bogus, juxtaposed as it was with full utilization of the rhetorical repertoire.[67] But it remains true that in the realm of Christian preaching,[68] and within the wide range of Christian literature, it was possible to cut across the barriers of class and genre in a way not open to classical writers. In its own way, the apocryphal literature did that too.

It was not that there was one voice for the high and another for the low. When it suited them, preachers and writers made much of the relation of "simple" and educated. However, the eagerness with which by the fourth century some sectors of the educated elite themselves took up these very "simple" genres and expressions of Christian literature needs an explanation. The *Life of Antony* provides the best-known model. A text of the mid–fourth century in its Greek form, it takes an aggressively "simple" stance in its depiction of the uneducated hermit in the Egyptian desert; from the beginning, it is clear that the contrast between Christian virtue and the corruption of the world has been extended to intellectual matters. Antony comes of a well-to-do family, yet he is said to have shunned schooling,

66. *De doctr. christ.* 4.2.3, 8.22.

67. Jerome is an offender here; see also E. Norden, *Die antike Kunstprosa vom VI. Jahrhundert v. Chr. bis in die Zeit der Renaissance,* vol. 2 (Leipzig: B. G. Teubner, 1909), 529 ff.

68. See H. T. Kerr, *Preaching in the Early Church* (New York: Fleming H. Revell, 1942); see also R. W. Smith, *The Art of Rhetoric in Alexandria: Its Theory and Practice in the Ancient World* (The Hague, 1974).

just as he rejected rich food; he was interested in faith, not in rhetoric, and was unimpressed when he received an imperial letter.[69] There is an element of disingenuousness about all this: "though he was without formal schooling, he was yet a man of ready wit and understanding," well able to argue with pagan philosophers or write a reply to Constantine and his sons.[70] The *Life* is by no means the artlessly simple text it may at first sight appear. After it had been rapidly translated into Latin and promoted by Jerome, it was read with earnest attention in the highest Roman circles, while Jerome himself adopted its mixture of apparent simplicity and actual sophistication in the hermits' lives that he composed in imitation of it.[71] It is only modern readers who have been embarrassed at the idea that a work which professes deliberately to reject the rhetoric of the learned could really have been written by the sophisticated Athanasius.[72]

Like these Christian *Lives* in the fourth century and later, the stories in the apocryphal *Acts* had an important part to play in the creation of a Christian universe of myth, which would be both totalizing in itself and capable of development at different intellectual and literary levels. The canonical Gospels had left many loose ends and required expansion from an early date; since they themselves constituted stories—at least in part—this expansion also naturally took story form. That it frequently resulted in multiple or contradictory versions was a considerable help in achieving the elasticity that proved in later years to be

69. *V. Ant.* 1, 80, 81.   70. *V. Ant.* 72, 81.
71. See further below.
72. For a Coptic original of the existing Syriac version, see R. Draguet, *La vie primitive de S. Antoine conservée en syriaque,* Corpus Scriptorum Christianorum Orientalium 417–18, Script. Syr. 183–84 (Louvain, 1980); on its authorship (as not by Athanasius but by someone in his milieu), see T. D. Barnes, "Angel of Light or Mystic Initiate?" *JThS,* n.s. 37 (1987): 353–68. Influential readers of the *Life* included Gregory Nazianzus, Jerome, and Augustine. For the problem of literary levels in relation to the Christian reading public of the late fourth century, see A.-M. Palmer, *Prudentius on the Martyrs,* 32–56.

Figure 9. Ascetic landscape with voices: SS. Antony and Paul. A. Dürer.
Early sixteenth century. (Photograph: Warburg Institute)

such a strength.[73] While second-century writers like Clement of Alexandria developed a presentation of Christian ideas in the terms of Greek philosophy, and Tertullian applied to Christian themes the skills of traditional rhetoric, these works, "popular" or even heretical by orthodox standards, created a set of Christian stories for the next generations. Not just in the canonical books, or through official church teaching, but in the whole spread of Christian inventiveness in the first centuries it was thus established what kind of reality Christianity would construct for the empire when the time came.

The model that these texts presented for the individual Christian was a life of asceticism.[74] The integrative Pauline rhetoric of the body is both diverted and confirmed by this equally emphatic negative focus. We can see the power of its appeal, for instance, in the history of the Thecla legend subsequent to the late-second-century *Acts*, which has been traced so persuasively by Dagron.[75] Here an early heroine from the apocryphal literature famous for her uncompromising asceticism (and of whose attraction Peter Brown has persuasively written)[76] becomes the subject of elaborate legend and cult—with a fifth-century *Life* of some rhetorical pretensions—and the object of the devotion of such figures as Gregory of Nyssa and Gregory of Nazianzus.[77]

73. For an interesting discussion of these issues by a New Testament scholar, see J. L. Houlden, *Connections* (London: SPCK, 1986), esp. 87–88, 94 ff.

74. For the Nag Hammadi collection, see Crossan, *Four Other Gospels*, 30–31. For the apocryphal *Acts*, see Y. Tissot, "Encratisme et Actes apocryphes," in Bovon et al., eds., *Les Actes apocryphes*, 109–119; P. Brown, *Body and Society*, 153 ff.

75. G. Dagron, *Vie et miracles de Sainte Thècle*, Subsidia Hagiographica 62 (Brussels, 1978); and R. Albrecht, *Das Leben der heiligen Makrina auf dem Hintergrund der Thekla-Traditionen* (Göttingen: Vandenhoeck & Ruprecht, 1986), 239 ff.

76. P. Brown, *Body and Society*, 156–57.

77. For the library at Seleucia where Egeria read the *Acts*, see Dagron, *Vie et miracles*, 55 ff.; Albrecht, *Leben der heiligen Makrina*, 286–87; the social milieu of the miracles recounted in the texts is upper rather than lower class

Even though the origins of the ascetic ideal preached in the apocryphal *Acts* and elsewhere may remain obscure and controversial,[78] by the second century the idea was evidently compelling. Moreover, the discourse of a religious system can, once established, have its own dynamic force. It is highly unlikely that the ascetic values so prominent in the apocryphal *Acts* and other Christian literature are separable from wider moral developments in society.[79] The apocryphal *Acts* cannot be marginalized; they too were integrally related to the general culture of the second and third centuries. But more specifically, they provided for Christians a set of texts in which the Christian self was expounded, first in narrative terms and then in terms of asceticism; the writing of Christian texts would shape Christian lives.[80]

These narratives are also important in terms of their relation to time, that is, the way they join with the canonical books and other early Christian writings to place the developing Christian mythology within a chronological world-view, by "an embedding of the present in a total time-sequence."[81] Since Christian discourse was based on events perceived to have happened in historical time, it was itself inescapably anchored in time, and furthermore, in a concept of time that united worldly events with the mythic past and future. Narrative was thus a particularly suitable form of expression for Christian discourse, since,

(Dagron, 123), even though the *Miracles* as a text is more "popular" in literary style than the *Life* (152 f.). For the long-term influence of the apocryphal texts, see also MacDonald, *Legend and the Apostle*, 90 ff.

78. P. Brown, *Body and Society*, 51 ff. emphasizes the fluidity of Christian groups and Christian identity in the first century and the consequent attraction of an option that served to define the latter more closely; on his reading of I Cor. 7, Paul was already arguing against such extremism. For the literary expression of asceticism, see chapter 5 below.

79. The connection is explored esp. by P. Veyne, "The Roman Empire" and "Famille et l'amour," though see P. Brown, *Body and Society*, 15 n. 51.

80. Harpham, *Ascetic Imperative*, 67 ff.

81. The phrase is Houlden's.

despite the efforts of semiotics to divorce it from time, narrative too stands in essential relation to time; stories have beginnings and endings, or they are not stories.[82] The stories in the Gospels, and the stories with which the bareness of the Gospel narratives was filled out, serve to bind Christian discourse ever more closely to linear time, and thus to an appropriation by the present of the past and the future, even while its figural and paradoxical aspects function on a synchronic level.

Consideration of the apocryphal *Acts* in terms of narrative theory leads to a further question touching on the traditional formulation of their relation to the ancient novel. What is fictional about these narratives? Why should they not simply be classified as novels too?

At first sight, they look very like secular fiction, with their immediately recognizable romance motifs—recognition scenes, travel narratives, wonders, young girls in trouble, and so on.[83] The speeches with which they are liberally supplied are anything but straightforward or artless utterances. Sometimes a hardly concealed erotic undercurrent is detectable alongside the more overt stress on virginity. And the fantasy element, whether in the story of Thecla's ordeal in the arena or, for instance, in the *Acts of Thomas*,[84] is as closely related to the novelistic literature as the theological interest of these texts is set apart from it. The very term "acts" (*praxeis*) links the texts with the Greek literary background.[85] And while they can be seen in social terms as rep-

---

82. E.g., in the implication of a conclusion: see F. Kermode, *The Sense of an Ending: Studies in the Theory of Fiction* (New York: Oxford University Press, 1967). In general, see P. Ricoeur, *Time and Narrative*, trans. K. McLaughlin and D. Pellauer, 2 vols. (Chicago: University of Chicago Press, 1984–85).

83. See esp. Söder, *Apokryphen Apostelgeschichten*.

84. Hennecke-Schneemelcher 2:428. See MacDonald, *Legend and the Apostle*, 18 ff.

85. See R. Mortley, "The Title of the Acts of the Apostles," *Cahiers de Biblia Patristica* 1 (1987): 105–12.

resenting a type of Christian discipleship advocated in the sub-apostolic period and characterized by asceticism, poverty, and displacement from home,[86] the actual events that they attribute to the apostolic age are in most cases clearly anachronistic and often entirely fanciful.

Still, while they are clearly not history, neither does it seem appropriate to label them as fiction and leave it at that; in some sense, if not in the same sense as in the case of history, they are different from fiction in the matter of their relation to truth.[87] They do not necessarily differ in the narrative structure itself, but in the supposition that what is narrated is in some sense true. It is not clear to what extent these Christian texts were thought of by contemporaries as historical narratives, but they certainly belong to the realm of intended truth and not, with the ancient novels, to the fictive. They cannot therefore be dismissed as a minor sub-branch of the novelistic genre. On the contrary, their narratives, so clearly in many cases the prototypes of the burgeoning later genre of saints' lives, deserve more of our attention—not just in terms of comparison with the ancient romance literature, or as indicators of the social aims and composition of second- and third-century Christian communities, but also for their role in the development of Christian discourse in the awkward early period when there were still so many gaps

86. See G. Kretschmar, "Ein Beitrag zur Frage nach dem Ursprung der frühchristlichen Askese," in *Askese und Mönchtum in der alten Kirche,* ed. K. S. Frank (Darmstadt: Wissenschaftliche Buchgesellschaft, 1975), 129–80; G. Theissen, "Wanderradikalismus. Literatursoziologische Aspekte von Worten Jesu im Urchristentum," in *Studien zur Soziologie des Urchristentums* (Tübingen: Mohr, 1979), 79–105. On the *Acts* as socially disruptive (against the Pastoral Epistles), see MacDonald, *The Legend and the Apostle,* 40 ff.

87. See Ricoeur, *Time and Narrative* 2:3; and Ricoeur, *History and Truth,* 165 ff.: Christian truth as eschatological truth, not historical truth. A writer of fictive literature might, however, employ devices used by historians so as to convey a sense of realism to his narrative; see J. R. Morgan, "History, Romance and Realism in the *Aithiopika* of Heliodorus," *Classical Antiquity* 1 (1982): 221–65.

to fill. The apologists, and the more theoretical Christian writers, might address themselves to technical matters of interpretation and exposition, necessarily reaching only small audiences, but we should not for that reason underestimate the place in the spreading of ideas occupied by imaginative development: religious storytelling.

Perhaps the nature of the evidence itself has distorted our perceptions of this literature. From the fourth century on and into the medieval period, the sheer bulk of hagiographical material is so vast that we tend to overlook this apocryphal literature as a serious influence on its origins. The texts in question are so few, and their context so hard to define, that it has been easier to leave them for the margins of scholarship, where they have traditionally had a hard time.[88] The orientation of scholarship now at last seems to be moving away from value judgments,[89] though it is still dominated by much the same questions as before. But these texts have something important to tell us, in terms of the sociology of knowledge, about how the Christian system was articulated in the early period, and thus about how it got itself established in the Roman Empire.

88. See, e.g., the harsh judgment of O. Bardenhewer, *Geschichte der altkirchlichen Literatur,* 2d ed., vol. 1 (Freiburg i. Breslau, 1913), 500–501.
89. See the historical survey by G. Poupon and discussion of present research by J.-D. Kaestli in Bovon et al., eds. *Les Actes apocryphes,* 25–47 and 49–67, respectively.

CHAPTER FOUR

The Power over the Past

Accommodation and Appropriation

With this chapter we move into the very different atmosphere of the great Christian oratory of the fourth century,
when imperial support placed Christians, and especially Christian bishops, in a new relation to political power. Even if Christians still remained numerically a minority, their representatives
could and did speak with a different voice. They had moved
onto the high ground, and knew it.

> The subject of religion falls under the head of *rhetoric* in the
> sense that rhetoric is the art of *persuasion,* and religious cos-
> mogonies are designed, in the last analysis, as exceptionally
> thoroughgoing modes of persuasion. To persuade men to-
> wards certain acts, religions would form the kinds of attitude
> which prepare men for such acts. And in order to plead for
> such attitudes as persuasively as possible, the religious always
> ground their exhortations (to themselves and others) in state-
> ments of the widest and deepest possible scope, concerning
> the authorship of men's motives.[1]

With the fourth century, the work of evangelizing took on a
new and powerful impetus, along with a range of modes designed, as we might now put it, to reach the widest possible
catchment area. To get the total picture we ought to be looking

1. Burke, *Rhetoric of Religion,* v.

at every level of Christian discourse, oral as well as written. For reasons of time and space, however, this chapter will concentrate on the high Christian rhetoric of the period, and on one aspect of it: the capacity of the great Christian preachers and writers to accommodate themselves to the modes of discourse that already prevailed, and thereby almost to take their audience by stealth, in particular by laying claim to past history. The energy that Christians put into the latter effort is summed up in Nietzsche's comment, only weeks before his collapse, that Christianity was "the vampire of the Imperium Romanum"; "the Church . . . falsified even the history of mankind into the pre-history of Christianity" and "robbed us of the harvest of the culture of the ancient world."[2]

This conquest of classical culture by Christianity, as Nietzsche saw it, made its greatest advance in the fourth century, once the constraints on the church had been removed and conversion became not only easy but often attractive. Nietzsche's description is of course a caricature. But Christianity did proceed to capture the centers of cultural power and thus to acquire their symbolic capital.[3] A jump was made: people crossed the divide, and they were increasingly people of influence and position. Not the least of the factors involved was the achievement of an adjustment between the Christian and the traditional rhetorics.

Unfortunately, modern criticism still largely polarizes the issue by starting from the assumption of a great divide between Chris-

2. F. Nietzsche, *The Anti-Christ,* in *The Twilight of the Idols and the Anti-Christ,* trans. R. J. Hollingdale (Harmondsworth, Eng.: Penguin Books, 1968), 180, 155, 183.

3. For the concept, see P. Bourdieu, *Outline of a Theory of Practice,* trans. R. Nice (Cambridge: Cambridge University Press, 1977), 159 ff. The process is signaled by G. W. Bowersock, "From Emperor to Bishop: The Self-conscious Transformation of Political Power in the Fourth Century A.D.," *Classical Philology* 81 (1986): 298–307; and see D. Kyrtatas, "Prophets and Priests in Early Christianity: Production and Transmission of Religious Knowledge from Jesus to John Chrysostom," *International Sociology* 3 (1988): 365–83.

tian and pagan; this has had the effect of obscuring the real
issues by implying that everything in fourth-century literature is
to be explained in terms of "conflict."[4] By contrast, as anthropologists and indeed theologians have realized in recent years, trans-
lating from one cultural system into another is not a straightforward process; it embraces many shades of relation, from
outright conflict to near-total accommodation.[5] In our own
case, the still common, and only partly acknowledged, triumphalist perspective has often led to the use of such inappropriate
terms as "victory" in reference to Christianity. One even gets
into problematic areas with the application of the very terms
"Christian" and "pagan," as though there were always firm and
easily detectable boundaries between them instead of a murky
overlapping area. But as anyone will at once discover on trying
to write about the process at all, we will often find ourselves
slipping unawares into statements not wholly immune from
these dangers. Our very difficulty mirrors the powerful role
played by language in Christianization.

I want to consider in this chapter some of the ways in which
Christian writers and speakers in the fourth century did indeed
convert their rhetoric into a power rhetoric in political terms,
and how they sought by using the past to suggest a more complete control of the present and the future. As I have said above,
this was only one side of the picture. Christianity appealed to
hearts as well as minds; its private side was at least as important
as its public one. That will be partly the concern of the next
chapter. For now we will concentrate first on the great public
Christian rhetoric of the fourth century and then briefly on an-

4. For an opposite view, see the key remarks of G. Dagron in his study of
Themistius, "L'empire romain d'orient au IVe siècle et les traditions politiques
de l'hellénisme: le témoignage de Thémistios," *Travaux et mémoires* 3 (1968):
1–242, esp. 1–2.
5. See, e.g., the remarks of J. Ball, "Anthropology as a Theological Tool, I:
Culture and the Creation of Meaning," *Heythrop Journal* 28 (1987): 249–62.

other characteristic Christian literary form that developed during the same period—the lives of saints. I propose to concentrate on two of the mechanisms used by Christian writers in the period: ambiguity and reenactment. Christian writers and speakers were able to use ambiguity to make their rhetoric fit the needs of the state; but in addition they claimed the past, not just through the adaptation of history, but characteristically through the writing and reading of *Lives*—the continual reworking and reenactment of idealized Christian biography, the pattern of Christian truth in action.

The first part of the chapter, then, will consider how Christians sought to legitimize their newly found political power and to ensure its transmission to future generations. Here rhetoric—not "mere rhetoric,"[6] but the formal control of central areas of public discourse—was a major tool. Through Christian rhetoric, as it was practiced in the fourth century, the cultural system implied by Christianity—Nietzsche's "consistently thought out and complete view of things," Gellner's totalizing discourse[7]—might better become established and its future be secured.[8] Language, and the control of language, are at the heart of the "struggle" between pagan and Christian culture in the fourth century.

The Public Arena

One of the most important areas of legitimizing political discourse is at once the most obvious and the most elusive: politi-

6. Cf., e.g., de Ste. Croix, *Class Struggle*, 399: "stupefying, inflated, verbose, bombastic rhetoric" (of Eusebius's *Tricennalian Oration*); by contrast, on the practical and symbolic importance of rhetoric for potential Christian leaders in the fourth century, see Spira, "Volkstümlichkeit und Kunst."
7. Nietzsche, *Twilight of the Idols*, 69; for Gellner, see above, chapter 1.
8. For the reproduction of a cultural system, see Bourdieu and Passeron, *Reproduction in Education, Society, and Culture*, vi ff.

cal theory, the theoretical discussion and justification of government—in practice, monarchy. It is here that we shall find the
greatest ambiguity.[9]

We may ask first what had happened to the cult of the emperors, apparently so characteristic of the pagan empire and so
unsuitable for the Christian. Far from coming to an abrupt end
with the conversion of Constantine, it is not hard to show that
in fact it continued. The modern historian finds this hard to explain. It seems to be difficult, for instance, to allow that the continued cult can still be held to be "religious"; it is far easier and
more convenient to suppose that it has become wholly secularized.[10] But then, how much more difficult it is to explain how the
Christian Theodosius can be said to be "adored by all peoples"
and to "receive private and public prayer all over the world," or
how there could be Christian *flamines* of the imperial cult in the
fifth century.[11] There would be nothing particularly surprising
or shocking to contemporaries about the idea of honors being
paid to the statue of Constantine in fourth-century Constantinople, even though the later sources, influenced by the concerns of
their own day, hardly permit a clear view of what sort of honors

9. The bibliography is very large; see in the first place K. M. Setton,
Christian Attitudes to the Emperor in the Fourth Century (New York: Columbia University Press, 1941); and F. Dvornik, *Early Christian and Byzantine Political Philosophy*, 2 vols. (Washington, D.C.: Dumbarton Oaks,
1966).

10. See G. W. Bowersock, "The Imperial Cult: Perceptions and Persis-
tence," in *Jewish and Christian Self-Definition*, ed. B. F. Meyer and E. P.
Sanders, vol. 3 (Philadelphia: Fortress Press, 1982), 171–241, esp. 178; and
S. Calderone, "Teologia politica, successione dinastica e consecratio in età
costantiniana," in *Le culte des souverains dans l'empire romain*, Entretiens
Hardt 19 (Vandoeuvres, 1973), 215–61.

11. *Pan. Lat.*, Pacatus 6.4; for the African evidence, see F. M. Clover,
"Emperor Worship in Vandal Africa," in *Romanitas. Festschrift J. Straub*, ed.
G. Wirth (Berlin: Walter de Gruyter, 1982), 661–74; F. M. Clover, "Le culte
des empereurs dans l'Afrique vandale," *Bulletin archéologique du C.T.H.S.*,
n.s. 15–16 (1984): 121–28.

they were.[12] Nevertheless, the highly organized public imperial cult of the early empire did eventually fade. For one thing, the social function it had performed in the principate now began to pass to the church as the latter became more important in civic life. Whereas in the early empire the temples and the organization of the imperial cult had served to mediate imperial power on an empirewide basis, it was now open to the institutional church under imperial support to take over that role. New forms of ceremony and the new physical settings provided by great churches gave Christian priests and bishops an increasingly public platform, while the temples slowly began to decline. The church developed its own ways of sacralizing the now-Christian emperors; one of them was the evolution of Christian political discourse, a theory, or rather a theology, of imperial rule.[13]

Of course, pagan imperial cult had not exactly been devoid of theory. The theoretical treatise on kingship and the formal praise of rulers constituted a literary type deeply engrained long before the Roman imperial cult as such began under Augustus. It continued to flourish—or rather, flourished all the more—alongside it.[14] The vocabulary and manner of praise of rulers had been settled in Greek for centuries before Seneca's *De Clementia* and Pliny's *Panegyricus* gave it formal recognition in Latin, and it was to receive a new impetus in the conditions of the empire in the hands of such writers as Dio Chrysostom and Aelius Aristides. The language was all-purpose, designed for repetition on innumerable public occasions. With the conversion of Con-

12. For the tangle of sources on this see in the first place Dagron, *Naissance d'une capitale*, 38 ff.; Averil Cameron and J. Herrin, eds., *Constantinople in the Eighth Century: The Parastaseis Syntomoi Chronikai* (Leiden: E. J. Brill, 1984), 263–64. The earliest are Philostorgius *HE* 2.17 and Theodoret *HE* 1.34.

13. de Ste. Croix, *Class Struggle*, 394 ff.

14. See Dvornik, *Early Christian and Byzantine Political Philosophy* 2:525 ff.

stantine came a new impetus altogether. Some writers—Eusebius, Themistius, Synesius—tackled the theme directly; many others had occasion to write in other kinds of works on the subject of the place of the emperor and empire within a Christian cosmos—Gregory of Nazianzus, John Chrysostom, and, from the pagan side (for the discussion was not simply one-sided), the panegyrists, Julian, Libanius, Ammianus, even in its way the *Historia Augusta*.[15] It was still continuing in the sixth century under Justinian, provoked by another strong emperor.[16] How are we to interpret this outpouring of theory, this "political" debate?

Remember that the debate was intensely *practical*. The range of writing that touched on the subject is vast, from the elaborate rhetoric of Themistius to the occasional glimpse of a far less formal world in the literature about the desert fathers. The prologue to the Greek *Historia Monachorum* sets out vividly the foundation of this general concern to place the Christian emperor within the context of the Christian system as a whole; the monks in Egypt remind the writer of society at large: "one can see them scattered in the desert waiting for Christ like loyal sons watching for their father, or like an army expecting its emperor, or like a sober household looking forward to the arrival of its master and liberator."[17] One of the best proofs of the power of a holy man was his power to prophesy correctly about the emperor. Here the author sets his whole description of John of Lycopolis within a frame of references to earthly power; he begins with examples of John's prophecies about Theodosius's successes against usurpers and barbarians and ends with a story

15. On this debate see esp. Dagron, "L'empire romain d'orient," e.g. 77 ff., 121 ff., 200 ff.

16. See my *Procopius and the Sixth Century* (London: Duckworth, 1985), 242–60.

17. Prologue, 7, in *Lives of the Desert Fathers*, trans. N. Russell (London: Mowbrays, 1981), 50.

that, though told by John of someone else, really related to himself, as the fathers who lived with him knew. Demons appeared to John in a vision and "showed him hosts of angels and a chariot of fire and a great escort of guards, as if an emperor was making a visit." And the "emperor" spoke, promising to take John up like Elijah, but the holy man replied, "You are not my king," and the demon disappeared.[18] In general, comparisons between Christ the king and the earthly ruler are extremely common in fourth-century Christian literature, just as later defenders of images often rested their justification on the respect paid to images of the emperor. From a rather different point of view, the *Life of Antony* is concerned to make the point that the holy man is superior to earthly rulers: when Constantine and his sons write to him asking for a reply, presumably as a sign of the favor of the holy man, Antony's response is first not to read the letter at all, and then, having been persuaded to read it, to urge Constantine to realize that Christ is the only true king.[19]

The thinking of Christian writers in the fourth century quite naturally took its examples and its terms of reference from the experience of living under an emperor—something we tend to forget when reading fourth-century political theory as a kind of patchwork of Christian and pagan elements in need of disentangling by modern scholarship. The dangers of the latter approach become obvious when we consider the case of Synesius of Cyrene, a writer at the other end of the scale from the *Historia Monachorum*, who, having been educated under the Neoplatonist Hypatia at Alexandria, ended his life as a bishop.[20] Can

18. Ibid., 64; for advice to emperors, 52.
19. *V. Ant.* 81.
20. Synesius is enjoying a vogue: see J. Bregman, *Synesius of Cyrene: Philosopher-Bishop* (Berkeley and Los Angeles: University of California Press, 1982); R. Lizzi, "Significato filosofico e politico dell'antibarbarismo sinesiano. Il *De Regno* e il *De Providentia*," *Rendiconti dell'Accademia di archeologia, letteratura e belle lettere di Napoli* 56 (1981): 49–62; J.H.W.G. Liebeschuetz,

we really know, from works of so high a literary polish as his, what he himself thought at any given time? The true Hellene, his own model, must, he says, also be "a man who is able to communicate and deal with people by being a competent practitioner of all forms of eloquence."[21] His three years as ambassador for his city in Constantinople and his call to the bishopric are deployed with equal rhetorical skill:[22] he rarely mentions the Scriptures or the name of Christ, even claiming that he will speak as a Christian in public but a philosopher in private;[23] but he was accepted by later generations as a Christian, and there is no sign that the speeches he delivered in Constantinople, in which he addressed in highly rhetorical and classicizing terms the subject of political power and kingship, were judged unsuitably pagan in character. Rather, the repertoire from earlier writers on kingship on which he drew, above all Dio of Prusa, formed a common stock shared by Christians and pagans alike. The court for which Synesius wrote his speeches was by now predominantly Christian, and the issues were not ones of Christianity versus paganism but sectarian issues within Christianity itself. Synesius can deploy with ease all the techniques and allusions of Greek rhetoric, with full panoply of mythological allegory and Platonizing language, with no fear of being misunderstood on religious grounds. Nevertheless, his hymns, which

"Synesius and the Municipal Politics of Cyrenaica in the Fifth Century A.D.," *Byzantion* 55 (1985): 146–64; J. H. W. G. Liebeschuetz, "Why Did Synesius Become Bishop of Ptolemais?" *Byzantion* 56 (1986): 180–95; J. H. W. G. Liebeschuetz, *Barbarians and Bishops: Army, Church, and State in the Age of Arcadius and Chrysostom* (Oxford: Clarendon Press, 1990); T. D. Barnes, "Synesius in Constantinople," *GRBS* 27 (1986): 93–112; D. Roques, *Synésios de Cyrène et la Cyrénaïque du bas-empire* (Paris: CNRS, 1987); Alan Cameron and J. Long, with L. Sherry, *Barbarians and Politics at the Court of Arcadius* (Berkeley and Los Angeles: University of California Press, 1992).
21. *Dion.* 1125A, 1128A–B.
22. Bregman, *Synesius of Cyrene*, 147.
23. Ibid., 155.

easily suggest lack of fervor, in fact represent an interesting and innovative blend of Greek poetic practice with a quite different, non-Hellenic tradition, which we shall meet again in later Greek Christian poetry.[24]

It had been different for Eusebius a century before, when no one could predict whether or not the Constantinian innovations would endure. But for Christians and pagans alike in the fourth- and fifth-century empire, writing about government meant writing about an emperor. Synesius adapts the old theme of rustic virtue and urban corruption in a way that points up that reality. It is a sign of real rusticity for him that his countrymen in Libya hardly know who the emperor is: "the emperor, his *amici,* and the wheel of Fortune . . . are just names that, like flames, have been kindled up to the height of splendor and then quenched."[25] Some even imagine (and here the literary tone of the passage comes out even more clearly) that Agamemnon is still king and Odysseus one of his *amici.* Synesius himself was of course far from rustic, though he might like to play on the theme of himself, the ambassador to Constantinople, as outsider. He knew how to write a mirror for the ruling prince, even if to us the *De Regno* seems to go dangerously near the edge in implicating the young emperor Arcadius in its condemnation of his advisers.[26] He knew, too, that political theory in the context of empire entailed panegyric. But the incorporation of the Greek philosophical and rhetorical tradition of ruler theory in a work designed for a Christian court was no longer a problem.

Between the reign of Constantine and the writing career of Synesius in the early fifth century considerable development had taken place in Christian public rhetoric. The greatest Christian

24. Ed. and comm. N. Terzaghi (Rome, 1949); C. Lacombrade (Paris, 1978); A. Garzya (Torino, 1989).
25. *Ep.* 148, 1549A.
26. Could the work have been delivered in Arcadius's presence as it now stands? We have no independent indication of its reception.

orators of the fourth century—John Chrysostom,[27] Basil, the two Gregorys, Ambrose—did not, of course, leave their Christianity in any doubt. They were able to speak with such confidence on major public issues not simply because the role of bishop now gave them a much wider platform than the pulpit itself might suggest; they could in fact restore to traditional rhetoric its popular platform, supported by institutional authority.

But they could also draw with great effect on a surrounding atmosphere of shared language. One of the standard techniques of persuasion lies precisely in the deliberate exploitation of areas of ambiguity, the appeal to and subsequent use, that is, of themes and language already familiar. In the spreading of ideas there is a tension between the need to show compatibility with an existing framework and the attraction of a complete change. Both these strategies can be seen at work in the Christian rhetoric of the period, but in Christian political discourse it is naturally the first that is more prominent. In these first generations of imperial support, Christians no longer preached revolution; on the contrary, we can observe a natural and powerful impulse toward demonstrating Christianity's compatibility with the political system of the empire. A realignment of Christian discourse toward the new political situation was essential, in particular if the degree of support shown by individual emperors toward the church was to be turned to ideological advantage. Just as the apocryphal literature of the second and third centuries had a serious evangelizing role, so too did the panegyrics and works of political theory of the fourth century and later; far from being just "empty rhetoric," they were essential instruments in the wider establishment of a lasting Christian political ideology.[28]

This is where the easy terms "Christian" and "pagan" can be

27. For the preaching of John Chrysostom and its relevance to the political situation in which Synesius was also involved, see also Liebeschuetz, *Barbarians and Bishops*, 166–88.

28. For this aspect of political oratory, see the suggestive contributions of G. Seidel, "Ambiguity in Political Discourse," in M. Bloch, ed., *Political Lan-*

particularly misleading. It has traditionally been seen as a problem that Synesius clothed his treatise on kingship in a Christian empire in the language of Dio Chrysostom, and that a pagan, Themistius, successfully represented the political position of successive Christian emperors. It is a temptation to suppose that Synesius was never really a Christian at heart, or else to deal with the difficulty by eliminating whole areas of discourse from consideration by designating their awkward features as "purely stylistic," as though literary style were somehow extraneous to content.

Gilbert Dagron was able to move the discussion onto new ground in his very interesting study of Themistius[29] by arguing that the pagan-Christian divide is not the main point at issue in this rhetoric of political rule; rather, it is about the nature and ideology of the Constantinian empire itself. On the one side stands Themistius, a pagan, advocating dynastic legitimacy (he came to the fore first as a spokesman of Constantine's son Constantius II), the authority of the emperor, and the unity of the empire—an ecumenical vision that is also the vision of Eusebius's *Life of Constantine*.[30] Paradoxically, it would seem, the Eusebian theory that evolved for the first Christian emperor is developed and reinforced, under even more aggressively Christian successors, by a pagan philosopher. On the side opposite Themistius stand the Emperor Julian, Libanius, and Synesius, supporting the traditional cause of the independence and regeneration of cities and the forceful suppression of barbarians; they are joined by Ammianus Marcellinus and the *Historia Augusta*.[31] The pagan-

---

guage and Oratory, 205–26; and D. Parkin, "The Rhetoric of Responsibility: Bureaucratic Communications in a Kenya Farming Area," in ibid., 113–39, esp. 116–117.

29. See above, note 4. I have also benefited from discussions on this subject with Scott Bradbury.

30. Dagron, "L'empire romain d'orient," 77–78.

31. This is in no way to suggest that the *Historia Augusta* is a work of pagan polemic: see Alan Cameron, *JRS* 55 (1965), 240–49; and R. Syme, *Ammianus and the Historia Augusta* (Oxford: Clarendon Press, 1968).

Christian division, therefore, cuts across other, political, differences; nor is it surprising that Themistius, whose career shows
remarkable tenacity and resilience in changing circumstances,
should have attracted the criticism of his pagan friends.[32] They
may employ it for different ends, but these writers actually have
in common a high level of shared vocabulary: the imagery of the
ruler as good shepherd, God as father of all, man made in the
image of God, the magnanimity of the good ruler—all are part
of the common language of ruler theory since Plato, and available to Christians and pagans alike.[33] Such a common vocabulary was a powerful asset for Christian writers in reaching into
existing cultural territory, just as it enabled in turn a pagan like
Themistius to speak for Christian emperors.

How this convergence of rhetorical vocabulary could work in
practice can be seen from what Themistius has to say on religious toleration. As a supporter and spokesman of Julian's enemy Constantius II, his career had been in temporary eclipse
during Julian's reign; presumably he lay as low as possible, even
though he was a pagan himself. But with the death of Julian and
elevation of Jovian in A.D. 363, Themistius comes back into
public view. In an important speech,[34] he argued against the
hard line being urged on the new emperor by Christian lobby-
ists. He claimed that if Jovian followed his advice, he would be a

32. Dagron, "L'empire romain d'orient," 62–63.
33. It has been customary, esp. in the light of N. Baynes, "Eusebius and the
Christian Empire" (in *Byzantine Studies and Other Essays* [London: Athlone
Press, 1955; repr. 1974], 168–72), to refer much of this terminology to lost
Hellenistic treatises on ruler cult, but it should be seen against a wider background of ultimately Platonic ideas; see S. Calderone, "Eusebio e l'ideologia
imperiale," in *Le trasformazioni della cultura nella tarda antichità. Atti del
convegno tenuto a Catania, Università degli Studi, 27 sett.–2 ott. 1982* (Rome,
1985), 1–26; and for Themistius, Dagron, "L'empire romain d'orient,"
158–59.
34. *Or.* 5, delivered at court six months after the death of Julian; see also
Socrates *HE* 3.26; and Dagron, "L'empire romain d'orient," 163–65.

new Constantine.[35] It is a Constantine we may not ourselves recognize, but in making the claim Themistius followed the instincts of a natural political orator. It also demonstrates the rhetorical requirements of the moment: over the next twenty years Themistius was to speak on behalf of emperors infinitely less tolerant than Jovian. Nor did his argument for the maintenance of an equilibrium between pagan cults and Christian church seem to damage him in the eyes either of Christian friends like Gregory of Nazianzus or of the Christian emperors who continued to employ him.[36] Themistius thus demonstrates the engagement of Christians and pagans alike after Constantine with the traditional categories of ruler theory and their desire to appropriate them for contemporary conditions. The uses to which the arguments were put might differ widely, but it was just this convergence of themes and vocabulary that made it possible for a Christianized political discourse to become established.

But complete unification was still far away; meanwhile the process of adaptation could not be anything but jerky and uneven. For one thing, the Emperor Julian, no mean rhetorician himself, attempted to bring about a dislocation in the flow of Christian discourse. Having practised it himself, in his orations on Constantius, he knew the power of rhetoric and endeavored to control Christian access to it by his abortive measures forbidding Christians to teach in rhetorical schools.[37] Perhaps Constantine himself, in the so-called *Oration to the Saints*,[38] and Eusebius in the *Life of Constantine* and the two major speeches from the last years of the emperor's life,[39] had taken the pace too quickly, pushing what Eusebius likes to call the "new strain" of

35. *Or.* 5.70D.
36. *Or.* 5.68D.
37. Cf. the criticism offered even by the pagan Ammianus in *Res Gestae* 25.4.
38. See Lane Fox, *Pagans and Christians*, 629–35.
39. See above, chapter 2.

Christianity too abruptly into the domain of traditional culture. Certainly there is a self-consciousness and a sense of incongruity about all these works that betrays the unease of their authors.[40] Christian orators of the later part of the fourth century seem to have been more cautious and more willing to make concessions to traditional ideas and language. Constantine's *Oration* puts the matter in the conventional Christian terms of a distinction between words and meaning: "Be indulgent, listeners, sincere worshippers of God and therefore the objects of His care; attending not to the language but to the truth of what is said; not to him who speaks but rather to the pious zeal which hallows his discourse."[41] As time went on, however, it would seem important to demonstrate that Christians could control the language as well as the content.

In a memorable passage, Eusebius describes the reception of Constantine's rhetorical strategy.[42] After explaining the severe regime of prayer imposed on the surprised court by the emperor, and his own pious practice, Eusebius gives a long account of the sort of discourses that Constantine would himself regularly deliver. Naturally they attracted large audiences, curious to hear an emperor in this unfamiliar role. If Constantine reached a particularly religious passage, he would drop his voice to a reverent hush and show by pointing upward that the acclamations with which he was hailed as emperor ought to be addressed only to God in Heaven. His orations usually followed a distinct pattern: first the errors of paganism, then the sovereignty of God and his providence and the divine plan. He played on the emotions of his audience, threatening them with their accountability to divine judgment; even some of his sophisticated friends and associates who were present felt the force of this, shuffling their feet

40. That is to take a sympathetic view; cf. de Ste. Croix, *Class Struggle*, 399.
41. *Oratio ad Sanctos* 2.
42. *VC* 4.29; cf. 17.

and looking at the floor—or so at least Eusebius alleges. But the real point came at the end, when he reminded his hearers that he had been given earthly rule by God, that they owed their own authority only to his gift and that his whole government was accountable to God, as it was also intended by him. A masterly handling of the theme, had the audience only been more receptive—had the convergence been yet more complete. As it was, Eusebius himself disarmingly records how flat the emperor's discourses fell as instruments of exhortation to the faith: "He himself both felt and uttered these sentiments in the genuine confidence of faith; but his hearers were little disposed to learn, and deaf to sound advice; receiving his words indeed with loud applause, but induced by insatiable cupidity practically to disregard them."[43]

Nevertheless, when practised by others, the Christian oratory of the fourth century was heard. More than that, the great Christian speeches of the later part of the century, like those by Gregory of Nyssa on Bishop Meletius or on Gregory's brother Basil, gave a new meaning to public oratory.[44] In the revived urban culture of the fourth century, Christian bishops succeeded to the place of the epideictic orators of the Second Sophistic; and their speeches were more political than the earlier ones ever could be. Gregory of Nyssa does not merely describe: he wishes to persuade, and he has the whole armory of classical technique at his disposal.

If many still held back from accepting the implications of the new state of affairs, these were orators whose commitment to their message was complete. Similarly, whereas earlier emperors could afford to joke about their prospects of divinity, their Christian successors were totally in earnest about claiming association with God's plan. Nor was it a matter of a limited discourse

43. *VC* 4.29 fin.
44. The point is well made by Spira, "Volkstümlichkeit und Kunst."

reaching only as far as the elite. Vegetius gives us the oath of a fourth-century army recruit: "By God and Christ and the Holy Spirit and by the emperor's majesty, which, by God's will, ought to be beloved and venerated by the human race. . . . For when the emperor receives the name of Augustus, faithful devotion must be given to him, as if to a deity present in the flesh. . . . For the civilian or the soldier serves God when he loves faithfully him who reigns with God's authority."[45] As the old imperial cult eventually declined, phrases such as these penetrated the consciousness more effectively than any number of sermons; by sheer reiteration and use they powerfully reinforced the political status quo.

One can see how the appropriation might work in practice by comparing the famous homilies delivered by John Chrysostom while still a priest in Antioch, on the offenses against imperial statues in the Antiochene riots of A.D. 387, with the speeches on the same subject by Libanius the pagan sophist. Chrysostom is able to elevate the mission of the aged Bishop Flavianus to be granted mercy from the emperor in Constantinople into an elaborate set piece on the theme of the relation of emperor and church, and by implication emperor and God.[46] In successfully appealing to the emperor, the bishop Flavianus "crowned Theodosius more brightly than with any diadem"; lest it be missed, John underlines the reason—first and foremost, because the emperor showed himself ready to grant such favors to clergy. But after all, says John, it was God's *philanthropia* that soothed his anger. He heard the details from someone else who was present, not from Flavianus himself, who "imitated the *megalopsychia* of St. Paul" and refused to take the credit that belonged properly to God and the emperor.[47]

In his address to the emperor, as John then reports it, the

45. Vegetius *Ep. rei milit.* 2.5.   46. *PG* 49.211–22 (*Hom.* 21).
47. *PG* 49.213.

bishop urges that Theodosius's response to the erring Antioch-
enes, stirred up by the devil, should resemble that of God toward Adam and Eve. Their fault proved to be the starting point
of man's salvation: "instead of paradise, he opened up heaven
for us."[48] One is surprised here as elsewhere by the boldness of
Christian writers, who unblushingly placed the emperor in the
role of God himself. But there is also a model for clemency from
the recent past: no less a person than Constantine, who, when
his statue was once stoned and his advisers were crying for pun-
ishment, is said to have fingered his face and commented with a
smile that he still seemed to be in one piece.[49] Chrysostom presents the bishop's embassy as affording material from which
pagans might learn the philosophy of Christianity: "What an
example of compassion! The pagans should be ashamed—or
rather, they should not be ashamed, they should learn from it,
give up their error (*planē*) and return to the power of Christianity (*Christianismos*), learning our philosophy from the emperor
and the bishop."[50]

Of the two, Chrysostom has the more forceful repertoire of
models on which to draw. Libanius, by contrast, although he
uses many of the same themes (the emperor as gentle father, for
instance)[51] and appeals like Chrysostom to the magnanimous
example of Constantine,[52] must turn to the apparatus of classical history[53] or the examples of past emperors, Diocletian and
Constantius,[54] the splendors of Antioch, and the education of her
upper classes.[55] He cannot use the strategy, so effective for his
Christian rival, of claiming the emperors, seen and known to be

48. *PG* 49.215.   49. *PG* 49.216.
50. *PG* 49.220.
51. *Or.* 19.18; cf. *PG* 49.220.
52. *Or.* 19.19; but 20 contrasts the severity of Constantine with the mercy
of Theodosius.
53. *Or.* 19.13: Athens and Sparta, Greece and Persia, Alexander the Great.
54. *Or.* 19.47–48.   55. *Or.* 19.51, cf. 5, 25.

beneficent toward the church, for the newer universe of Christian rhetoric.

In the words of the pagan Porphyry quoted by Eusebius, Christianity was a "barbarian insolence," in contrast to Hellenism, "the rule of law."[56] Julian could seriously believe that Christians could not explain Homer without hypocrisy.[57] What was being fought over by pagans and Christians in the fourth century, therefore, was the right to interpret the past. Each side approached the task through hermeneutics; in the words of E. R. Dodds, "Christians and pagans were alike schoolmen: they could not challenge the authority of the ancient texts; they could only evade it by reading back their own thoughts into them."[58] The implications and the advantages for Christians in the fourth century were clear—like pagans, they laid claim to classical literature and mythology;[59] but simultaneously, they could set about the wholesale reinvention of history in terms of Christian typology.

From certain points of view it is a very well told story.[60] Although their own attitudes remained ambivalent, the cultured Christian oratory of the Cappadocians could match that of any previous century.[61] Many, including John Chrysostom, were wor-

56. *HE* 6.19.7.

57. See E. L. Fortin, "Christianity and Hellenism in Basil the Great's Address *Ad Adulescentes*," in *Neoplatonism and Early Christian Thought*, ed. H. Blumenthal and R. A. Markus (London: Variorum, 1981), 189–203, esp. 199.

58. Lane Fox, *Pagans and Christians*, 131.

59. So Basil argues in his essay to his nephews on the utility of Greek literature; see N. G. Wilson, *St. Basil on the Value of Greek Literature* (London: Duckworth, 1975).

60. See, e.g., E. Norden, *Antike Kunstprosa*, vol. 2; and Laistner, *Christianity and Pagan Culture*. Extensive recent bibliography on the relation between Christian literature and Greek *paideia* can be found in P. Allen, "Some Aspects of Hellenism in the Early Greek Church Historians," *Traditio* 43 (1987): 368–81.

61. See Kennedy, *Greek Rhetoric*, 215 ff.; R. R. Ruether, *Gregory of Nazianzus: Rhetor and Philosopher* (Oxford: Clarendon Press, 1969);

ried about the effects of pagan literature on their children, yet few Christians were willing to abandon the traditional classical curriculum.[62] Jerome was still wrestling with the problem at the end of the fourth century, and Augustine returned to it at the end of his life: both the *Confessions* and the *City of God* represent a sustained meditation on the relation of secular and Christian learning. As with the claim to simplicity, it was open to Christian writers to exploit or decry pagan culture as seemed most advantageous. For the most part, though, classical culture was too important in relation to the power structure of society to be discarded. Inevitably, therefore, they took it over, and the extent to which its importance was already recognized is shown by the outcry that followed Julian's attempt to deprive Christians of the chance to teach.[63] The many—often agonized—contemporary Christian discussions of the relation of classical to Christian learning should be read as necessary attempts to defend the extent to which Christians had in fact endorsed an educational system that could be represented as contrary to their professed beliefs. Taking the longer view, it was essential, if the growing influence of the institutional church was to be maintained and increased, to control the educational system, either by drastic change or by adaptation and justification; on the whole at this stage, it was the latter course that was chosen. The old formulation of the process in terms of the relation, or supposed conflict, between Christianity and classical culture can thus now give way to a theory of discourse in modern terms as a means to power.

This is especially true in the context of Roman imperial society, where contemporaries placed an overwhelming emphasis

---

C. Klock, *Untersuchungen zu Stil und Rhythmus bei Gregor von Nyssa. Ein Beitrag zum Rhetorikverständnis der griechischen Väter*, Beiträge zur klassischen Philologie 173 (Frankfurt a. Main: Athenaeum, 1987); Spira, "Volkstümlichkeit und Kunst."

62. See Laistner, *Christianity and Pagan Culture*, 85 ff.

63. See above, n. 37.

on rhetoric in public life and education. The fourth century, with its enlarged bureaucracy, saw an increased need for educated men, the vast majority of whom were produced by the standard rhetorical schools; at the same time, Christian orators, who had themselves usually been educated in the same way, were able to take good advantage of their own higher profile and new public platforms. Since everything conspired to make of the fourth century a time when rhetoric did indeed convey power, Christians needed to make it their own.

It is perhaps surprising that Christian history—history written from the Christian point of view, that is, not the more specialized history of the church—is conspicuously absent from the fourth-century list of Christianized literary forms. Eusebius's *Church History* sprang into new popularity with Rufinus's Latin translation and had a clutch of imitators in the church historians of the early fifth century, but important as its innovations were,[64] it did not inspire the development of a new and perhaps more pragmatic Christian history. When Eusebius himself, at or near the end of Constantine's reign, came to write a considered account, he did so in the shape of a hybrid between panegyric and biography. Indeed, the use of traditional historiography as a pagan vehicle by Eunapius and the Greek writers who followed may be related to the fact that this was one area that Christians had not made their own. Its revival in Latin by Ammianus followed sentiments of literary and political tradition and was unimpeded by any Christian examples; nor, in the conditions that followed in the West in the fifth and sixth centuries, did Ammianus have any successors who wrote on the same scale. But the result of this gap was that in Greek, where no such cultural

64. See A. Momigliano, "Pagan and Christian Historiography in the Fourth Century A.D.," in Momigliano, ed., *Conflict Between Paganism and Christianity,* 79–99. See also B. Croke and A. Emmett, eds., *History and Historians in Late Antiquity* (Sydney: Pergamon Press, 1983).

break occurred, a very traditional form of secular history continued and indeed enjoyed something of a vogue over the next two hundred years,[65] so that when Christians did attempt it they found it increasingly hard to reconcile a Christian approach with the rigid secular form.

Lives as Image

Christians had other ways of thinking about the past. History as a literary genre was perhaps too recalcitrant; as is all too obvious from Augustine's *City of God*, it forced the writer into unambiguous positions, and in a Christian form it was unlikely to reach beyond a limited audience. *Lives*, in contrast, provided a more congenial and flexible genre as well as greater opportunities. Funerary encomia even of members of the imperial family began to be the preserve of bishops such as Ambrose or Gregory of Nyssa. The latter, like his namesake Gregory of Nazianzus, wrote both on public figures and on members of his own family; indeed, both wrote encomiastic orations on Basil, who was one of Gregory of Nyssa's many siblings.[66] But the writing of *Lives*, which in the nature of things tended to combine the features of biography and encomium, offered Christians the possibility of integrating public and private in a new way. They could at once employ the devices and themes of classical rhetoric either for public subjects or to express the intimacy of family and personal feeling. We can even see the same feature in Gregory of Nazianzus's poetry, among which, alongside epigrams on Christological themes, there are a great many about his mother, Nonna.[67]

65. See R. Blockley, *The Fragmentary Classicising Historians of the Later Roman Empire*, vols. 1–2, Classical and Medieval Texts, Papers, and Monographs 6, 10 (Liverpool: ARCA, 1981, 1983). For Ammianus, see John Matthews, *The Roman Empire of Ammianus* (London: Duckworth, 1989).
66. See Kennedy, *Greek Rhetoric*, 215 ff.
67. See below, chapter 5.

Figure 10. St. Gregory of Nazianzus. Russian fresco, A.D. 1199. (Photograph: Phaidon Press)

Through *Lives,* Christian writers could present an image not only of the perfect Christian life but also of the life in imitation of Christ, the life that becomes an icon.

Lives thus offered far more to Christian writers than the *Life of Antony,* with its concentration, if disingenuous, on ascetic "simplicity," might at first sight seem to suggest.[68] To a degree greater than with any other possible literary form, *Lives* could embrace all subjects—male, female, high, low—and all literary levels. With their combination of story, pattern for emulation, public and personal, intellect and heart, nothing could have better suited Christian literary opportunism.

In asking ourselves why Christian *Lives* were so popular from the fourth century on, it is not enough to point to such phenomena as the literary origins of hagiography or the influence of the classical encomium on Christian writers. Even when at their most rhetorical, *Lives* represented the appeal to the heart, the private instead of—or as well as—the public.

In Christian encomia the genres merged: Gregory of Nazianzus's great encomium on St. Basil[69] demonstrates how that form could be turned, in a creative use of tradition, to the integration with Christian content of the highest forms of classical rhetoric. The subject himself exemplified the union of Christian and classical discourse: "an orator among orators, . . . a philosopher among philosophers." The speech is as self-conscious about its oratory as Synesius was about his Greek style or the apocryphal *Acts* about the power of preaching; the experience of Basil and Gregory as students of rhetoric in Athens provides one of its main themes. The other sides of Basil—Basil the ascetic, Basil the liturgist, Basil the founder of monastic discipline—are sub-

68. On its authorship, see above, chapter 3; and see F. M. Young, *From Nicaea to Chalcedon* (London: SCM Press, 1983), 81–82.

69. *Or.* 43, in *Grégoire de Nazianze: discours funèbres en l'honneur de son frère Césaire et de Basile de Césarée,* ed. F. Boulenger (Paris: Picard, 1908); on this speech, see Kennedy, *Greek Rhetoric,* 228 ff.

ordinated here to Basil the Christian orator and statesman; the subject is made to mirror the speech. If Christians were still claiming "simplicity," "the language of fishermen," over the style of the classical authors, Gregory's great encomium unites the two characteristics of grandeur and simplicity, as prescribed for panegyric by the rhetorical handbook of Hermogenes,[70] but in a different way: this "simplicity" is glossed by "purity"— "thoughts common to mankind, reaching, or believed to reach, everyman, with nothing deep or sophisticated about them."[71] On the other hand, "grandeur" obviously includes most of the features that in our own usage we would naturally call "rhetorical." Yet it remains an encomium on an individual for whom the inner life was at the heart of his Christian faith; even though it uses every rhetorical artifice available and more, it still seems "vibrant with sincerity."[72] The speech on Basil constitutes not only a near-perfect panegyric but also the integration of classical rhetoric with that *simplicitas* which Christians continued to want to claim as their own.

But most of the Christian *Lives* written during this period were of a different kind and purpose. I argued earlier that Eusebius's *Life of Constantine*, finished soon after Constantine's death in A.D. 337, was to be read as a demonstration, a verbal icon, as much as a historical text. Eusebius had already written in the *Church History* about his predecessor Origen in ideological rather than historical terms. His "task was not a quest for a historical Origen. Like that of other biographers, his aim was to create a convincing portrait of a magnificent man by capturing in prose the ideals which that man represented."[73] It will be re-

70. Hermogenes *On Types* 404, ed. Rabe (Leipzig: B. G. Teubner, 1913), trans. in D. Russell and M. Winterbottom, *Ancient Literary Criticism* (Oxford: Oxford University Press, 1972), 575.

71. Ibid., 572, 566–67.

72. Kennedy, *Greek Rhetoric*, 237.

73. Cox, *Biography in Late Antiquity*, 101.

membered that he describes his aim in the *Life of Constantine* as that of giving a "verbal portrait."[74] Other Christian *Lives*, whether of holy men like Antony, public figures like Basil, characters from the Christian or Christianized past, like Paul or Moses, whose lives were written by John Chrysostom and Gregory of Nyssa, operated in a similar way, showing how the Christian life was to be lived. Sacred lives functioned as ideological and literary exemplars. Moses is the model for Constantine: in turn, seeing Constantine as Moses enabled the audience to see Constantine more clearly.[75]

Pagans also engaged in this creative use of history, taking exemplary figures from their own past and making them into literary models of the pagan life; they continued the precedent with lives of their own holy men, even to the extent that Christian and Neoplatonist rivalries could seem to be expressing themselves in a war of biography.[76] But the writing of *Lives* was inherent to Christian literature in a way that it was not to pagan. We have seen it from the earliest phase—in the Gospels, in the apocryphal *Acts*, in martyr literature. The existence of a vast modern bibliography on the relation of biography to the aretalogies of great men does not in the least alter the fact that Christian mythology was built on biography, that its most characteristic metaphors were drawn from the human body, and that it persistently used written *Lives* as models for Christian behavior. The *Life* itself becomes an image; Christian lives of the present are interpreted in terms of their relation to sacred lives of the

74. *VC* 1.10; see chapter 2 above.
75. *VC* 1.12, 19–20, 28–29. For Christian writings as verbal icons, see V. E. F. Harrison, "Word as Icon in Greek Patristic Theology," *Sobornost* 10 (1988): 38–49.
76. See also G. Fowden, "The Pagan Holy Man in Late Antique Society," *JHS* 102 (1982): 33–59; G. Fowden, "The Platonist Philosopher and His Circle in Late Antiquity," *Philosophia* 7 (1977): 359–83; A. Meredith, "Asceticism—Christian and Greek," *JThS*, n.s. 27 (1976): 313–32.

past, and their written forms, having taken on that shape, also acquire its evocative power.

These *Lives* are far from bare records. They are full of meaning, signs by which Christians taught one another how to interpret the present and past and how to live in the future. A good case has been made recently for the interpretation of another of Gregory of Nyssa's *Lives* along these lines—that of Origen's pupil Gregory Thaumaturgus.[77] It was achieved at differing literary levels,[78] but the object and the symbolic technique were the same. The *Lives,* from the most classicizing, the most deeply suffused with the motifs and language of secular literature, to the simplest and seemingly most artless narrative, present a Christian model for the virtuous life and a blueprint for the interpretation of history.

In the fourth century, therefore, we can see a confident progress of Christian discourse toward the appropriation of those areas that pagans had thought their own. In political theory and public oratory, Christians adapted old themes and styles to their own purpose, and spoke from positions of authority. But often the same writers also composed Christian *Lives,* in which a more symbolic appropriation of the past—this time the sacred past—was attainable. Even more importantly, the narration of Christian *Lives* spoke to the individual and to the heart—not just to theory, but also to practice.

Let us briefly consider the implications for the future of this concentration on *Lives.* As I have stressed already, it was not

77. Van Dam, "Hagiography and History," 289: *Lives* as constituting a cognitive logic of symbols; similarly, B. Flusin, *Miracle et histoire dans l'oeuvre de Cyrille de Scythopolis* (Paris: Etudes augustiniennes, 1983).

78. R. Browning, "The 'Low-Level' Saint's Life in the Early Byzantine World," in *The Byzantine Saint,* ed. S. Hackel, Studies Supplementary to Sobornost 5 (London: Fellowship of St. Alban & St. Sergius, 1981), 117–27; I. Ševčenko, "Levels of Style in Byzantine Prose," *JÖB* 31 (1981): 289–312.

simply theoretical. The patterning of the *Lives,* in all its variety, had connotations for one's own life. The *Lives* presented ideals of behavior for Christians to follow. The theoretical implied the moral and the practical. Without suggesting that all, or even many, Christians actually tried to put into practice in their own lives the precepts implied in Christian *Lives* or preached in Christian sermons,[79] they were nevertheless at the receiving end of models of behavior that were all the more powerful for being often repeated. In the practice of Christian asceticism, for instance, the lessons of many *Lives* were acted out. Methodius, Gregory of Nyssa, and Jerome held out as an ideal of Christian womanhood the heavily charged life of Thecla, the heroine of the *Acts of Paul and Thecla,* with the implication that their readers should imitate her in her ascetic life.[80] The argument from *Life* to action was always there.

Second, it is clear that the *Lives* are not to be dismissed as indicative of a general softening of the intellect or an effusion of popular piety. They ranged over the entire literary spectrum and appealed to readers of all educational levels; in the same way, they could be and often were written by the same men who also composed works of abstruse theology or elevated rhetoric. One of the greatest advantages of Christian over pagan literature was precisely this, that it could and did break out of the mold of traditional elite culture and develop types of writing that could be diffused far more widely, and yet that did not lose the essential appeal to the elite audience. It is a feature of the late fourth cen-

79. The gap between the prescriptive literature and the actuality (admitted in the tone of a good many sermons) is well discussed by Patlagean, *Pauvreté économique et pauvreté sociale à Byzance (4e au 7e siècles)* (Paris: Mouton, 1977), 128 ff.

80. For the models presented in literature to fourth-century Christian women, see the study by F. E. Consolino, "Modelli di comportamento e modi di santificazione per l'aristocrazia femminile d'occidente," in Giardina, ed., *Società romana e impero tardoantico* 1:273–306. On *Lives* and human life in general as enacted narrative, see Harpham, *Ascetic Imperative,* 67 ff., 86 ff.

tury unimaginable in a pagan context that educated and aristocratic Christians could engage in intense activity directed toward the collecting, reading, and copying of earlier texts, while
also enthusing in their palaces over the life of an Egyptian hermit.[81] For intelligible reasons, it is also now that a notable group
of Christian women—aristocrats, it is true—come to our notice
both as devotees of the ascetic life and as patrons of learning.
According to her biographer (another *Life*), the younger Melania
"read the Old and New Testaments three or four times a year"
and copied them out herself. She also read all the lives of saints
that she could get hold of; "so overwhelming was her love of
learning that when she read in Latin, it seemed to everyone that
she did not know Greek, and on the other hand, when she read
in Greek, it was thought that she did not know Latin."[82] A vivid
example of Christian biographical patterning comes in the account of Melania's death: when she felt death approaching, it
was the day after Christmas, St. Stephen's Day, and she read out
from the Acts of the Apostles the account of Stephen's martyrdom.[83] Melania also acted as guide in the Holy Land to the Empress Eudocia, herself a poet and supposedly the daughter of a
pagan philosopher.[84]

The experience of Christian women, and their new prominence in our sources, especially from the later fourth century,

81. See P. Brown, "Aspects of the Christianization of the Roman Aristocracy," *JRS* 51 (1961): 1–11; Alan Cameron, "The Latin Revival of the Fourth
Century," in *Renaissances Before the Renaissance,* ed. W. Treadgold (Stanford: Stanford University Press, 1984), 42–58; *V. Mel.* 26; C. P. Hammond
Bammel, "Products of Fifth-Century Scriptoria Preserving Conventions Used
by Rufinus of Aquileia," *JThS,* n.s. 35 (1984): 347–93; and cf. ibid. 29
(1978): 366–91; 30 (1979): 430–62.

82. *V. Mel.* 26.

83. Ibid., 63.

84. See Alan Cameron, "The Empress and the Poet," *Yale Classical Stud-
ies* 27 (1982): 217–89; and K. Holum, *Theodosian Empresses: Women and
Imperial Dominion in Late Antiquity* (Berkeley and Los Angeles: University of
California Press, 1982), 112 ff., 183 ff.

are indicators both of the impact of the models presented in the *Lives* and of the openness of Christian culture to groups, of which women were one, outside the traditional elite. Of course, we hear most at this stage about the women of the senatorial class or even of the imperial family, who were in the best position to take up this possibility, besides being likely because of their position and social milieu to attract attention from contemporary writers.[85] But as the body of hagiographical literature grew, especially in Greek, it is possible to see that this was a much wider phenomenon altogether.[86] Why is it that women feature so largely in Christian *Lives?* Is it merely a reflection of the social prominence of these late-fourth-century Christian ladies?

That Gregory of Nyssa should choose to write about his sister at all is in itself sufficiently remarkable,[87] but the *Life of Macrina* is only a notable individual example. For an explanation, we should look again to the distinction between the public and private spheres. Personal consciousness and the small details of daily life are not prominent in classical literature, as we know. But Christianity, with its emphasis on the inner person, the spiritual rather than the external, brought the private sphere to the fore. With this emphasis new classes received attention, in particular women, classic dwellers in the private sphere, and the poor, previously scorned as an object of attention in their own right; there are plenty of poor people in saints' lives, just as there are women. In the hands of a sophisticated author, alive to the rhetorical possibilities, both categories could provide good material for a clever comparison; nevertheless, this fact should not

85. See, e.g., A. Yarborough, "Christianisation in the Fourth Century: The Example of Roman Women." *Church History* 45 (1976): 149–65.

86. Women of varying social levels feature quite large in the stories in the *Apophthegmata Patrum*, for instance, despite the generally misogynistic tone.

87. A. Momigliano, "The Life of St. Macrina by Gregory of Nyssa," in *The Craft of the Ancient Historian*, ed. J. Ober and J. W. Eadie (Lanham, Md.: University Press of America, 1985), 443–58.

obscure the element of real innovation in subject matter of the *Lives,* or the significance of that choice.

Consideration of the Christian *Life* as image has an obvious relevance both to my argument so far and to later developments in Christian discourse. I have emphasized one of the major characteristics of Christian writing, namely its figural quality. That figural tendency centered notably on the concept of the life of a sacred or saintly person, presented in symbolic tones as a pattern for Christians to live by. The basic metaphor of the body was thus translated into a literary and thus an imaginative model, and underlined in practical terms by the much-vaunted practice of asceticism. We have seen how natural it was, following Plato and many others after him, to borrow the language of visual art in order to express this figural meaning. Notwithstanding the prohibition inherited from Judaism, the step toward a Christian representational art was a very short one indeed. Our earliest surviving examples of pictorial cycles in churches date from the fifth century, but many individuals were already using Christian images on rings and seals, on embroideries, and on pictures in their houses, and Christian scenes were being painted in martyria and even on secular buildings.[88] From now on, the visual presentation of Christian themes was to become a very important instrument in their diffusion, a fact that was not lost on contemporaries. Nilus of Ancyra writes of the advantages to be found in decorating churches with Christian pictures: the church should be painted with scenes from the Old and New Testaments, "so that the illiterate, who are unable to read the Holy Scriptures, may, by gazing at the pictures, become mindful of the manly deeds of those who have genuinely served the true God, and may be roused to emulate those glorious and cele-

88. See the convenient collection of sources in Mango, *Art of the Byzantine Empire,* 32 ff. The practices drew comment, both approving and disapproving; see the passages from John Chrysostom and Epiphanius of Salamis quoted at 39–43.

Figure 11. Relics being granted an imperial reception, Constantinople. Ivory, Cathedral Treasury, Trier. Fifth century A.D. (Photograph: Bildarchiv Foto Marburg)

brated feats."[89] What the pictures showed was people; they constituted narrative art—that is, they told stories about people. These were scriptural examples; at other times the pictures were of Christian saints and martyrs or scenes from their lives.[90] Thus the *Life,* represented in literature as a pattern to follow, is also seen as such in visual art. As the Platonic language of representation used in so many Christian texts was translated into concrete expression, Christians were presented with a pictorial world thickly populated by holy people. It would not be long before they became as familiar and as beloved as living friends.

It was entirely predictable that pictures would become more and more important as a means for representing Christian truth.

There was much in the rhetoric of Christianity, both in its Platonizing language of representation and in its emphasis on lives
as images or verbal icons, to make the steady development of
religious images in art entirely predictable. It was not, however,
accidental that the greatest increase in the use of and devotion to
these images took place from the middle of the sixth century onward, and thus that it coincided first with a decline and then
with a virtual cessation in all but a few places of access to the
old educational system.[91] Icons thus stepped into the role assigned by Nilus of Ancyra to pictorial cycles from the Bible: they,
not literary texts, were now the main mode of access to the
Christian faith.

This chapter has tried to show how, notably from the start of
imperial support in the fourth century, Christian rhetoric increasingly moved into central areas of political discourse, and
how that process was helped by the changed relation of Christian speakers, especially bishops, to their potential audiences.
Gradually, therefore, it became more common, and more acceptable, for important public speeches to be given by Christians, and for Christian writers to use and assimilate to their
own purposes the rhetorical modes that had been the preserve of
the educated elite. At the same time, we have seen a concentration on the writing of *Lives*, invested with both symbolic and
practical implications for their readers and reinforced, as time
went on, by complementary pictorial representations. It all
added up to a wholesale taking over and reinterpretation of tradition at the intellectual, the moral, and the emotional levels.

The writers of *Lives*, like the authors of the apocryphal *Acts*,
knew what they were doing. They are often self-conscious about
it, like the author of the *Life of Melania*, who patterns the life of

91. See further below, chapter 6.

his subject on earlier models and represents Melania herself as reading those earlier *Lives* in order to pattern herself on them. Again the texts talk about text, but at the same time the Christian audience is encouraged to internalize the subject itself.

Christians in this period had a considerable range of choice in tackling the question of what model they should choose in order to learn how best to live a Christian life. Even in this story from the *Apophthegmata Patrum,* the degree of consciousness in the choice is illustrated. Arsenius, a man of senatorial rank and formerly tutor to the two sons of Theodosius I, but now a desert father, is visited by "a very rich and god-fearing virgin of the senatorial class" from Rome.[92] She for her part confidently expects a warm reception for her piety in coming all the way to the Egyptian desert; furthermore, she is evidently used to getting her own way. But to him she is merely a woman, the repository of evil, and especially so in view of her rank and status; he sends her harshly away: "Do you not realize that you are a woman, and cannot go just anywhere? Or is it so that on returning to Rome you can say to other women: I have seen Arsenius? Then they will turn the sea into a thoroughfare with women coming to see me."

The story seems to epitomize the situation of Christian culture at the turn of the fourth and fifth centuries. Those who have chosen "simplicity" have to guard their ideal against the corruption of exposure to the world, while the rich elite vie with one another to court them. There was much rhetorical mileage in this contrast, but the social contrast was real: the same Abba Arsenius, who "when he was in the world was the father of the emperor, surrounded by thousands of slaves with golden girdles, all wearing collars of gold and garments of silk," fell prostrate

---

92. Trans. in B. Ward, ed., *Sayings of the Desert Fathers* (London: Mowbrays, 1975), 13–14.

on the ground and would not get up simply because a visitor came to his cell with whom he might have to converse.[93] Arsenius's neighbor among the hermits was Abba Moses, who had previously been a thief. With all its streams of visitors, and with its social mix, that "city" of the Egyptian desert was as inclusive as the Christianity that made it so.[94]

93. Ibid., 17. Cf. Browning, "The 'Low-Level' Saint's Life," 127, on the popular saint as "the direct antithesis of the ideal citizen of classical antiquity."
94. Cf. D. Chitty, *The Desert a City* (Oxford: Oxford University Press, 1966); cf. Browning, "'Low-Level' Saint's Life," 118.

CHAPTER FIVE

The Rhetoric of Paradox

The Other Side of Christian Discourse

They walked by the estuary,
Eve and the Virgin Mary,
And they talked till nightfall,
But the difference between them was radical.

Stevie Smith

Yet convergence and accommodation had their price: they might seem to endanger the essentially paradoxical aspect of Christian discourse—that aspect which made it a religious discourse. That the educated elite in the late fourth century showed such enthusiasm for the more exotic forms of asceticism, and with it for the writings in which its values were extolled, demonstrates in itself that the essential appropriation of traditional rhetoric and argument by the Christian bishops of the period not only failed to drive underground the paradoxical elements inherent in Christian discourse since its inception but actually encouraged their parallel development. The same people often formed the audiences for kinds of Christian writing that were at first sight poles apart from each other; again, it was often the same preachers and writers who were the authors both of public orations for great occasions and of rococo treatises on virginity. Therein lay the paradox of late-fourth-century Christian discourse: that it was capable of embracing just such apparent opposites. We must now therefore explore that other side—the rhetoric of paradox. It will be seen that this too, far from being the strange aberration it seems to modern taste, constituted a strength that contributed a great deal toward the process of Christianization.

It sometimes seems that religious conversion can be a matter of reason. In his account of his move toward the Roman Catholic church, Newman gave an important place to the reflections suggested by reading he had done four years earlier on the doctrinal controversies of the early church. "This thought," he wrote of his new conviction that the truth lay with Rome and not with the Anglican church, "arose in the first instance from the Monophysite and Donatist controversies, the former of which I was engaged with in the course of theological study to which I had given myself."[1] At this point in Newman's profoundly intellectualized account, he claims to have been persuaded by reason and argument.

Yet this very reasoning concerned the language of Christian doctrine, which many historians and philosophers would feel uneasy recognizing as belonging to the realm of rational argument at all.[2] A great deal of Christian discourse is of this kind. It necessarily attempts to express the paradoxical, to describe in language what is by definition indescribable.[3] Fourth-century writers, in particular the Cappadocians, were highly conscious of this: Gregory of Nazianzus and Gregory of Nyssa debated the issues confronted today by philosophers of religion. How was it

1. J. H. Newman, *Apologia pro vita sua*, ed. Maisie Ward (London: Sheed & Ward, 1976), 149.

2. See, e.g. (from a large bibliography), A. Macintyre, "Is Understanding Religion Compatible with Believing?" in *Faith and the Philosophers*, ed. J. Hick (London: Macmillan, 1964), 115–33.

3. This is a commonplace in recent discussions of religious language; see, e.g., Macquarie, *God-Talk*, 229; and R. W. Hepburn, *Christianity and Paradox* (London: Watts, 1958). The same idea lies behind the current preoccupation with the analysis of parable (a technique for expressing a truth in nonrational terms) and the role of metaphor in theology; see above, chapter 2; and see, e.g., S. Laeuchli, *The Serpent and the Dove* (Nashville: Abingdon Press, 1966), 228 ff.

possible to speak of God at all, when by definition he could not be circumscribed in language? It would not at any rate be a matter of the usual categories and methods of rational logic.[4] Such thinking through "apophatic" theology, deeply indebted among others to Gregory of Nyssa, is fundamental to the approach of the Orthodox church.[5] But this was not purely a Christian problem; on the contrary, it went back to Plato, and in particular to the *Timaeus*, a work much discussed in this context by the patristic writers; it was also a theme of Middle Platonism. Not simply the status of propositions about God, but the very nature of language were at issue; often enough those Christian writers who were most aware of the logical difficulties were also themselves accomplished rhetoricians and the most closely involved in the formation of a more public Christian discourse.

These difficulties were not only felt in the East. Augustine's long career in the intimate relationship of a bishop to his congregation developed in him an exceptional sensitivity to both the practical and the theoretical aspects of Christian language. His debt to Platonism combined with his early practice of Latin rhetoric and his own experience with audiences at all intellectual levels to make him vividly aware of the power and the limitations of language. In an unforgettable phrase, he wrote that God had "struck him with his Word";[6] in the end, after years of mental struggle, he saw the ultimate source of meaning as lying not in human reason or logical argument, but in divine inspiration.[7] The tension was basic to Christian writing, as we can see,

4. See further Young, "God of the Greeks"; and esp. Mortley, *From Word to Silence*. M. Canevet, *Grégoire de Nysse et l'herméneutique biblique* (Paris: Etudes augustiniennes, 1983), is valuable on Gregory of Nyssa.

5. See, e.g, V. Lossky, *The Mystical Theology of the Orthodox Church*, trans. members of the Fellowship of St. Alban & St. Sergius (London: James Clarke, 1957; repr. 1973), esp. chap. 2, "The Divine Darkness."

6. *Conf.* 10.6.

7. The crucial work is the *De doctrina christiana*, but cf. also the *De magistro*.

too, from the works of so accomplished a rhetorician as Gregory of Nazianzus, who with John Chrysostom and Gregory of Nyssa was instrumental in bringing Christian oratory into public and indeed imperial occasions.[8] The pull that these authors— usually bishops, and therefore practical men—perceived between the traditional, classical oratory and Christian spirituality often comes out explicitly in their works, as it does in Gregory of Nyssa's *Life* of his sister Macrina, where in an enhanced and highly literary polarization Macrina can stand (as a woman, but also as an ascetic) for the "true philosophy," symbolized by the lack of worldly education. The ambiguities implicit in the contrast between this and the intellectual background of her brother, the great St. Basil, whom she is said to have converted to the ascetic life, are an important element in the *Life* in terms both of content and of form. Here and elsewhere we see how Christian writers could exploit to rhetorical effect the contradictory aspects in Christian discourse even while themselves continuing to struggle with their philosophical and religious implications.

That paradoxical element can be seen already in the Gospels, which indeed insist on its importance. The disciples often misunderstand. "Why do you talk to them in parables?" they ask, to which Jesus replies: "Because it is given unto you to know the mysteries of the kingdom of heaven, but to them it is not given."[9] He must speak in parables in order to fulfill prophecy: "I will open my mouth in parables; I will utter things which have been kept secret from the foundation of the world."[10] But the concept of a central mystery or mysteries is crucial. For St. Paul, who

8. The same role was played by Ambrose in the West at the same period. The point is made for the Greek writers by Momigliano, "Life of St. Macrina."
9. Matt. 13:10–11. On parables, see chapter 2 above.
10. Matt. 13:35; cf. Ps. 78:2, 49:4; Is. 6.9–10. See R. Girard, *Des choses cachées depuis la fondation du monde* (Paris: B. Grasset, 1978); and on hidden meanings in relation to the Gospels, esp. Mark, see Kermode, *Genesis of Secrecy.*

first formulated the paradoxes of Christology later to be developed to such baroque limits, the greatest mystery of all was that of the cross: "For the Jews require a sign and the Greeks seek after wisdom; but we preach Christ crucified, unto the Jews a stumbling block and unto the Greeks foolishness; but unto them which are called, both Jews and Greeks, Christ the power of God and the wisdom of God. Because the wisdom of God is wiser than men, and the weakness of God is stronger than men." [11] The language of the cross may be illogical, [12] for the wisdom of God is hidden in a mystery, which is perceived only through a glass darkly. [13]

We have already seen something of the implications of this insistence on mystery for Christian thought and its expression. If it is the nature of the ultimate truth to be hidden, it will be revealed only through signs, linguistic or otherwise; in other words, Christian language and Christian rhetoric will be of their very essence figural. However, the realization that religious experience and religious language are built on paradox has also been expressed in wider terms. Christianity itself, not just Christian language, is sometimes seen as resting on impossible opposites, an idea that reappears in definitions of the holy. [14] In addition, in the field of sociology of knowledge, theology has been assigned the role of mediator between "rationality" and the irrational, or rather the nonrational realm occupied by religion.

The allegorical interpretation so much favored in early Christian writing is just one way around the problem of how to translate the essentially paradoxical into language that conforms to more normal logical expectations. Yet while under the Christian emperors from Constantine on Christian discourse necessarily adapted itself to some degree to the expectations of the society

11. I Cor. 1:22–25.   12. I Cor. 1:18.   13. I Cor. 2:7, 13:12.
14. R. Otto, *The Idea of the Holy*, trans. J. W. Harvey (London: Oxford University Press, 1929). See also R. Girard, *Violence and the Sacred*, trans. P. Gregory (Baltimore: Johns Hopkins University Press, 1977).

around it, it could not deny or eliminate that very paradoxical quality which made it a religious discourse.

In this chapter I want to explore, not the philosophical problems inherent in Christian language, important though they were, but the major role of paradox in Christian literature of the fourth century and later.

We can best observe how important this was to be if we consider the later development of Christian writing in the Eastern Empire, where the tradition was continuous. That aspect of Christian writing which gloried in and made a virtue of paradox prevailed in particular in the long, unbroken tradition of Greek homiletic. Week by week, preachers of all levels of sophistication expounded the familiar themes and scriptural passages to their congregations, drawing according to their abilities on both learned and popular tradition. Heavily influenced though they were by the more abstruse precepts of Greek rhetoricians,[15] even the learned homilists of the middle Byzantine period drew as well on an earlier and more complex tradition, in which paradox was already being pushed to its limits. Of course, we can often see the influence of rhetorical antithesis at work; but for centuries a long series of preachers had already drawn on sets of oppositions as a means of hinting at what was essentially inexpressible. It was after all no more than a reworking in more palatable and immediate terms of the theological language employed in the Christological and other disputes of the fourth century and later. We should look there, therefore, not for intriguing but peripheral details, but for an indication of Christian discourse in action. Just as the apocryphal Acts helped to form the thought-world of early Christians, so the weekly or at times daily homilies reinforced their consciousness of the familiar texts and fixed the mysteries of the faith in their minds.

15. See Kustas, *Studies in Byzantine Rhetoric;* Kennedy, *Greek Rhetoric,* 291 ff.; H. Maguire, *Art and Eloquence,* 13 ff.; on antithesis and paradox in Byzantine literature, see ibid., 53 ff.

I shall return to homiletic, but it was of course not only here that the central role of paradox can be observed. In the Christian epigrams of Gregory of Nazianzus, for instance,[16] paradoxical language is pushed to its limits. As perhaps the most rhetorically accomplished of all the Greek patristic writers, Gregory draws heavily on the classical rhetorical technique of antithesis;[17] but it is also Gregory who with his contemporary, Gregory of Nyssa, struggles to find ways of expressing Christian truth in language and wrestles with the problem of linguistic representation of God.

The same paradoxical element is to be seen conspicuously in the Syriac Christian writing that received such a great impetus in the late fourth century from the works of Ephrem the Syrian; undoubtedly, in a world where translation back and forth rapidly became the norm, and where the two languages often overlapped in use, the mass of Greek homiletic of the fifth and sixth centuries in which these qualities are also characteristic is thoroughly influenced by contemporary Syriac writing.[18] The hymns of Ephrem probably also influenced the sixth-century Greek liturgical hymns of Romanos, the deacon of St. Sophia in Constantinople.[19] But Christian language had always, and naturally,

16. F. E. Consolino, "Σοφίης ἀμφοτέρης πρύτανιν: gli epigrammi funerari di Gregorio Nazianzeno (A.P. VIII)," *Athenaeum*, n.s. 65 (1987): 407–25, with bibliography. It has been customary to see Gregory's epigrams in too literary a context, important though that is; they should be set not only against contemporary Christian writing of other kinds, but also in the context of the development of the inscribed Greek verse epigram in late antiquity.

17. For antithesis in his epigrams, see Spira, "Volkstümlichkeit und Kunst," 70–73; on his rhetorical skill generally, see Ruether, *Gregory of Nazianzus*.

18. On Ephrem, see R. Murray, *Symbols of Church and Kingdom: A Study in Early Syriac Tradition* (Cambridge: Cambridge University Press, 1975); and S. Brock, *The Luminous Eye* (Rome: ACIIS Publications, 1985).

19. See below, chapter 6. As with Gregory of Nazianzus, it is also possible to emphasize the rhetorical elements in both Ephrem and Romanos; the exact balance is a matter of controversy. For rhetoric in Romanos, see H. Hunger, "Romanos Melodos, Dichter, Prediger, Rhetor—und sein Publikum," *JÖB* 34 (1984): 15–42.

tended to emphasize mystery and hiddenness; we do not need to look to the influence of Syriac literature, whatever it may be, for the whole explanation. In the sixth and seventh centuries, the prose theological works of "Dionysius the Areopagite" and Maximus Confessor stressed the mystical and paradoxical side of Christianity more than ever;[20] in this tradition, Christian language itself, like religious images, could be held to carry the mystery of the faith.[21]

It has been argued, indeed, that the ps.-Dionysian corpus, with its emphasis on contemplation and acceptance of a divine order, marks the end of a process that can be characterized as the decline of the tradition of *logos,* rational argument.[22] On that basis it would be appealing to understand the enormous weight placed in early Byzantine society on the symbolic visual representation as an alternative means of expressing religious truth when words failed.[23] But the "rise of icons" was always accompanied by verbal explanation. The Byzantines did not fall silent; far from it—they continued to struggle, even more than before, to provide exactly the verbal definitions of the faith that had proved so difficult for so long, and specifically to capture in words the relation of images to the truth that they were held to represent. The "rise" and subsequent importance of icons in Byzantine religious life took place in the context of an outpouring of verbal explanation, attack, and defense.

This mystery of representation will form part of the subject of my final chapter. Here, I wish to demonstrate the long process whereby the early emphasis on mystery and paradox in Christian discourse resisted the impetus to assimilation with public

20. See below, chapter 6; and Lossky, *Mystical Theology.*
21. See Harrison, "Word as Icon," pointing to the analogy between word and icon drawn by the Seventh Ecumenical Council of 787.
22. See Mortley, *From Word to Silence,* 2: *Way of Negation,* 221 ff., with bibliography.
23. See below, chapter 6.

rhetoric that we traced in the last chapter and survived as a powerful element in Byzantine religious thought.

In the later fourth century, then, the Christological verse of Gregory of Nazianzus brought the contradictions of Christianity sharply into focus: "He was human, but God, of the line of David, but the creator of Adam. He was in the flesh, but outside the flesh, born of a mother, but a virgin."[24] On one level, this is a play on words.[25] But, being implicit in the subject matter itself, such paradoxes were common to a wide range of Christian writings of very different types and literary levels. We meet them in the learned homilies of the early-fifth-century patriarch Proclus of Constantinople,[26] and in many less finished productions of uncertain authorship from the fourth to sixth centuries. On the Jews, a favorite topic in these homilies, "Eusebius" exclaims: "O disobedience! How evil it is! Into what pit of destruction it has led men! Hate disobedience, which hates you and wants to destroy you; love obedience, which loves you and wants to save you."[27] It is the same with more elevated authors: when the

---

24. *PG* 37.406, 62–63.

25. Cf. Claudian *De Salvatore* 13–15: "He who embraces the whole world, and cannot be contained in all the space of the earth, the waters of the sea or in heaven, was reduced to the size of a child."

26. *PG* 65.681: "bridge, loom, spinner, wool, thread, shuttle"; 720: "mother and servant and cloud and benefactor and ark of the Lord." On Proclus's homilies, for possible Syriac influence, see F. J. Leroy, *L'homilétique de Proclus de Constantinople*, Studi e Testi 247 (Vatican City, 1967); against: M. Aubineau, "Bilans d'une enquête sur les homélies de Proclus de Constantinople," *Revue des études grecques* 85 (1972): 572–96.

27. *PG* 86.1.524. The importance of this large body of material has yet to be brought into the general cultural history of the period, and much remains unedited or available only in unsatisfactory old editions; see, e.g., M. Van Esbroek, "Jalons pour l'histoire de la transmission manuscrite de l'homélie de Proclus sur la Vierge (BHG 1129)," in *Text und Textkritik. Eine Aufsatzsammlung*, ed. J. Dummer (Berlin: Akademie Verlag, 1987), 149–60; in general, see Datema and Allen, *Leontii presbyteri Constantinopolitani homiliae*, intro. The "Greek Ephrem," a mass of such material in Greek claiming to be translated from Ephrem's Syriac, remains equally unstudied.

fifth-century homilist Hesychius of Jerusalem praises Easter Day, he writes in a very typical passage of "a sepulchre which gives birth to life, a tomb exempt from corruption and purveyor of incorruptibility, a marriage bed which has held the sleeping spouse for three days, a bridal chamber which saw the bridegroom wake as a virgin after his marriage." Hesychius goes on, like so many others, to play on scriptural and Christological phraseology, when he writes that "the same who descended into Hell as one of the dead has liberated the dead as God," or "You will say in fact that this one and that one are the same, not two, neither one and the other, nor one in another, nor one for another, for 'the Word made flesh,' being one, has assembled both these and those elements into one, as He wished, in a manner indescribable: the flesh He has delivered . . . He has made use of divinity for signs and prodigies."[28]

In the late sixth century, the patriarch Gregory of Antioch follows earlier precedent in including in a homily a dialogue between the women and the angel at the empty tomb, of which both the style and the language are familiar: "Do you wish to know whom it is that you seek? The truth is verified . . . I will express to you the inexpressible." The angel continues: the resurrection is a mystery, like the cross. "He broke neither the virginity of His mother by His birth nor the tomb by His resurrection."[29] And the tradition continued unbroken; centuries later, George of Nicomedia, another homilist, gives these words to the

28. M. Aubineau, ed., *Les homélies festales d'Hésychius de Jérusalem*, 2 vols. Subsidia Hagiographica 59 (Brussels: Société des Bollandistes, 1978–80), 1:112–14 (*hom.* 4.2–3). The same homily is also edited with introduction and detailed commentary in M. Aubineau, *Hésychius de Jérusalem, Basile de Seleucie, Jean de Béryte, Pseudo-Chrysostome, Léonce de Constantinople: homélies pascales (cinq homélies inédites)*, Sources chrétiennes 187 (Paris: Cerf, 1972), 103–66. For Hesychius's style, see Aubineau, *Homélies festales*, xxxv–ix; and *Hésychius de Jérusalem*, 43–46.

29. PG 88.1860–61.

Virgin as she gazes at the body of her son: "You lie there now, and are devoid of life, you who are the fount of all life."[30]

We could go on multiplying examples. In the nature of the subject, they tend to concentrate so often on the twin themes of the nature of Christ and the virginity of Mary his mother. What theme could be more full of paradox than that of the Incarnation, the subject of fourth- and fifth-century doctrinal debate? And the paradox of the Incarnation implied the centrality of Mary. It is worth looking, therefore, at the special discourse that formed itself around the theme of the Virgin, in particular from the late fourth and early fifth centuries on.

The Virgin as Mystery

At the very end of the fourth century and in the context of Christological and ascetic discourses we begin to find attention focused on the Virgin in earnest, culminating in the adoption at the Council of Ephesus in A.D. 431 of the title Theotokos, Mother of God. In this process, the exact details of the birth of Christ and its physical implications for Mary occupied a principal place.[31] Such questions—including another of burning importance in contemporary Christian writing: whether or not Adam and Eve were sexual beings in the Garden of Eden[32]— arose not just from an intense curiosity, but from the urgent

---

30. *PG* 100.1488.

31. See, e.g., Jerome *Against Helvidium* 18; *Ep.* 22.39; and later, *Dial. Against the Pelagians* 2.4.

32. For an introduction to the extensive literature, see E. A. Clark, "Heresy, Asceticism, Adam, and Eve: Interpretations of Genesis 1–3 in the Later Latin Fathers," in *Ascetic Piety and Women's Faith*, ed. E. A. Clark (Lewiston, N.Y./Queenston, Ont.: Edwin Mellen Press, 1986), 353–85; E. A. Clark, "'Adam's Only Companion': Augustine and the Early Christian Debate on Marriage," *Recherches augustiniennes* 21 (1986): 139–62; E. Pagels, *Adam and Eve*.

need to define Christological doctrine with ever increasing precision. Other factors of course later entered the scene to form and maintain the importance of the Virgin as a cult figure to our own day;[33] in this period, however, the whole subject, like that of asceticism, was intimately connected with the history of Christian discourse.

On the eve of the Council of Ephesus, Proclus of Constantinople wrote several homilies on the Virgin in which she appears as the very type of Christian mystery. As both mother and virgin, she can be said to have "opened Heaven for Adam"—that is, made the impossible possible.[34] She is at one and the same time mother and servant; cloud, room, and ark; Heaven, bridge, and basket;[35] "the figurative Paradise of the second Adam."[36] As with the epigrams of Gregory of Nazianzus, we find here an interweaving of rhetoric with biblical typology to form an inclusive system. Even more than in the case of Christ himself, the person of his mother furnished a subject around which it was possible to create a whole world of paradox and symbolic language, capable of sustaining the Byzantine imagination for centuries to come. Only now, however, did this symbolic world come into its own. Even in the *Life of Macrina*, Thecla remains the model for female sanctity.[37] But from the end of the fourth century we encounter for the first time a developed discourse focused on the subject of the Virgin and concerned with the most intimate details of her physicality.

33. Michael P. Carroll has recently restated the perennial psychological/psychoanalytic argument in *The Cult of the Virgin Mary: Psychological Origins* (Princeton: Princeton University Press, 1986).

34. *PG* 65.709; on the authenticity of the homilies attributed to Proclus, see Aubineau, "Bilans d'une enquête."

35. *PG* 65.720, 684; cf. also 756.

36. *PG* 65.681.

37. *V. Macr.* 2.21–22. See in detail Albrecht, *Leben der heiligen Makrina;* and for Thecla, above, chapter 3.

It was not, however, her tender or maternal qualities that were the main point of attention, but the logical paradoxes implicit in her role as instrument in the birth of Christ. The terms of the Incarnation made Mary into a figure emblematic of Christian paradox. At the beginning of the fifth century, Ennodius, in one of the earliest hymns to the Virgin, asserted that to praise her was to pass beyond the limits of logic:

quid, mens, requiras ordinem?
natura totum perdidit.[38]

In the art of the period, to judge from the fifth-century Virgin-empress of St. Maria Maggiore in Rome, Mary appeared not as suffering or as loving, but as powerful and imposing; in the same way in literary contexts she appeared not as the human mother but as a divine and mysterious personage. Only later, or in some more popular texts, would she acquire the more familiar and sympathetic traits. George of Nicomedia in the middle Byzantine period might describe her in extravagant terms as an afflicted mother weeping beside the cross,[39] Byzantine icons might become progressively tender and maternal as time wore on, but the Virgin as she appeared before the Council of Ephesus was a different kind of figure altogether.

Even for the patriarch Proclus, to sing her praises was to make verbal play with every paradox of Christology: to explain the mystery of the Incarnation, of which Mary was the "vessel";[40] to enumerate the details of biblical typology and the array of female examples from the Old Testament—Sarah, Re-

38. *Carm.* 1.19.
39. Cf. Maguire, *Art and Eloquence*, 96 ff.; the Virgin's lament appears in a sixth-century *kontakion* of Romanos, on which see Alexiou, *Ritual Lament*, 62–63, 142–44.
40. *PG* 65.681, 688–89. For the image applied to human beings in general, e.g. by Gregory of Nyssa, see Harrison, "Word as Icon," 40–43.

becca, Leah, Deborah—of whom Mary and her cousin Elizabeth were regarded as the successors,[41] as well as Eve, whose sin
Mary was held to have canceled. The Virgin of Proclus is a Virgin of the intellect, not the emotions. In the same way, two homilies in honor of the Virgin attributed to Hesychius of Jerusalem
assemble a veritable array of biblical texts, while rehearsing
again all the familiar themes discussed at the Council of Ephesus
and just before.[42] She is termed "God-bearer" ("mother of
God");[43] the birth of Christ, it is claimed, did not damage her
virginity, a theme we shall see taken up with gusto elsewhere.
Hesychius produces a list of praises of the Virgin, which is in
fact a set of paradoxes deeply rooted in scriptural allusion:
among them, she is called "mother of the light," "star of life,"
"throne of God," "temple bigger than the heavens," "seat wider
than that of the Cherubim," "unsown garden."[44] When they
reach the physical details of conception and parturition the paradoxes reach their heights: thus Mary is said to have given birth
without opening her womb, conceived without rupturing the
hymen, nursed the child without change to her breasts. Rococo
as it may seem now, the rhetoric of Jerome and others on the
same theme follows in the same pattern of contradictions. At
times they seem to go too far, as when Hesychius claims that
Mary became pregnant without knowing who was the father of
the child. When he turns to address Christ, however, the Christological relevance of these Marian paradoxes becomes fully apparent: "if you are the pearl, she must be the case; since you are
the sun, the Virgin must be called the sky; since you are the

---

41. *PG* 65.719.

42. Aubineau, *Homélies festales* 1:158–68 (*hom.* 5), 194–204 (*hom.* 6).

43. See the title of *hom.* 5, ibid., 158, and several examples in the homily
itself. The term was recognized officially at the Council of Ephesus in A.D. 431;
Hesychius's homily is dated just after the Council by Aubineau, ibid., 147–49.

44. *Hom.* 5.1–2, ibid., 158–62; on the style, see 145–47, and more generally, 142–45.

flower that never fades, the Virgin must be the plant of incorruptibility, and the paradise of immortality."[45]

The Virgin of these texts is in a real sense a rhetorical construction arising from contemporary Christological definitions. When writing on the Incarnation, Athanasius had met the same problem of having to describe in words what is by definition indescribable.[46] The ultimate paradox lay in the nature of Christ: as the Logos, he represented reason, yet he could not be circumscribed in conventional description.[47] The Word defied words. It is hardly surprising even on the theoretical level that fourth-century Christianity, faced with such a paradox, shows a preoccupation with the philosophical and theological problems of representation, or that the extended disputes about the nature of Christ should have produced ancillary discourses such as that concerning the status of the Virgin.

What is interesting, however, is the way we find these discourses becoming objectified and the Virgin developing into a cult figure on a scale far different from that of earlier times. Cult followed language, and at least in part it arose out of it. We shall see in the next chapter that it was not only verbal but also visual representation that posed problems for Christians of the post-Constantinian era; and here, too, representations of the Virgin provide a striking example of the range of difficulties encountered.

At this period the question of Christological definition was possessed of a fundamentally important political dimension. On the one hand, a unified faith—which meant an agreed and therefore a verbalized faith—was a prime aim of all Christian emperors from Constantine on, whichever side they might incline to themselves. But on the other, the exact nature of that agreed

45. *Hom.* 5.3, ibid., 164.
46. See Ramsey, *Religious Language.*
47. See Laeuchli, *Serpent and Dove*, 61–62; cf. 79–80.

definition carried political implications. It has of late again been argued that the Trinitarian theology of the creed of Nicaea, artfully omitted by Eusebius from his account of the Council,[48] provided theological support for an autocratic political order, just as Eusebius himself presents in his panegyrical works on Constantine a view of descending hierarchical authority from God through the Logos and the emperor to the rest of the human sphere.[49] Such an interpretation leads to a view of Arianism as representing an anti-authoritarian and individualistic position, and holds its dangers for the church of today, as it did for Christians of the fourth century. Not all supporters of Nicaea took Eusebius's view of its political implications.[50] Much more was at stake than mere theoretical questions of definition or description; not just the practical political implications of relations between state and church in an age in which persecution had been replaced by imperial support, but also the formation of a Christian world-view concerning the relation of the individual to authority both secular and divine was involved. In the doctrinal disputes of the fourth century we see a continuing series of struggles to resolve these issues—focusing exactly on the religious language we have been studying, and inevitably involving the reopening of the traditional Platonic questions of language, meaning, and description. But increasing recourse was also made even in learned writings to such figurative tropes as metaphor and simile, and with them to paradox, those very features so deep-seated in all the less formal types of religious discourse and inherent in Christian language.

48. Cf. the bland statement at *VC* 3.14.

49. For an interesting discussion and criticism, see R. Williams, *Arius: Heresy and Tradition* (London: Darton, Longman & Todd, 1987), 14–15, 236–37; see also V. Lossky, *In the Image and Likeness of God*, ed. J. H. Erikson and T. E. Bird (Crestwood, N.Y.: St. Vladimir's Seminary Press, 1974), 13 ff.

50. In particular, not Athanasius; see Williams, *Arius*, 238–39.

The Discourse of Virginity

The theme of the Virgin must, however, also be set against the background of a further and equally paradoxical discourse on the general theme of virginity, which as a subject of treatises and exhortations achieved its greatest success precisely in the fourth century, especially the second half, when scarcely any major Christian figure neglected to write about it.[51] This, too, can be seen as a discourse of paradox, within which the Virgin herself is in an obvious sense simply a special case; it was posed in terms of logical contradictions and rhetorical tropes rather than in relation to real life. For Gregory of Nyssa, himself married, death, which had "reigned since Adam," was finally broken when it "hit the virginity of Mary as if it had hit a rock."[52] The supreme miracle would lie in the restoration of virginity to one who had lost it. Not to be a virgin was always to be the poor relation or the servant at the banquet. Yet the theme also provided endless scope for the play of antithesis; critical issues were indeed in dispute,[53] with individuals ranged along battle lines in the debate about sexuality, celibacy, and the implications of this enthusiasm for virginity for the understanding of marriage.[54]

51. For a list, see T. Camelot, "Les traités *De virginitate* au IVe siècle," in *Mystique et continence: travaux scientifiques du VIIe congrès international d'Avon* (Paris: Etudes carmélitaines, 1952); they are discussed by A. Rousselle, *Porneia* (Paris: Presses universitaires de France, 1983), 171 ff., who remarks on their theoretical rather than practical tone.

52. Greg. Nyss. *De virginitate* 14.

53. Cf. esp. Augustine's agonized and prolonged wrestling with the nature of marriage and sexuality, in which he was frequently also reacting against a background of intense argument by others, and particularly to Pelagianism: see P. Brown, "Sexuality and Society in the Fifth Century A.D.: Augustine and Julian of Eclanum," in *Tria Corda. Scritti in onore di Arnaldo Momigliano*, ed. E. Gabba, Biblioteca di Ateneo 1 (Como: Edizioni New Press, 1983), 49–70; and E. A. Clark, "'Adam's only companion.'"

54. See also P. Brown, *Body and Society;* and P. Brown, "Late Antiquity," in Ariès and Duby, eds., *History of Private Life* 1:235–312.

Figure 12. *The Creation and Fall.* M. Albertinelli, Florence, fifteenth century.

But the argument was fought out in the field of discourse, where it held out virtually limitless possibilities for virtuosity.

No one was better at handling the theme than Jerome—or, at his most extreme, more perverse. He dealt with it both in treatises—*Against Helvidius* and *Against Jovinian,* crushing counterblasts directed at those who had attempted to argue in the other direction—and in many letters addressed to his Roman friends, and especially the young girls and women whom he influenced so strongly.[55] On many occasions, and especially in the notorious Letter 22 addressed to the unfortunate young Eustochium,[56] his sheer rhetorical bravura led him to absurd lengths: marriage, he claims, is worth praising as a means of producing more virgins; the mother of a consecrated virgin, because she

55. For the context of Jerome's writing on the subject, see J. N. D. Kelly, *Jerome* (New York: Harper & Row, 1975), 91 ff., 104 ff., 179 ff.
56. Another sister, Blesilla, actually died as a result of excessive ascetic zeal; see *Ep.* 39.6; Kelly, *Jerome,* 98 ff., 108.

(Courtauld Institute Galleries, London)

has become the mother-in-law of Christ.[57] Yet special case though he may be, and although Jerome the rhetorician may often get in the way of Jerome the Christian writer, his advocacy of virginity and the terms in which it is conducted cannot be so easily set aside, for they belong within a much wider and very deeply rooted contemporary discourse. Ambrose and Augustine in the West, as well as Gregory of Nyssa and John Chrysostom in the East, not to mention the targets of Jerome's own polemics and Augustine's opponent Julian of Eclanum, concerned themselves with the same issues. These now presented themselves in terms of an absolute polarity of opposites: if in the divine sphere the Incarnation represented the impossible, the negation of nature, it might seem that virginity did likewise in the human sphere. It was seen, for example, as overcoming the disadvantages of female gender: if the Virgin Mary canceled the sin of Eve, for

57. On this letter see Kelly, *Jerome*, 100 ff.

which sexuality and marriage were the penalties, she did so precisely by her virginity; thus virginity in human women was represented as a means of transcending the taint of Eve.[58] In real terms, its achievement was a badge denoting the denial of the human condition and the attempt to get back to the "angelic life";[59] in Christian discourse, it stood for the impossible, and thus for a form of religious truth. Jerome, who had engaged in polemics with no holds barred over the details of Mary's virginity, usefully makes explicit the connection between this topic and the theme of virginity in general in his defense of his excessively outspoken denunciation of marriage in *Against Jovinian:* "Christ and Mary," he says, "both virgins, consecrated the pattern of virginity for both sexes."[60] Earlier, he had exhorted the virgin Eustochium to make Mary her example.[61] His blistering attack on Helvidius, who claimed that Mary and Joseph had a normal married life, reaffirmed the increasingly accepted view of celibacy as a higher state than marriage. As in the case of the later attack on Jovinian on similar grounds, Jerome's opponent lost the battle, even if the violence of Jerome's attack and his extreme views brought him into disrepute; in each case the virginity of Mary was related to contemporary views of marriage.[62]

58. Justin *Dial.* 50, 66–67, 84, and esp. 100; Irenaeus *Dem.* 31–32. On gender polarities in biblical imagery, see Frye, *Great Code*, 140 ff.

59. For the theme, see Albrecht, *Leben der heiligen Makrina*, 96 ff.

60. *Ep.* 49 fin. Mary also featured as the "enclosed garden" and "sealed fountain," exemplifying virginity in contemporary exegesis of the Song of Songs; see E. A. Clark, "The Uses of the Song of Songs: Origen and the Later Latin Fathers," in Clark, ed., *Ascetic Piety and Women's Faith*, 405 f., where the point in question was again her virginity during parturition (see below). Further on the importance of the Song of Songs, see P. Brown, *Body and Society*, 274; P. Cox, "Pleasure of Text, Text of Pleasure: Origen's *Commentary on the Song of Songs*," *Journal of the American Academy of Religion* 54 (1986): 241–51; F. E. Consolino, "*Veni huc a Libano:* La *Sposa* del Cantico dei Cantici come modello per le vergini negli scritti esortatori di Ambrogio," *Athenaeum*, n.s. 62 (1984): 399–415; see H. Crouzel, *Origen*, trans. A. S. Worrall (Edinburgh: T. & T. Clark, 1989).

61. *Ep.* 22.38.

62. Jerome does not attempt to answer Jovinian's contention that Mary's virginity had been impaired during parturition; rather, he holds her out as

The late-fourth-century discourses on virginity and on the virgin mother of Christ, with all their concentration on the paradoxical side of Christian expression, also belong within an elaborate nexus of ideas and practice, in which virginity had come to stand for the highest form of asceticism, and human sexual behavior had become the most crucial arena for the practical display of the Christian life. Ideas of human sin and its redemption through the Incarnation were worked out into a detailed scenario in which Eve and Mary both played major roles.[63] The theoretical treatises on virginity, and the long series of homilies and hymns on the Virgin that now begins, should both be read in this connection.

It was a discourse that worked by metaphor and paradox, and that boldly exploited the very imagery it was ostensibly denying. Thus since the second century, virgins had been seen as brides of Christ; by a bold paradox, the "true" marriage was virginity, just as the "true" philosophy was asceticism. In the *Acts of John*, those who refrain from marriage are said to be bound "in an indivisible, true, and holy matrimony, waiting for the one incomparable and true bridegroom from Heaven, even Christ, who is a bridegroom forever."[64] There was yet another, deeper paradox behind this language: Mary, the virgin Eve before the Fall, and all virgins thereafter were understood as figures of the church, the bride of Christ. As virginity is the perfect state, so virginity is a figure for Christianity itself.

Such connections, fed on a constant reinterpretation of the biblical Song of Songs, and especially on Origen's commentary on it, encouraged an overtly erotic language in Christian writing about the relation of a virgin to Christ. Methodius draws on

---

a shining example of virginity (*Against Jovinian* 1.32); see Kelly, *Jerome*, 180 86.

63. Pagels, *Adam, Eve, and the Serpent.*

64. Hennecke-Schneemelcher 2:210; cf. *Acts of Paul* 3.5 – 6; *Andrew* 5; *Peter* 9:34; *Thomas* 1:12, 14; see in general Davies, *Revolt of the Widows*, 32 – 33.

bridal imagery in his *Symposium*,[65] and by the late fourth century Jerome is able to write more explicitly still; in his letter to Eustochium he imagines Christ as a jealous lover, or as putting a hand through a crack in the wall and touching the sleeping girl in the night.[66] Even contemporaries thought that Jerome went too far; but Gregory of Nazianzus can write of his respectable married sister Gorgonia that in death she "desired to be purely joined with her fair One and embrace her Beloved completely, and I will even add, her Lover."[67] We should not, it is clear, read this language in our straightforward modern way as erotic. It may appear more seemly to us, for instance, for widows, rather than young girls, to be represented as "wedded to God,"[68] but in the rhetorical context virgins, widows, and even particularly virtuous married women belonged together as desirous brides, at once the subjects and the objects of this paradoxical erotic discourse.

It was indeed a discourse in which women occupied a special place. They were usually the unspoken targets of writings of virginity, a category that often expanded, following the strictures of St. Paul on women's deportment and behavior, to include writings on their dress and general appearance.[69] There was ample scope for paradox here also. For Jerome, neglect of personal clothing and appearance, even to the point of never washing, is a point of pride in a true ascetic and naturally in a virgin,

65. *Symp.* 3–6. In the Song of Songs and Origen, see Crouzel, *Origen,* 118–19, 141–42, 219–20; in Ephrem, Murray, *Symbols of Church and Kingdom,* 131–58; Brock, *Luminous Eye,* 99 ff., 102 ff.

66. *Ep.* 22.25–26. Jerome translated Origen's commentary on the Song of Songs, see Clark, "Uses of the Song of Songs," 402–6; and P. Brown, *Body and Society,* 367.

67. Greg. Naz. *Gorg.* 19.

68. Tertullian *Ad Uxorem* 4; *Exhort. Cast.* 2.1–2. See Laporte, *Role of Women,* 26–27.

69. See, e.g., Tertullian *De virginibus velandis, De cultu feminarum,* and *De pudicitia;* Cyprian *De cultu virginum.* On dress as deception, see H. Bloch, "Medieval Misogyny."

while conversely, fine clothes denote corruption.[70] The rich Roman lady, nominally Christian, but still fond of her silks and jewels, is one of his most characteristic targets; the Christian girl-child must not be adorned with baby jewels and pretty clothes, for she is destined to receive the most precious pearl of all.[71] It was an extremely self-conscious discourse. Like Jerome, Gregory of Nyssa plays on the contrast between treatises on virginity and the real thing, between text and reality: "Persons who compose long and detailed panegyrics and think that thus they add something to the wonder of virginity deceive themselves. . . . The only sufficient praise of virginity is to make it clear that it is beyond praise and that purity of life is more wonderful than the spoken word."[72]

One of the earliest in this series of writings on virginity is also to our eyes the strangest. The *Symposium* of Methodius, a bishop martyred under Maximin Daia in A.D. 312,[73] is cast in the form of a reported dialogue between women at a banquet in an idealized country mansion, the home of a beautiful lady called Arete. Ten virgins recline at the banquet, and after dinner Arete proposes that each in turn should deliver a panegyric on virginity. Of the ten, Thecla wins the crown, and she then leads the rest in a hymn to the heavenly Bridegroom. Scholars have not found the work easy to classify; Musurillo, for instance, called it "one of the most peculiar phenomena in patristic literature."[74] Its Pla-

---

70. See, e.g., *Epp.* 23 (Lea), 22.27 (Eustochium), 45 (Paula and Melania), 130 (Demetrias); cf., e.g., Greg. Naz. *Gorg.* 10; Paulinus of Nola *Ep.* 39.12–13 (Melania); *Life of Olympias* 13. On dirt as characteristic of holiness, see *V. Ant.* 47, and below, note 77.

71. Jerome *Ep.* 107.5.

72. *De virginitate* intro.

73. Methodius, *Symposium*, ed. H. Musurillo and V. Debidour, Sources chrétiennes 95 (Paris: Cerf, 1963); Eng. trans. by H. Musurillo, *St. Methodius, The Symposium*, Ancient Christian Writers 27 (London: 1958). See also P. Brown, *Body and Society*, 183 ff.

74. *St. Methodius*, 17; according to Brown (*Body and Society*, 184), it is a "bare-faced pastiche."

tonizing form and language place it at a time when virginity already presented itself as an important theme, but before the
authors of the later fourth century had developed a recognized
mode of treatment. Methodius's Platonizing tendencies (he also
wrote a work directed against Porphyry), his use of the symposium theme in this female connection, and his reference to
Thecla link his work with Gregory of Nyssa's *Life of Macrina*.[75]
Like Jerome, both these authors could employ a highly literary
manner in conjunction with the themes relating to virginity or
gender so characteristic in late-fourth-century writing.

The contrast between worldly learning and Christian simplicity was simultaneously developed in cultural terms. It was
not just that Eustochium must refrain from such typically female pleasures as fine clothes; the difference between holy virginity and the worldly life was defined in terms of the world of
the intellect as well. The dedicated virgin would confine herself
to the study of Scripture, especially the Psalms; she might even
learn Hebrew, as Blesilla and Eustochium did; and she should
keep away from sophisticated married women who might lead
her astray: "What has Horace to do with the Psalter, Vergil with
the Gospels, Cicero with Paul?"[76]

By the later fourth century, the topic of virginity had become
a central point of political division for Christians. It posed in
acute terms the problem of the possibility of reconciliation between the stricter, uncompromising side of Christianity and its
need to fit in with the secular world. Jerome's aristocratic Roman friends may not have been typical, but they were being
asked to renounce the accepted signs of secular culture in a way

75. Macrina recalls Plato's Diotima in the *Symposium*, although the
Phaedo is in fact a more prominent influence.
76. *Ep.* 22.29; cf. 107.12: the young girl must keep away from jeweled
and illuminated codices and learn to love first the Psalms, Proverbs, Eccle-
siastes, and Job, then the Gospels (copies of which should never leave her
hands), Acts, and the New Testament Epistles.

that differed from the similar choices being urged on the less exalted only in its heightened drama and visibility. Just so, the treatises on virginity by such men as Methodius, Ambrose, Gregory of Nyssa, and John Chrysostom reflect in themselves polarities implied in the choice: they preach virginity and celibacy in rigorous terms, denouncing the worldly seductions of secular culture while practising the high rhetoric they affect to decry.

The fourth-century discourse on virginity can be read in multiple ways. In the first place, it is a specialized type of the religious discourse that flourished side by side with the public accommodation sought by many of the great Christian orators of the period; like those of Christology or the Virgin, the theme of virginity gave rise very naturally to metaphor and paradox, and could sometimes call forth almost baroque excesses. Yet this literature was typically a learned literature, whose practitioners had usually themselves received the best classical education available at the time. While encouraging virgins to avoid the classics, read Hebrew, and become learned in the Scriptures, they extolled uneducated "simplicity." Their praise of the unwashed and uncultured over and against the social advantages of civilization and learning, which they did not hesitate to display themselves in their own writing, is indicative of an area of deep ambiguity and uncertainty in contemporary Christian culture.[77] Virginity as a rhetorical theme also stood for the actual polarities that remained between Christian and pagan, or between Christian and Christian. Christians at all social levels differed sharply from one another on the degree of rigorism that was obligatory in ordinary life. At the same time, as is perfectly obvious from the sermons of John Chrysostom addressed to his congregation in Constantinople, assimilation of lukewarm

77. Washing had been seen by ascetic Christians since the *Life of Antony* as an emblem of worldliness; thus, Melania the Younger gave it up in order to advertise her religious commitment: see *V. Mel.* 2; cf. E. A. Clark, *Life of Melania the Younger*, 28.

Christians to worldly standards was perceived to be one of the real dangers of success.

We have so far been considering the paradoxical element in Christian discourse mainly in relation to learned writings. The theoretical arguments of the treatises on virginity will have had little effect on—indeed, will hardly have reached—the vast majority. But they quickly made their way into forms of discourse that did have a wider impact, and especially into the homiletic tradition that was the real conveyor of Christianity to the population at large. And they encouraged the development of a whole discourse about the Virgin through which she now rapidly became—and remained—a major object of actual cult. It was not surprising that the passions of contemporary rivalry should have showed themselves in this arena too. These were not mere theoretical issues: they concerned every aspect of human life and emotion.[78]

The learned writings of the fourth century, then, while being the precursors of an unbroken Byzantine tradition of theological writing, also contributed to the spread of that essentially paradoxical and figurative trait in Christian discourse which could not find easy expression in the kind of writing discussed in the last chapter. It is striking to see how in the late fourth century the most highly cultivated of Christian writers—those who practised the most accomplished form of public oratory—simultaneously devote themselves to the themes that will spill over into more popular Christian literature and become the basis of devotional discourse. Accommodation was essential, but too much accommodation might have risked that part of Christian discourse which was "the sacramental language of religion."[79]

The question of the relation of Christian discourse to the pub-

---

78. P. Brown, *Body and Society*, 366 ff., is predictably good on Jerome and Augustine.

79. The phrase comes from an article by J. S. Whale, *The Times*, 23 November 1987, emphasizing the religious limitations of logical synthesis.

lic and private spheres is one that has been briefly raised already, and that has often been implicit in the argument. From the fourth century on we find both the appropriation of the public sphere, in the ways suggested in the last chapter, and a powerfully increasing appeal to inward and private feeling. This is not the whole story, by any means. That feature of late antique culture, for instance, which scholars have confidently termed "irrationality" can be seen not just in terms of an appeal to the emotions over reason, but also in relation to a greater emphasis in discourse on the figurative and metaphorical. In philosophical terms, the outcome of the profound difficulties of fourth-century writers about the use of language might result in negative theology—in silence. But Christian writing in the Eastern Empire continued entirely unabated. Nevertheless, "religious language" in late antiquity went through a movement from "religious expression as and within an intellectual system towards religious expression that is less intellectual and more purely metaphorical."[80] The writings considered in this chapter mark an important step in the change.

It was also during the fourth century, as we have seen, that Christian *Lives* can be said to have settled into a literary genre. Why was this literature so eagerly read and so greatly admired by many in the circles we have been discussing—even the most highly cultivated of late-fourth-century Christians, and especially among the Roman circles influenced by Jerome? Although it is not clear that Gregory of Nyssa, for instance, had read it when he composed his *Life of Macrina*,[81] the *Life of Antony* was rapidly translated into Latin by Jerome's friend and early patron Evagrius of Antioch, and became highly influential among

80. J. Soldati, "Talking Like Gods: New Voices of Authority," in *Pagan and Christian Anxiety: A Response to E. R. Dodds,* ed. R. C. Smith and J. Lounibos (Lanham, Md.: University Press of America, 1984), 178.

81. Albrecht, *Leben der heiligen Makrina,* 52; Albrecht emphasizes the relation of the *Life of Macrina* to martyr acts and apocryphal writings, while also seeing it as marking the beginning of female hagiography.

the Christian ladies of Rome such as Marcella, who were already adopting Eastern ascetic and monastic practices in the 370s.[82] But again, things were not entirely straightforward. The *Life of Antony* is not the "simple" work it may misleadingly appear at first sight, and typically, it drove Jerome himself to try to go one better: his *Life of Paul the First Hermit* claimed that Antony had had a predecessor as an Egyptian ascetic in Paul of Thebes (d. 341). Jerome's own *Life* was equally successful, being immediately translated into Greek, Syriac, Coptic, and Ethiopic. Interestingly, in contrast to Antony, his hero is well read, even though Jerome himself claims to have adopted a "simple" literary style.[83] Considerably later, during his first stay at Bethlehem after his enforced withdrawal from Rome, and simultaneously with his great outpouring of biblical commentary and translation, he produced two other *Lives,* those of Malchus and Hilarion, of which the first, also translated into Greek[84] and composed around 390,[85] extolled the virtues of virginity in a narrative of contrived simplicity, while the second employed a more rhetorical treatment of its subject, a follower of Antony who had died in Cyprus in 371. In the short *Life of Malchus,* a Gothic tale of a monk of well-to-do origins from Nisibis who was captured by nomadic Arab tribesmen and successfully preserved his chastity despite being forced to marry a fellow slave, Malchus, whom Jerome claims to have met as an old man, is allowed to tell his own story. Inevitably the story betrays Jerome's own prejudices: riding on camels, Malchus and a woman taken in the same raid in the desert between Aleppo and modern

82. Marcella *Ep.* 127.

83. See further E. Coleiro, "St. Jerome's Lives of the Hermits," *Vigiliae christianae* 11 (1957): 161–78, and see P. Rousseau, *Ascetics, Authority and the Church in the Age of Jerome and Cassian* (Oxford: Oxford University Press, 1978), 133–39.

84. See P. Van den Ven, "S. Jérôme et la vie du moine Malchus," *Le muséon,* n.s. 1 (1900): 413–55; 2 (1901): 208–326.

85. See Kelly, *Jerome,* 170.

Figure 13. St. Jerome in the wilderness reading. Follower of Bellini. Fifteenth or sixteenth century. (Photograph: National Gallery, London)

Urfa (Edessa) eat "half-cooked meat" and drink camels' milk;[86] thrown together into a cave, they address each other with passionate defenses of chastity; and, having made a thrilling escape, they eventually reach the monastery at Maronia, thirty miles from Antioch, where they are received by the male and female religious respectively. The purpose of the work is clear—to provide yet another exhortation to the virgin life—and although there is plenty of appealing narrative detail, there is little room for the typical features of hagiography. Jerome's art is not in question. Years before, when he composed the *Life of Paul*, Jerome had used the argument that he was putting new wine into old bottles, and he ends the work with a familiar string of contradictions between the worldly and ascetic life styles:

> I should like to conclude this little work by asking those whose heritage is so vast that they cannot keep account of it, who veneer their houses with marble, who string upon one thread the value of whole estates, if there was anything wanting to this naked old man? You drink from jeweled goblets; he satisfied nature with the hollow of his hands. . . . Paradise opens to him, a pauper; hell awaits you, robed in luxury.[87]

Even so, there is a difference between these two *Lives* and that of Hilarion, where Jerome (stylistically, at least) is more his normal self. The introduction invokes classical models, notably Sallust, and defends his work from detractors who had attacked his *Life of Paul*. But the main body of the work combines scriptural allusions with the continuing classical ones, and so in its account of Hilarion's miracles of healing makes the comparison between the life of the saint and the life of Christ.[88]

In these three works by Jerome we can see some of the ambi-

---

86. *Life of Malchus* 4.
87. *Life of Paul* 17.
88. See, e.g., *Life of Hilarion* 17, 18, 22, 23, 27, 29.

guities inherent in the evolution of hagiography, especially in the hands of a highly sophisticated writer. Nevertheless, *Lives,* like some other forms of Christian communication, had the power of speaking to the individual. The holy men of these *Lives* inhabited a world several stages removed from realism, and are described in language evocative of that extra dimension; but real or not, they worked out in their lives both the model presented by the life of Christ and the contemporary ideals of asceticism and, in so doing, brought home the possibilities for every Christian individual. This was a period when a variety of Christian roles, including that of bishop, were evolving, and when Christian writing played an important part in defining ideals for lay as well as clerical audiences; these ideals, embodying the extremes of religious paradox, had an effect on society just as powerful as the public rhetoric in which Christianity took on an apparently more imperial and familiar guise.[89]

The polarities implicit in writing about Christian ideals (especially when identified with asceticism) in relation to worldly life gave an easy reinforcement to the habit of cultivated writers, and especially Jerome, of drawing an over-rigid distinction between the "simplicity" of Christian discourse compared with the results of a classical education;[90] we can indeed see the consciousness of that distinction very clearly at work in the *Lives* written in this period. That Christianity had used, and continued to use, "the language of fishermen" could be a severe embarrassment to a highly trained author of literary ambition, even allowing for considerable exaggeration in their complaints. Yet as Augustine knew best of all, it was also one of the greatest strengths of Christian discourse that it could in some sense reach

89. For bishops, see R. Lizzi, *Il potere episcopale nell'oriente romano. Rappresentazione ideologica e realtà politica (IV–V sec. d.C.)* (Rome: Edizioni dell'Ateneo, 1987).
90. See above, chapter 1.

all levels of society and all levels of education—that is, it could form horizontal as well as vertical links in society. This was also one of its greatest advantages over pagan literature, which for the most part was directed at the perpetuation of the elite. Without that capacity, it is doubtful whether Christianization could ever have progressed as far as it did. As it was, given the Christian emphasis on the articulation of the faith, all classes had to be able to absorb the religious message as well as follow the rules and receive the material benefits of membership.

The connection of Christianity with a new emphasis on the individual has already been noted. It could lead, as it did in the case of Augustine, to a preoccupation with the psychology of the inner life that was altogether new in ancient thought. Similarly, it required new attention to be paid to classes of society hitherto successfully ignored. This in turn had repercussions for Christian writers and preachers. Jerome still resolutely fixed his attention on the upper class, but other Christian leaders in the late fourth and fifth centuries show a striking degree of interest in the problems of reaching an audience at all levels. For Augustine, the average congregation is full of confused masses, the "straw" of the Lord's "threshing floor";[91] these pose a problem just as difficult to deal with as the Jews, pagans, and heretics whom one met outside the churches. It was only natural that religious art came to be seen as a means of reaching such people. An encomium of St. Theodore attributed to Gregory of Nyssa says of the picture of Theodore's martyrdom on a church wall that "painting, even if it is silent, is capable of speaking from the wall and being of the greatest benefit."[92]

Both in preaching and in visual art, the needs of the audience were kept firmly in mind by the practitioners. As far as literature was concerned, the conventional distinctions of popular and

91. *De rudibus catechizandis* 7.11.
92. PG 46.737 (trans. Mango).

"high" literature that lie behind modern claims for the irrationality of late antiquity seem inadequate to explain the fact that horizontal bonds partly dependent on aspirations toward personal fulfilment did manage to become established, even in an increasingly hierarchical society.

The apparent change of taste among cultivated Christian readers that can be seen in some circles in the late fourth century is itself something of an index to these new articulations. Significantly, we often know best about women's reading; both Melania the Elder and Melania the Younger, for instance, were enthusiastic readers of Scripture, commentaries, and ascetic literature,[93] while Jerome sometimes found the demands that Marcella made on him for elucidation of difficulties in her rigorous reading program more than his patience could bear, and Paula's devotional approach easier to cope with.[94] This was a highly self-conscious milieu, and it is possible to sense in the reports of these women something of the enthusiasm with which they threw themselves into their self-imposed task and their thirst for new things to read, as if they had been starved of such intellectual sustenance before. Not only Jerome, but the other Christian writers of the period as well, give the impression of entering on a new world with their exploration of the possibilities of combining Christian literary expression with traditional rhetorical forms. It was not a takeover of high culture by something essentially more popular; rather, new lines of communication were opened up, in which the absorption of those elements that had in fact been inherent in Christian discourse for centuries played a role—the emphasis on the figurative, the use of paradox and now again of

93. *Life of Melania* 23, 26; Palladius *Lausiac History* 55. See E. A. Clark, *Life of Melania the Younger*, 63 and passim; P. Brown, *Body and Society*, 369–70. Rufinus found such zeal for learning alarming in upper-class Christian women; see ibid., 385.

94. *Epp.* 28, 29, 34, 37; on Paula, see *Epp.* 30, 108; cf. *Ep.* 45.2 (a "turba virginum" asks him for lectures).

story. The old barriers were far from down, but the circles in which they could be enthusiastically and even touchingly ignored were growing all the time.

Thus, through its insistence on mystery and religious paradox on the one hand, and through its appeal to the imagination on the other, Christian discourse after Constantine resisted the danger of overassimilation into the public realm. Especially in the Greek world, with the writings of the Cappadocians, Christian discourse as religious language survived a potential imperial takeover. The final chapter will explore the continuation of these more subversive aspects in the Eastern Empire of the sixth century, ending with some suggestions about their contribution to the characteristic thought of Byzantium.

CHAPTER SIX

Toward a New Representation

The Implications of Christianization

The consent of language
This loved Philology
Emily Dickinson

With the growing split between East and West in the
fifth century, it is harder to trace the development of the figural
and narrative rhetoric of early Christianity across both parts of
the empire. In the West, the towering figure of Augustine can
make it seem that an end has been reached; at the same time, his
sheer intellectual stature threatens to obscure for us how far he
actually differed from his contemporaries.[1] There was far more
continuity in the East. We must therefore ask what the nature of
the link is in terms of Christian discourse between late antiquity
and the early Byzantine world of religious images.

I shall attempt to do so here by drawing attention to three
main features apparent in this transitional phase between the
classical world and the Christian empire of Byzantium. The first
of these continues the theme of chapter 4 and is concerned with
the much greater degree of penetration of public life by Christian discourse and Christian ideas.

---

1. Thus P. Brown, *Body and Society*, having reached Augustine, effectively comes to an end; the epilogue (428 ff.), though brilliantly written, does
no justice to the continuity into the Eastern Empire of the themes studied in
the book.

The Christian State

It may seem at first sight that by the sixth century, especially the reign of Justinian in the East, Christian discourse had already come to prevail; the Christian society and the "thought-world of Byzantium" had arrived.[2] But this would be premature. The emperor, who saw himself as a crusader for the faith, felt unsure enough about his position to persecute pagans and "intellectuals,"[3] and Christians were still drawing themselves up along the old battle lines: "Athenians will be worsted by Galilaeans" and "Nazareth will shake Corinth," writes the deacon Romanos; the disciples were "fishermen before Christ and they are fishermen after Christ. Those who formerly dealt with sweet water now utter sweet eloquence."[4] The old claim to Christian "simplicity" continues to be opposed to the corrupt eloquence of the classical world.

Even if disingenuous, these Christian fears were not altogether ill founded. Paganism had not yet disappeared, and Justinian, even while struggling to control division within the church, had to launch several major offensives against pagans.[5] In the capital, some of the most accomplished writers of the day took pains to adopt a purist classical manner, and the emperor himself presented his legal innovations in the guise of restoration of

2. For the term see N. Baynes, "The Thought-World of East Rome," in *Byzantine Studies and Other Essays* (London: Athlone Press, 1955; repr. 1974), 24–46; and cf. C. Mango, *Byzantium: The Empire of New Rome* (London: Weidenfeld & Nicolson, 1980), 149 ff.; C. Mango, "Discontinuity with the Classical Past in Byzantium," in *Byzantium and the Classical Tradition*, ed. M. Mullett and R. Scott (Birmingham: Centre for Byzantine Studies, 1981), 48–57.

3. See P. Lemerle, *Le premier humanisme byzantin* (Paris: Presses universitaires de France, 1971), 68–73.

4. *Sancti Romani Melodi Cantica. Cantica Genuina*, ed. P. Maas and C. A. Trypanis (Oxford: Clarendon Press, 1963), cantica 31, p. 247.

5. On the continuance of paganism, see, e.g., F. Trombley, "Paganism in the Greek World at the End of Antiquity: The Case of Rural Anatolia and

the Roman past.[6] It was an age of cultural contradictions, which in turn mirrored the uncertainty that people felt about the policies of the emperor and the situation of the empire in a changed world. What we see under Justinian, the emperor who aspired to be the "restorer" of Roman glory within a Christian empire, is the last and confusing manifestation of cultural diversity in Byzantium for a long time to come.[7]

All the same, between the end of the fourth century and the accession of Justinian in A.D. 527, the growing public role of bishops and the higher profile of the Christian leadership was a major feature of the undiminished urban life of the Eastern Empire.[8] After the official condemnation of paganism under Theodosius I, Christian patronage could be exercised with the confidence of active imperial support, and cities began to look and sound Christian.[9] As churches proliferated, a repertoire of pic-

Greece," *Harvard Theological Review* 78 (1985): 327–52; T. E. Gregory, "The Survival of Paganism in Christian Greece: A Critical Survey," *American Journal of Philology* 107 (1986): 229–42, with further bibliography; G. W. Bowersock, *Hellenism in Late Antiquity,* Jerome Lectures (Cambridge, 1990), chap. 6; on missions to pagans, see my *Procopius,* 120 ff.

6. For the latter, see M. Maas, "Roman History and Christian Ideology in Justinianic Reform Legislation," *DOP* 40 (1986): 17–31.

7. See my *Procopius,* chap. 2, where I attempt to make sense of the usually puzzling Procopius of Caesarea; cf. also my "Byzantium in the Seventh Century: The Search for Redefinition," in *The Seventh Century: Change and Continuity,* ed. J. Fontaine and J. Hillgarth (London: Warburg Institute, forthcoming).

8. On the Eastern bishops, see Lizzi, *Potere episcopale;* on fifth-century urbanism, see Patlagean, *Pauvreté économique;* and C. M. Rouaché, *Aphrodisias in Late Antiquity* (London: Society for the Promotion of Roman Studies, 1989), 60 ff.

9. This is not the same as Brown's "silent withdrawal of the [classical] city" (*Body and Society,* 439 ff.), an evocative but one-sided view of a process that he seems to date too early. The replacement of pagan euergetism by Christian charity is part of the story, but so is the positive exercise of Christian patronage by individuals and by the church; for the latter in the West, see B. Ward-Perkins, *From Classical Antiquity to the Middle Ages: Urban Public Building in Northern and Central Italy, A.D. 300–850* (Oxford: Oxford University Press, 1984).

Figure 14. Gold marriage belt, with medallions showing Christ between the bride and groom. Byzantine, sixth century. (Byzantine Visual Resources, copyright 1990, Dumbarton Oaks, Washington, D.C.)

torial decoration came into being.[10] As monasteries increased in number, monks increasingly attracted attention from the lay public, while individual holy men were influential in urban as well as rural contexts.[11] Pilgrimage and cult centers, with their building complexes, attracted a flourishing trade in souvenirs

10. For Christian, Jewish, and pagan art in late antiquity, on which the bibliography is vast and often contentious, see K. Weitzmann, ed., *The Age of Spirituality: Catalogue of the Exhibition at the Metropolitan Museum of Art, November 19, 1977, Through February 12, 1978* (New York: Metropolitan Museum of Art, in association with Princeton University Press, 1979).

11. The classic article on holy men by P. Brown, "The Rise and Function of the Holy Man in Late Antiquity," *JRS* 61 (1971): 81–101, stresses their rural role, but a number of scholars have subsequently focused on their integration with urban life; see, e.g., H. J. W. Drijvers, "Hellenistic and Oriental Origins," in Hackel, ed., *Byzantine Saint*, 25–33; S. A. Harvey, "The Politicisation of the Byzantine Saint," in ibid., 37–42; J. Seiber, *Early Byzantine Urban Saints*, British Archaeological Reports, Supplementary Series 37 (Oxford, 1977).

to satisfy the large numbers of visitors,[12] and sometimes gained imperial attention and patronage.[13] In visual terms alone, these developments contributed powerfully to the same revolution of consciousness that centuries before had helped the Augustan regime to find acceptance.[14]

These changes to the physical environment called forth a commentary in words, a Christian discourse of representation, while at the same time the very opportunities for Christian discourse, literary and oral, were greatly extended, in both quantity and type. New circumstances called forth new genres and new ways of expression; indeed, much Christian discourse was now actually *about* Christian images. The new physical setting of a late antique or early Byzantine city called forth its own Christian and mimetic discourse just as surely as the confident Romanized architecture of Greek cities in the second century had prompted the panegyrical descriptions of the contemporary Greek sophists.[15]

There is much to suggest an intensified self-consciousness

---

12. See E. D. Hunt, *Holy Land Pilgrimage in the Late Roman Empire, A.D. 312 to 460* (Oxford: Oxford University Press, 1982); and the splendid survey by P. Maraval, *Lieux saints et pèlerinages d'orient: histoire et géographie des origines à la conquête arabe* (Paris: Cerf, 1985).

13. The notable example is that of the Empress Eudocia's stay in the Holy Land; see Holum, *Theodosian Empresses*, 217 ff.

14. See F. Millar, "State and Subject: The Impact of Monarchy," in *Caesar Augustus: Seven Aspects*, ed. E. Segal and F. Millar (Oxford: Clarendon Press, 1984), 37–60; for the enormous importance of Augustan art and architecture in bringing this acceptance about, see A. Burnett and S. Walker, *The Image of Augustus* (London: British Museum, 1981); and esp. P. Zanker, *The Power of Images in the Age of Augustus* (Ann Arbor: University of Michigan Press, 1988).

15. See, generally, my "Rome and the Greek East: Imperial Rule and Transformation," in *The Greek World: Classical, Byzantine, and Modern*, ed. R. Browning (London: Thames & Hudson, 1985), 203–14; for the Eastern Empire in the fifth century, see also my "Le società romano-barbariche e l'oriente bizantino: continuità e rotture," *Storia di Roma* 3 (Turin: Einaudi, forthcoming).

during the reign of Justinian (A.D. 527–65) about the relation
between what was "classical" and what was Christian. The emperor saw himself both as upholder of Roman tradition and as
crusader for the faith; the prefaces to his laws appealed to ancient custom even while he earned among contemporaries the
reputation for tireless innovation.[16] The ambivalence is familiar:
so too the rhetorical play in the deacon Romanos's diatribes
against classical literature recalls precisely the sentiments expressed by Ephrem the Syrian in the fourth century.[17] Indeed,
the rhetorical stance persists so tenaciously that it can be described as one of the "commonplaces of Byzantine literature."[18]
Yet it was exactly now that the liturgical hymns of Romanos
and others, performed in the Great Church of St. Sophia in
Constantinople, came to serve the purpose of official communication and occupy the territory of imperial panegyric.[19] The curious traveler Cosmas Indicopleustes consciously set up his flat-

16. Like contemporaries, modern writers tend to take up partisan positions for or against Justinian; against are T. Honoré, *Tribonian* (London:
Duckworth, 1978), chap. 1; and Mango, *Byzantium*, 135; for the opposite
view, see A. Gerostergios, *Justinian the Great: The Emperor and Saint* (Belmont, Mass.: Institute for Byzantine and Modern Greek Studies, 1982). The
historian Procopius provides material for both interpretations by portraying
Justinian both as the Devil incarnate and as the emperor beloved by God.
    17. See the discussion in S. Griffith, "Ephraem," esp. 40–41; S. Brock,
"From Antagonism to Assimilation: Syriac Attitudes to Greek Learning," in
Garsoian, Mathews, and Thomson, eds., *East of Byzantium*, 17–34; for Romanos's imagist manner and its Syriac background, see P. Brown, *Body and
Society*, 329. A detailed discussion of Romanos's debt to Ephrem may be
found in W. L. Peterson, "The Diatessaron and Ephrem Syrus as Sources of
Romanos the Melodist" (Diss., Utrecht, 1984); see also A. de Halleux, "Hellénisme et syrianité de Romanos de Mélode," *Revue d'histoire ecclésiastique*
73 (1978): 632–41; but see Hunger, "Romanos Melodos"; and J. Grosdidier
de Matons, *Romanos de Mélode et les origines de la poésie religieuse à Byzance* (Paris: Beauchesne, 1977).
    18. See, generally, Mango, *Byzantium*, 131–32.
    19. See E. C. Topping, "Romanos, On the Entry into Jerusalem: A Basi-
likos Logos," *Byzantion* 47 (1977): 65–91; and E. C. Topping, "On Earthquakes and Fires," *Byzantinische Zeitschrift* 71 (1978): 22–35.

earth account in contrast to the Aristotelian cosmology favored in contemporary philosophy[20] even as the members of the Athenian Academy voyaged to Persia in fruitless quest of Plato's philosopher king.[21]

The term "classical revival" has been much used in relation to this period.[22] Unfortunately, the label is responsible for many distortions, among them the anachronistic picture of Justinian as a patron of the arts, presiding over a Christianized concept of humane letters and visual art.[23] But such readings are a measure both of our unwillingness to admit the actual complexity of the period and of its capaciousness to serve the contemporary concerns of the interpreter. Justinian was presented by the young Raphael in the *Pandects* fresco of the Stanza della Segnatura in

20. The recent bibliography on late Athenian and Alexandrian Neoplatonism, and particularly on Simplicius and John Philoponus, is both extensive and lively; see, e.g., H. J. Blumenthal, "Simplicius and Others on Aristotle's Discussions of Reason," in *Gonimos: Neoplatonic and Byzantine Studies Presented to Leendert G. Westerink at 75* (Buffalo, N.Y.: Arethusa, 1988), 103–19.

21. The related questions of the closing of the Academy by order of Justinian in A.D. 529 and the subsequent whereabouts of its leading figures, especially Simplicius, have given rise to much controversy; see Alan Cameron, "The Last Days of the Academy at Athens," *Proceedings of the Cambridge Philological Society* 195 (1969): 7–29; and H. Blumenthal, "529 and After: What Happened to the Academy?" *Byzantion* 48 (1978): 369–85. A recent theory locates Simplicius's activity at Ḥarrān (Carrhae), where al-Masudi is taken to testify to the existence at least later of a Platonic school; see M. Tardieu, "Sabiens coraniques et 'Sabiens' de Ḥarrān," *Journal asiatique* 274 (1986): 1–44; and I. Hadot, "La vie et l'oeuvre de Simplicius d'après des sources grecques et arabes," in *Simplicius: sa vie, son oeuvre, sa survie. Actes du colloque international de Paris (28 sept.–1er oct. 1985)*, ed. I. Hadot, (Berlin: Walter de Gruyter, 1987), 3–39.

22. See esp. E. Kitzinger, *Byzantine Art in the Making* (Cambridge, Mass.: Harvard University Press, 1977). For critical discussion of the concept, see Treadgold, ed. *Renaissances Before the Renaissance.*

23. This view is particularly evident in the various writings of G. Downey, e.g., "Justinian's View of Christianity and the Greek Classics," *Anglican Theological Review* 40 (1958): 13–22, and "Julian and Justinian and the Unity of Faith and Culture," *Church History* 28 (1959): 339–49.

the Vatican as the emperor who gave Roman law and thus authority to the Middle Ages and the High Renaissance, parallel and prototype for Raphael's patron, Pope Julius II.[24] The very converse of such a conception is the image of Justinian's laws in some writings of his own contemporaries as symbolic not of order but of its exact opposite, disorder, of "throwing things into confusion." It was not surprising that when the manuscript containing the *Secret History* of Procopius, where such ideas receive their most sensational expression, was discovered in the early seventeenth century by the Vatican librarian, he and others who had grown up with the image of Justinian as painted by Raphael, which they took to be confirmed in Procopius's *Wars*, denied that the new text could possibly be genuine.[25]

It is difficult to give a fair account of such a rich and contradictory age. While claiming to uphold "Roman" ideals, Justinian was also an energetic defender of the faith; some intellectuals of Procopius's class—rhetors and lawyers in particular—were arraigned and even put to death.[26] Large-scale missionary success was claimed in Asia Minor, and heretics in the Eastern provinces were forced into hiding.[27] In the towns, the majority of the population, including the educated classes, was now Christian, at least in observance. But the church had not yet succeeded in neutralizing the effects of an intellectual

24. For the Roman imperial symbolism in Raphael's portrayals of Julius, see L. Partridge and R. Starn, *A Renaissance Likeness: Art and Culture in Raphael's Julius II* (Berkeley and Los Angeles: University of California Press, 1980), 42–59; Constantine was another model; see ibid., 53.

25. For the circumstances, see S. Mazzarino, *The End of the Ancient World*, trans. G. Holmes (London: Faber, 1966), 102 ff.

26. See F. Nau, "L'histoire ecclésiastique de Jean d'Asie," *Revue de l'orient chrétien* 2 (1897): 481–82; pagan books were also burnt: Malalas, p. 491 Bonn.

27. See E. Honigmann, *Évêques et évêchés monophysites de l'Asie antérieure au VIe siècle* (Louvain: Corpus Scriptorum Christianorum Orientalium, 1951); and I. Engelhardt, *Mission und Politik in Byzanz. Ein Beitrag zur Strukturanalyse byzantinischer Mission zur Zeit Justins und Justinians*, Miscellanea Byzantina Monacensia 19 (Munich, 1974).

tradition still maintained by an educational system based on the classical authors. The real issues were often obscured, especially for the traditionalists who continued to take classical writers as their models. The Fifth Ecumenical Council of A.D. 553, which took place in Constantinople amid great controversy and excitement just as Procopius was completing his *History of the Wars*, goes entirely without mention from him, although the Eutychius who was unceremoniously bundled into the patriarchate as the bishops were already preparing for the council is the same who is praised by the classicizing poet Paul the Silentiary.[28]

These writers, like the artists of the period, were struggling to make sense of the contradictions in their society. At first sight their themes often seem familiar. The role of the emperor and his style of government, the place of cities, the survival of the landed (and educated) elite—all these are standard themes. Familiar, too, is the apparent contrast between exponents of traditional literary culture and the authors of saints' lives, homilies, ecclesiastical histories, and so on. But the situation now was very different. Christians are in the majority, even within the upper class, though the charge of paganism was readily available for a multitude of purposes, and in particular to indicate dissidence. Even prominent churchmen were not exempt. As late as the end of the sixth century, Gregory, the patriarch of Antioch, author of several surviving homilies, and previously hegumen of

28. For the Council and for Eutychius's role, see my "Eustratius's Life of the Patriarch Eutychius and the Fifth Ecumenical Council," in *Kathegetria: Essays Presented to Joan Hussey for Her 80th Birthday*, ed. J. Chrysostomides (Camberley, Eng.: Porphyrogenitus, 1988), 225–47; and further below. The enormous political importance of this council is brought out by Herrin, *Formation of Christendom*, esp. 119 ff. On Paul the Silentiary, see Mary Whitby, "The Occasion of Paul the Silentiary's Ekphrasis of S. Sophia," *Cambridge Quarterly* 36 (1985): 215–28; Mary Whitby, "Eutychius, Patriarch of Constantinople: An Epic Holy Man," in *Homo Viator: Classical Essays for John Bramble*, ed. Michael Whitby, P. Hardie, and Mary Whitby (Bristol: Bristol University Press, 1987), 297–307; R. Macrides and P. Magdalino, "The Architecture of *Ekphrasis*: Construction and Context of Paul the Silentiary's *Ekphrasis* of Hagia Sophia," *BMGS* 12 (1988): 47–82.

Fara and Sinai, was brought to Constantinople on such a charge. No doubt the grievance had more to do with local politics than with any actual religious leaning, but the crowd in the capital was easily excited and demanded forceful action.[29] However, what actually mattered far more was an individual's position in matters of doctrine—Monophysite or Orthodox, Chalcedonian or Origenist, Tritheite or Aphthartodocetist.[30] Although Procopius affected to deplore such wranglings,[31] they were now what counted. The end of classical urban culture took place to the accompaniment of an ever-increasing level of theological controversy, against which Procopius's criticisms seem oddly beside the point.

By now, despite the persistence of traditional forms, even secular works written by members of the traditional elite are increasingly permeated with Christian ideas and imagery. Imperial panegyric, for instance, is firmly Christian; Paul the Silentiary writes,

> Can anyone find a better day than this,
> on which God and the emperor are honored
> together? It is not possible. We know that
> Christ is Lord, and we know it in every way;
> for you, by your words, sire, make it known
> even to the barbarians.[32]

In Paul the Silentiary's poem, God is Justinian's helper in all the traditional divisions of an emperor's life according to conventional encomium: legislation, founding cities, building churches, making war, drawing up treaties, and embarking on battle.[33] His accompaniment therefore will be perpetual victory.[34] Old and new Rome are invoked together with Christ, and the pa-

29. Evagrius Schol. *HE* 5.18.
30. See my "Eustratius's Life of the Patriarch Eutychius."
31. *BG* 1.3.6.   32. Paul. Sil. *H. Soph.* 1–5 ff.   33. Ibid., 6–9.
34. Ibid., 10.

rade of tamed barbarians jostles with that of Christ.[35] More striking still, the emperor is praised in equal measure with the patriarch, as though the church and the state have finally come together. The poem addresses each in turn, moving from the court of the earthly king, as the poet puts it, to the "hearth of the king of all";[36] toward the end they are invoked together in the same Homeric hexameters in which the church itself has been described.[37] There is no embarrassment here about turning the learned conceits of late Greek poetry to Christian and imperial use.

The same composite of Christian and imperial themes is found in the *Buildings* of Procopius, where the author eulogizes Justinian's building works. Its opening draws on the tired repertoire of classical ruler praises—Homer, the king as the father of his subjects, Cyrus of Persia.[38] But the greatest of Justinian's works in Constantinople is for Procopius the rebuilding of St. Sophia after the Nika revolt of A.D. 532. Justinian becomes the emperor inspired by God, the destruction foreordained in order to make the rebuilding possible, the architects divinely chosen.[39] The rabble, lower class and worthless in Procopius's view, "took up arms against God Himself," and God allowed their impiety so that the church could be rebuilt with even greater splendor.[40] Procopius's determined classicism, affecting ignorance of things Christian, sits uneasily with the more representative theme of the *Buildings*—the emperor's special relation with God: in St. Sophia, "whenever anyone enters this church to pray, he understands at once that it is not by any human power or skill but by the influence of God that this work has been so finely turned."[41] Another church rebuilt and enlarged by Justinian stands "like an acropolis" across the Golden Horn, reminding people of the

35. Ibid., 145 ff., 193, 227–42. 36. Ibid., 81 ff.
37. Ibid., 921 ff. 38. Proc. *Buildings* 1.1.6–19.
39. Ibid., 1.1.21–24; on St. Sophia, see further below.
40. Ibid., 1.1.20, 21. 41. Ibid., 1.1.61; cf. 31.

emperor's generosity.[42] When God inspires the emperor the results may seem well-nigh impossible, yet God works in this way,
beyond the rationality of men.[43] The *logos* demands belief; indeed, its credibility is strengthened, Procopius claims, when it
seems to go counter to the skills of worldly craft.[44] The discourse
is truly totalizing: whether the emperor receives an apparently
"irrational" inspiration or chooses his advisers from the best
available talent, he is always associated with the providence of
God. Just as the patriarch is "all to all people"—judge, doctor,
adviser, teacher, shepherd[45]—so the emperor, repository of secular power, is identified in all things with the overriding power
of God. Even in more deliberately secular works, such as Procopius's *Wars* or John the Lydian's antiquarian treatises, acceptance of the Christian framework is often apparent: "God does
all for a purpose," miracles can save cities, the emperor has a
special relation with God, God can be expected to punish the
wicked in the next world if not in this. The generally accepted
thought patterns, even among the conservative critics of Justinian, are now Christian ones.

The many contemporary examples of a more devotional style
both in literature and in the visual arts are indicative of more
than just some popular feeling that now begins to oust the classicizing tradition. It has been easy enough in the past to dismiss
in this way such writers as John Malalas, whose world chronicle, written in a more popular Greek, seems miles removed
from a history like Procopius's *Wars*.[46] It was now, too, that the

42. Ibid., 1.6.5–8.   43. Ibid., 5.6.19–21.   44. Ibid., 2.3.8–9.
45. See below.
46. The editors of the recent translation of the *Chronicle* give some examples of this view; see E. Jeffreys, M. Jeffreys, R. Scott et al., eds., *The
Chronicle of John Malalas* (Melbourne: Australian Association for Byzantine
Studies, 1986), xxii, with n. 2, citing among others A. H. M. Jones, *The Later
Roman Expire* (Oxford: Basil Blackwell, 1964), 267: "John Malalas, whose
narrative, though childish, has at least the merit of being a contemporary
record."

stories about the semilegendary past of Constantinople, some of
them reflected in Malalas, seem to have become established—
part of a subhistorical world of the imagination that flourished
the more as real knowledge and access to it receded from view.[47]
But these developments and others like them should be seen as
part of a continuum, rather than in terms of a vertical stratification of culture.

Similarly, the appearance in the latter part of the sixth century
of the first of the "icons not made with human hands" has often
been seen as part of an upsurge of popular religious feeling.[48]
The period certainly saw major religious developments; in particular, the Virgin came to occupy the special place in contemporary religious life that she was to retain throughout the medieval period,[49] and that seems to be mirrored in, for example, the
famous Sinai icon of the Virgin and saints.[50] It was also now that
the Marian feasts of the Eastern church took shape, especially
that of her Dormition,[51] and Marian miracle stories now in-

47. See esp. G. Dagron, *Constantinople imaginaire: études sur le recueil
des "Patria"* (Paris: Presses universitaires de France, 1984).

48. See esp. E. Kitzinger, "The Cult of Images in the Period Before Iconoclasm," *Dumbarton Oaks Papers* 8 (1954): 85–150; and P. Brown, "A Dark-
Age Crisis: Aspects of the Iconoclastic Controversy," *EHR* 88 (1973): 1–34;
for the view against, see Averil Cameron, "Images of Authority: Elites and
Icons in Late Sixth-Century Byzantium," *Past and Present* 84 (1979): 3–35.
Concern about images was not a new development; see H.-G. Beck, *Kirche
und theologische Literatur im byzantinischen Reich* (Munich: C. H. Beck,
1959), 296 ff., who emphasizes the long theological antecedents of icon theory.

49. For developments in the sixth and seventh centuries, see my "The Theotokos"; and "The Virgin's Robe: An Episode in the History of Early Seventh-
Century Constantinople," *Byzantion* 49 (1979): 42–56; also "The Construction of Court Ritual: The Byzantine Book of Ceremonies," in *Rituals of
Royalty: Power and Ceremonial in Traditional Societies*, ed. D. Cannadine
and S. Price (Cambridge: Cambridge University Press, 1987), 103–36.

50. See Kitzinger, *Byzantine Art*, 117 ff.

51. Niceph. Call. *HE* 17.28; see Averil Cameron, "The Theotokos," 95.
For a recent discussion, with full bibliography, of the difficult question of the
introduction of eastern Marian feasts, see E. Russo, "L'affresco di Turtura nel
cimitero de Commodilla, l'icona di S. Maria in Trastevere e le più antiche feste
della Madonna a Roma," *Bullettino dell'Istituto storico italiano per il medio*

creasingly feature in the sources.[52] The "relics" of the Virgin venerated at Constantinople in the early seventh century are themselves an index of the hold that the cult had now taken on the contemporary religious mentality.[53]

But resort to a vertical explanation proceeds from a modern sense of superiority and relegates religious phenomena forever to the popular category. As we have seen throughout this book, it was indeed a mark of Christian discourse, and thus of Christian ideas, to be able to work horizontally in a society where few channels of horizontal communication existed. There are many indications in our sources that people of all classes venerated icons and were devoted to the Virgin, just as there are many stories in contemporary saints' lives of ordinary people coming to be cured or helped by the saint.[54] Holy pictures could be small and personal as well as impressive and public, a visible sign of how Christian cults reached into the private sphere. It is not surprising, then, that the stories associated with them in this period often concern women, who are inhabitants of the private sphere

---

evo e archivio muratoriano 89 (1980–81): 71–79. The Western evidence (ibid., 79–150) is of a different order, and much clearer; all the same, it is agreed that the three Marian feasts of the Purification (2 February), Annunciation (25 March), and Dormition (15 August) were all observed in the East by the end of the sixth century.

52. E.g., Niceph. Call. *HE* 18.33 (reign of Maurice); Evagrius *HE* 5.18. On the Virgin in the siege of Constantinople in A.D. 626, see Averil Cameron, "The Virgin's Robe" and "Images of Authority," 18 ff. For Marian miracles in the medieval West, see Benedicta Ward, *Miracles and the Medieval Mind: Theory, Record, and Event, 1000–1215* (London: Scolar Press, 1987), 132 ff.

53. B. Ward stresses the difference between the Western medieval cult of the Virgin (essentially devoid of relics) and that of the saints, usually centered on shrines. The public attention given to Marian relics in this period in Constantinople should be seen as a clear attempt to give this cult a public function.

54. One such occurs in *The Life of St. Nicholas of Sion,* ed. I. Ševčenko and N. P. Ševčenko (Brookline, Mass.: Hellenic College Press, 1984), chap. 69 (the Virgin appears to Nicholas and tells him where to build a church dedicated to her).

par excellence.[55] But now in particular, as the public role of Christianity grew, so we must expect to find religious expression and religious feeling at the top levels of society too. The religious images of the period, it must be emphasized, existed in a context not just of private but also of public Christian discourse.

It is difficult to trace in detail the development of the Christianized imperial ceremonial so fully recorded in the tenth-century *Book of Ceremonies,*[56] but a good deal was certainly already in place under Justinian.[57] The imperial presence at St. Sophia was a well established and regular part of public life when Romanos and others wrote their liturgical hymns celebrating the overthrow of the Nika revolt of A.D. 532. These compositions, with their probable Syrian influence, their openly expressed hostility to classical Greek literature, their blending of Old and New Testament themes within an elaborate metrical system, and their direct allusion to political topics, accompanied the imperial ceremonies conducted in and around the great new cathedral. The dedications of the first Justinianic St. Sophia in A.D. 537 and of the church as restored in A.D. 562 after the dome had been damaged by earthquake were among the great public occasions of the reign; similarly the natural culmination of the proceedings of the Fifth Council in A.D. 553 was a united eucharist in

55. J. Herrin, "Women and the Faith in Icons in Early Christianity," in *Culture, Ideology, and Politics,* ed. R. Samuel and G. Stedman Jones (London: Routledge & Kegan Paul, 1982), 56–83. On women and the private sphere, see J. B. Elshtain, *Public Man, Private Woman* (Princeton: Princeton University Press, 1981).

56. See Averil Cameron, "Construction of Court Ritual"; for the development of ceremonial and the Christianization of Roman imperial practice, see also M. McCormick, *Eternal Victory* (Cambridge: Cambridge University Press, 1986).

57. See my "Images of Authority," 6 ff.; Justinian's successor was crowned by the patriarch in November, A.D. 565, in a ceremony that marked a distinct advance toward the prescriptive formality of later Byzantine imperial rituals.

St. Sophia.[58] Justinian presented himself as the new Solomon.
An elaborate liturgical hymn apparently written to celebrate the
restoration of the dome weaves a complex structure of interlocking images—temple, tabernacle, the Virgin as the temple of
Christ incarnate, the real light of the church and the light of
wisdom (*sophia*), the waters of creation and of baptism.[59] After
a comparison with Bezaleel, the architect of Moses, building the
Tabernacle and the ark, the hymn continues: "We have the Sav-
iour as our lawgiver, as all-holy Tabernacle this divinely constructed temple, we propose our believing *basileus* for Bezaleel's
office."[60] The church of St. Sophia surpasses the temple of Solomon: "That Temple was commonly known as the Place of God,
to which appeal was made by all . . . but they [would] certainly
have to give us credit for surpassing them."[61]

The liturgical hymns of Romanos and others display to the
full the figural qualities not merely of Syriac poetry but of Chris-

58. Eustratius *V. Eutych.; PG* 86.2.2308D–2309A, 2309C.
59. For the Greek text, see C. A. Trypanis, *Fourteen Early Byzantine Cantica*, Wiener byzantinische Studien 5 (Vienna, 1968); for an English translation and discussion, see A. Palmer, with L. Rodley, "The Inauguration Anthem
of Hagia Sophia in Edessa: A New Edition and Translation with Historical
and Architectural Notes and a Comparison with a Contemporary Constantinopolitan Kontakion," *BMGS* 12 (1988): 117–67. On Solomon, see strophes
3, 13–14; cf. also *Narratio de S. Sophia* 27 (French translation and commentary: Dagron, *Constantinople imaginaire,* 191–314.)
60. Strophe 12 (trans. Palmer); cf. Exod. 31:1–11. The concluding stanza
prays for only one *basileus,* suggesting a date after the death of Theodora in
A.D. 548, thus the second dedication of the church; Palmer's analysis of the
themes of the *kontakion* relates it to John 1, the Christmas Gospel (the re-
dedication in 562 took place over the Christmas period and lasted until Epiph-
any 563). On the other hand, there is no specific reference to the restoration of
the dome, and strophe 2 (interpreted by Palmer as referring to the Church of
the Nativity at Bethlehem) suggests rather a new dedication; Dagron, *Constantinople imaginaire,* 192 n. 4 expresses doubt as to 562. Palmer points out
that it is Christ, not Justinian, who is likened to Moses.
61. Strophe 14 (trans. Palmer). There was another side to this: Justinian's
first dedication of St. Sophia had been made possible only because of a riot
bloodily suppressed; its ceremonial, naturally a religious one, placed the emperor firmly in charge; cf. Theoph., p. 217 de Boor.

tian discourse in general. A similar technique is to be found in another literary composition for an imperial occasion in St. Sophia, the publicly delivered funerary eulogy of the patriarch Eutychius, cast in the form of a *Life* and spoken in the presence of the Emperor Maurice, probably in A.D. 580. This is a work highly literary in character, yet conspicuously limited in its range of models; apart from scriptural allusions, the models are almost exclusively specific works by the Cappadocian fathers, among which the oration on Basil and the *Life of Moses* by Gregory of Nyssa are particularly prominent. With such models, the *Life of Eutychius* predictably follows a prescribed rhetorical pattern, the rules of the classical encomium having long been adopted with hardly a change by the more elevated kinds of hagiography.[62] But the function of its use in the *Life of Eutychius* is rather different: it is to produce a kind of collage of reminiscences from the Cappadocians, mingled with scriptural images—Moses, Job—that together set the subject in the middle of a whole complex of interlocking images, just as the liturgical hymn weaves a figural setting. In the extravagance and excess of its imagery, the *Life of Eutychius* goes far beyond modern limits of taste and scale. Yet it is testimony to the available mechanisms as well as to the thought patterns of the late sixth century.

The work, written for an occasion of state and concerned with what were in fact matters of high politics (for the patriarch Eutychius had been a highly controversial figure), offers a curious continuation of themes apparent throughout early Christian literature. Its epilogue offers yet another elaborate play on the old idea of the two rhetorics, the divine, "simple" eloquence, and the rhetoric of the "wise," who yet do not have true wisdom: "Those who journey through life without much travel

62. See, for some brief remarks, Kennedy, *Greek Rhetoric*, 215–41; on the *V. Eutych.*, see A. M. Wilson, "Biblical Imagery in the Preface to Eustratios' Life of Eutychios," *Studia Patristica* 17 (1985): 303–9.

money, that is, eloquence and understanding, and who are in need of skill for the harmonious balance of their discourse, should turn to the living water and drink from the water from its vessels and wells, for it is not seemly to go to an alien kind of education and learning."[63] The action is set throughout on the sacred plane; both emperor and patriarch are advised and helped in prophetic dreams, but the power that Eutychius receives (before the Fifth Council, for which this is in fact the major literary source) is inevitably the power of rhetoric: "holiness rested upon him as if on one of the holy apostles, given to them by fiery tongues, and filled by the Holy Spirit he began to speak."[64] Similarly, the orator himself calls on the power of God for eloquence: "The material for building the tower of David is plentiful, but I am an ignorant architect and an inexperienced builder. But the Lord God is all-powerful. He makes the ignorant wise and gives words . . . to those who preach the good news, opening the ears of the deaf with His own finger, that is the Holy Spirit, and clearing the way before a clumsy tongue."[65] Having taken Gregory of Nyssa's speech on Basil as a primary model throughout, the orator hopes at the end to have "laid the poor fare of his speech before banqueters and connoisseurs."[66] Like the great Basil, his subject has embraced all the secular and sacred virtues: "all praise him [Eutychius] for being all to all people," that is, both to the clergy and the lay.[67] The totalizing discourse is finally claimed.

What does it mean that the Christian discourse becomes in practical terms the prevailing one? One enormously important factor affected both East and West from now on, namely the increasing limitations on the availability of the system of education that had been shared for centuries by nearly all members of the upper class. Books ceased to be readily available,

63. *PG* 86.2.2388C.   64. *PG* 86.2.2305B.   65. *PG* 86.2.2273C.
66. *PG* 86.2.2388A.   67. Ibid.

Figure 15. The Patriarch Eutychius, with Constantine and Helena. (Mykonos, Cathedral of Theotokos Pigadiotissa)

and learning became an increasingly ecclesiastical preserve; even those who were not ecclesiastics were likely to get their education from the Scriptures or from Christian texts.[68] In this situation, whereas an important factor in the spread of Christianity from early times had been its opportunistic quality—its ability to ride on the back of contemporary trends and to draw, if in

68. In the West the situation was the more complex: Cassiodorus's schema for his monastery at Vivarium preserves classical authors even while relegating them to second place. In the East, the position after the mid–seventh century seems to have been much worse: see Cameron and Herrin, eds., *Constantinople in the Eighth Century*, 34 ff.; Mango, *Byzantium*, 136 ff.; C. A. Mango, "The Availability of Books in the Byzantine Empire, A.D. 750–850," in *Byzantine Books and Bookmen* (Washington, D.C.: Dumbarton Oaks, 1975), 29–45; N. G. Wilson, *Scholars of Byzantium* (London: Duckworth, 1983), 61–62. On books in the West, see G. Cavallo, "La circulazione libraria nell'età di Giustiniano," in *L'imperatore Giustiniano: storia e mito. Giornate di Studio a Ravenna, 14–16 ott. 1976*, ed. G. G. Archi, Circolo toscano di diritto romano e storia del diritto 5 (Milan, 1978), 201–36; and A. Giardina, ed., *Società romana e impero tardoantico*, vol. 4: *Tradizione dei classici, trasformazioni della cultura* (Rome: Laterza, 1986).

new ways, on existing patterns of discourse—the balance now
tipped the other way. Those elements that are most characteristic of Christian discourse and least like classical rhetoric come
to the fore.

Ways to Truth

Procopius was exceptional in believing that people should be
allowed to believe what they liked. Most of his contemporaries
were convinced that absolute truth lay in Christianity; this conviction explains the very intensity of the doctrinal arguments
that characterize the period and the unwillingness of most parties to compromise. It also lies behind the increased emphasis on
images and signs as ways to understanding religious truth, and
behind the various attempts that we now see to arrive at comprehensive systems of religious knowledge.

The sixth century saw the beginnings of a kind of religious
scholasticism. It was an age of florilegia, collections of approved
passages, mostly made for polemical purposes and destined
to form the staple source of references in the theological disputes of the next two centuries.[69] In the case of the *Life of
Eutychius,* this attitude made it essential for those in the next
generation who supported his views to claim the authority and
legitimacy of the Fifth Council and his association with the
great orthodox Fathers.[70] But we can also see in this curious *Life*
the enormous importance attached to signs and images, indications by which divine intervention in the world could be
recognized.

In the minds of contemporaries, miracle was one of the clear-

69. See H. Chadwick, *Reallexicon für Antike und Christentum* (Stuttgart,
1969), vol. 7, cols. 1131–60; E. Mühlenberg, *Theologische Realenzyklopädie*
(1983), 11:215–19; on sixth-century attitudes to the Fathers, see P. Gray,
"'The Select Fathers': Canonizing the Patristic Past," *Studia Patristica* 23
(1989): 21–36.
70. For the latter, see esp. *PG* 86.2.2373D.

est signs of God's intervention. Accordingly, we now see a great increase in miracle stories and those forms of Christian writing—saints' lives, for example—in which the emphasis is on the visible signs of the working of God in individuals and in the world. Both collections of miracle stories such as those of SS. Cyrus and John in early-seventh-century Egypt, and the narrative of the miracles attributed to Eutychius during his exile, combine the impulse to codify with the emphasis on divine signs; holy places attracted their own collections of stories to similar effect. From this period dates a great proliferation of collections of miracle stories relating to particular shrines. It was not enough simply to possess relics; the relics had to be given their own discourse.[71]

But as well as strikingly illustrating the importance attached to the possibility of divine intervention in the natural world, miracle stories express in graphic terms the idea that God is knowable through divine signs. Certain biblical signs were placed in a special category, among them the Virgin Birth and, from the Old Testament, incidents from Exodus associated with Moses, Elijah, and Elisha.[72] In addition, the Virgin, who had already in earlier periods represented the mystery and paradox of the Incarnation, and thus the possibility of God's intervention in the human world, now acquired a still more enhanced status in her symbolic role as indicator of divine power. The growing

71. On the *Miracula* of Cyrus and John, see N. Fernando Marcos, *Los "Thaumata" de Sofronio. Contribución al estudio de la "Incubatio" cristiana* (Madrid: Consejo superior de investigaciones científicas, 1975); on holy places and pilgrimage centers as centers of story collections (Oxeia, Thessaloniki, Euchaita, Choziba, and elsewhere), see Maraval, *Lieux saints,* 17 ff. (and see below). See also Averil Cameron, "The History of the Image of Edessa: The Telling of a Story," in *Okeanos: Harvard Ukrainian Studies* 7 (1984): 80–94.

72. See the suggestive discussion in Ward, *Miracles and the Medieval Mind,* 20 ff. Lists of such signs began early (e.g., Cyril of Jerusalem *Catech. Hom.* 10.19; see R. M. Grant, *Letter and Spirit*) and later become a component in iconophile argument; one of the most important of these "signs" was the Virgin, as signifying the miracle of the Incarnation.

number of images and icons of the Virgin from this period presented this signifying role in visible terms. These and other religious pictures, whether of Christ, the Virgin, or the saints, reinforced the idea of a possible contact with God; by extension,
they were often believed to have the miraculous properties of
their subjects. Conversely, pictures or statues of pagan deities
were held to be capable at any time of causing injury: one of the
miracle stories in the *Life of Eutychius,* significantly, concerns
the healing of a mosaicist whose hand had become inflamed
when he removed a mosaic depicting Aphrodite.[73] This suspicion of pagan representation and the converse tendency to attribute miraculous powers to religious images of all kinds can be
seen in a multitude of stories from the late sixth to eighth centuries. But the range of miracle stories is wide, and they appear
in every kind of text, from the simpler saints' lives to the more
ambitious, and from church history to classicizing history. Even
Procopius subscribed to the view that God's will is made known
through signs; in the famous passage where he expresses his be-
wilderment at the sack of Antioch in A.D. 540, he concludes that
God's providence is mysterious, not that it does not exist.[74] Unlike classical historians when they write of *fatum* or *fortuna,*
Procopius is sure of a beneficent purpose and sure that it is
sometimes manifested through a miraculous event.

We find, then, catalogues of miracles in works such as those
in the *Life of Eutychius* or the contemporary *Life of St. Symeon
the Younger,* told in order to guarantee the sanctity of the hero
by demonstrating that God's power worked through him. Although miracles are often associated with asceticism, it is not
the saint or holy man who works the miracle, but rather God
who works it through him.[75]

73. *PG* 86.2.2333 ff. For statues, see C. Mango, "Antique Statuary and the
Byzantine Beholder," *DOP* 17 (1963): 53–75.
74. *BP* 2.10.4–5.
75. See *V. Ant.* 38; *PG* 26.897B ff.

Miracles could also happen quite unexpectedly through ordinary people, or through inanimate objects, as we can see in the almost casual way authors of all kinds in the late sixth and early seventh centuries include miracle stories.[76] Equally, they could be attached to places or institutions, especially monastic ones. The prominent place that Cyril of Scythopolis, author of several monastic lives written in Palestine in the reign of Justinian,[77] gives to miracle in his works demonstrates a world-view in which, since the world itself is the miraculous creation of God, all is potentially miraculous.[78] History becomes a matter of revelation through signs, and signs the mechanism of history. But miracles are often localized, as in the works of Cyril, where they are associated with the foundation of the Great Lavra; they might equally be attached to shrines like that of SS. Cosmas and Damian outside the Theodosian wall of Constantinople, where Justinian himself experienced a healing miracle.[79] With earlier exceptions, such as the miracles attached to the shrine of Thecla at Seleucia, collections of miracle stories focused on specific shrines seem characteristically to develop in the East in the sixth and seventh centuries.[80] In the majority of cases the miracles consist of cures associated with the shrine itself, as in the cases of SS. Cosmas and Damian and St. John the Baptist at Oxeia (site of the relics of Artemius) in Constantinople, SS. Cyrus and John at Menouthis in Egypt, and others where incubation was practiced.[81] They vary greatly in origin and mode of collection, and cannot be dismissed as merely representing simple tales for

76. Several examples related to images are included in Mango, *Art of the Byzantine Empire*, 134 ff.

77. See Flusin, *Miracle et histoire*, 32 ff.

78. This is essentially the view of Augustine (*Civ. Dei* 21.9).

79. Proc. *Buildings* 1.6.5–8.

80. Maraval, *Lieux saints*, 17–18. Cosmas and Damian (Constantinople); Cyrus and John (Menouthis); Demetrius (Thessalóniki); Menas (south of Alexandria); Artemius (Constantinople); Ptolemaeus (Hermopolis Magna).

81. Maraval, *Lieux saints*, 224 ff.

the pious: Sophronius, for example, the editor of the *Miracles of Cyrus and John,* was later patriarch of Jerusalem and one of the major and most accomplished writers of the seventh century. Not only are martyria and shrines with relics of saints thick on the ground all over the Eastern Empire; the miracles associated with them now had to be recorded and codified as well.

Certain distinguishable types begin to appear among the individual stories of the wider repertoire. Among them are miracles associated with the Eucharist and the Virgin. The church historian Evagrius tells how in the reign of Justinian a boy, who happened to be the son of a Jewish glassblower, was sent among a group of Christian boys according to custom to consume the remainder of the consecrated elements after a service. His father punished him by shutting him inside his furnace, but although the boy spent three days in the furnace before his mother found him, the flames had not harmed him; on being questioned he said that a lady dressed in purple had kept bringing him water so that he could quench the flames.[82] The upshot of the story was that the boy and his mother were converted, whereas Justinian had the father impaled as a child killer. Then, as often in recent times, the Virgin was identified in visions only as a beautiful lady.[83] Just as now she is sometimes believed to bring warning messages for the world, so in the sixth century she could

82. *HE* 4.36; cf. Gregory of Tours *De gloria martyrum* 9, and 8, 10, 18, 19. In a letter of St. Symeon Stylites the Younger to the emperor (probably Justinian), a call is made for repression of Samaritans on the grounds that they have profaned an image of the Virgin (Mansi 13.159–62; *PG* 86.2.3216–20).

83. On stories of the Virgin in the late sixth century, see H. Chadwick, "John Moschus and His Friend Sophronius the Sophist," *JThS*, n.s. 25 (1974): 65–66; on modern apparitions of the Virgin, see Carroll, *Cult of the Virgin Mary,* 115 ff. M. Walsh, *The Apparitions and Shrines of Heaven's Bright Queen,* 4 vols. (New York, 1904), gives a conspectus of Marian apparitions from the beginning to the twentieth century. Although in some recent apparitions the Virgin was seen as she was represented in a familiar depiction, equally often, as at Paris in 1830, La Salette in 1846, and Lourdes in 1858, the

punish her enemies as well as protect those whom she favored.[84] Visions of beautiful children, in contrast, may signify the Eucharist, although when the patriarch Eutychius sees such a vision his panegyrist identifies the boy as representing the church.[85]

The East did not rival the West in collections of Mary miracles, but the restoration of the Virgin's robe to Blachernae after removal for safekeeping in A.D. 619 and the role attributed to the Virgin in the siege of Constantinople in 626 both called forth contemporary reports of her miraculous intervention.[86] Moreover, Constantinople claimed two Marian relics, her robe and her girdle, whose finding stories were updated as events seemed to warrant. During Iconoclasm the icons of the Mother of God were frequent subjects of Iconoclast abuse and Iconophile justification, but the Iconoclasts never attacked her preeminent position as "higher than the heavens and holier than the cherubim,"[87] and the restoration of her image in the apse of St. Sophia in A.D. 867 sealed the final ending of Iconoclasm. In the figure of the Virgin, or as she was more commonly called in the East, the Mother of God, the power of image and mystery was ratified once and for all.

The reliance on Christian imagery and scriptural typology in works designed for public and indeed imperial occasions, the growth and codification of miracle stories with their emphasis on signs, and the increasing devotion to icons all continue the tendencies in Christian discourse that I have stressed in earlier

---

lady was not at first identified. Needless to say, the "bewildering variety of titles" and types under which the Virgin is known to modern Catholics (Carroll, *Cult of the Virgin Mary*, 180) was not yet a complicating factor in late sixth-century apparitions.

84. Nic. Call. *HE* 18.33.

85. *PG* 86.2.2301.

86. See Averil Cameron, "The Virgin's Robe."

87. As recognized in the so-called *horos* of the Iconoclastic Council of A.D. 754; Mansi 13.277D.

periods; now, with the loosening of "classical" structures, they come into full prominence. We should also expect to find continued just that element of mystery and paradox that was the subject of the last chapter.

These trends now found a theoretical base in the writings of one of the most influential authors of the period, who is also in all senses one of the most mysterious. The works attributed to "Dionysius the Areopagite"[88] seem to belong to the early sixth century; for the author of the *Life of Eutychius* he is already one of the fathers. Nevertheless, it is far from easy to characterize the basis of his thought, since although he writes of Christ and the hierarchy of the church, and indeed of the liturgy, he does so very much in the context of the later Neoplatonists.[89] For our present argument it is sufficient to emphasize some of the main elements and to remember how influential his works were on the next generations, in order to realize how far the writings of the ps.-Dionysius actually put into theoretical terms tendencies long apparent in the wider Christian discourse. The two fundamental ideas are those of hierarchy, according to which all things human and divine are arranged in a fixed order of authority, the underlying principles being *taxis* (order) and harmony, and mystery, the gap between human and divine and the consequent need for revelation through signs. Neither of these

88. The *Celestial* and *Ecclesiastical Hierarchies,* the *Divine Names,* and the *Mystical Theology* (PG 3.119–1064), and *Letters* (PG 3.1065–1122); the works are translated with notes and introduction by C. Luibheid and P. Rorem, *Pseudo-Dionysius: The Complete Works,* Classics of Western Spirituality (London: SPCK, 1987). See A. Louth, *Denys the Areopagite* (London: Geoffrey Chapman, 1989); Mortley, *From Word to Silence,* 2: *Way of Negation,* 221 ff.; R. Roques, *L'univers dionysien: structure hiérarchique du monde selon le Pseudo-Denys* (Paris: Cerf, 1983).

89. Cf. Mortley, *From Word to Silence,* 2: *Way of Negation,* 229: "The archetypal Christian mystic . . . his work illustrates the apophatic way at its most highly developed, and constitutes the end of the long voyage from Parmenides through to the closure of the Athenian academy in the sixth century A.D."

ideas was new. Origen, in his *De Principiis* had expressed the conception of a unified world order under the will of God and the need for revelation through God's signs. There are further similarities: both writers see divinization as the human goal, culminating in complete participation in God, and achievable only through the tradition of the church, and above all through the Scriptures.[90] But unlike those of Origen, the works of the ps.-Dionysius rapidly acquired quasi-canonical status and exerted an enormous influence in the next formative period. Indeed, it would be hard to exaggerate the extent to which they contributed to the totalizing Christian discourse which was now becoming the discourse of the whole of society.[91]

Like many later mystics, the ps.-Dionysius asserts the contradictory.[92] God is to be known both by affirmative (*kataphatic*) and negative (*apophatic*) means. Rational language, the language of Greek philosophy, will not suffice to describe the attributes of God; it will be necessary to go beyond it, in the direction of mystical contemplation. The Scriptures are naturally not to be taken literally, but rather as full of symbols used in the effort to get near to understanding the indescribable. Letter 9 discusses scriptural imagery explicitly: "Among uninstructed souls the fathers of unspeakable wisdom give an impression of outstanding absurdity when, with secret and daring riddles, they make known that truth which is divine, mysterious, and, as far as the profane are concerned, inaccessible." The Scriptures use "sacred pictures" to represent God, which are "the protective

90. On Origen, see J. Daniélou, *Origen,* trans. W. Mitchell (London: Sheed & Ward, 1955); R. P. C. Hanson, *Allegory and Event: A Study of the Sources and Significance of Origen's Interpretation of Scripture* (London: SCM Press, 1959); K. J. Torjesen, *Hermeneutical Procedure and Theological Method in Origen's Exegesis,* Patristische Texte und Studien 28 (Berlin, 1986). I am grateful to Robert Brogan for this comparison.

91. For the lasting influence of the corpus on orthodox thinking, see, e.g., Lossky, *Mystical Theology.*

92. See Mortley, *From Word to Silence,* 2: *Way of Negation,* 237–38.

Figure 16. The ranks of the heavenly host surrounding the baptism of Christ. Venetian, late sixteenth century. (The Governing Body, Christ Church, Oxford)

garb of the understanding."[93] Symbols are thus all-important; the paradox, the mystery, the sign, the sacrament—these are the ways in which God can be known. The precise images demand their own explication: "Why," the author asks, "does the Word of God seem to honor the depiction of fire above all others?"[94] He is thinking of the imagery of the seraphim, and answers that this is the most appropriate way in which to show that the intelligent beings of Heaven are like the Deity; the image of fire reflects the characteristics of the Deity. The language is the language of resemblance: heavenly beings resemble the divine and are imitators of God.[95] But ultimately God remains a mystery, to

93. *Letter* 9 (trans. Luibheid and Rorem, 281–83).
94. *Celestial Hierarchy* 328C (trans. Luibheid and Rorem, 183).
95. Ibid., 329A–C.

be known only in the mystical "cloud of unknowing,"[96] where the "mysteries of God's Word lie simple, absolute and unchangeable in the brilliant darkness of a hidden silence."[97]

The Closed Tradition

The ps.-Dionysius is at once the interpreter of the signs through which God can be known and one who insists on man's inability to penetrate the ultimate mystery. The correct signs have been established by a chain of authorities who constitute the tradition.[98] It is a closed tradition, formed of the Scriptures, the Apostles, the "ancient teachers" (the Fathers), baptism, and the sacraments of the church. It is not simply that all the elements of a total discourse are now firmly in place; even knowledge and discourse themselves are limited to the dim perceptions allowed in the human world, through the signs and messengers that God chooses to vouchsafe.

Logically, the effect should have been silence. But the ps.-Dionysius represents both the tendencies in Christian discourse that I have emphasized: the stress on mystery and signs, and the impulse toward codification. Just as it was necessary for miracles to be codified, for a theory of images to develop, for a theology of the Virgin to be created complete with liturgical feasts and finding-stories for her relics, so it was necessary for this systematic Christian discourse to be articulated. The ps.-Dionysius does more: he presents us with a fully worked out Christian system, from the practicalities of the liturgy to a theory of angels. Not surprisingly, then, the paradox of Christian discourse was exactly that even after the writings of the ps.-Dionysius it con-

96. *Mystical Theology* 1001A (trans. Luibheid and Rorem, 137): "the truly mysterious darkness of unknowing."
97. *Mystical Theology* 997A (trans. Luibheid and Rorem, 135).
98. *Ecclesiastical Hierarchy* 568A.

tinued to try to say the impossible; the first commentary was already in existence before the middle of the sixth century, but in practice the most important and influential was that written a century later by an equally great theologian, Maximus Confessor.[99] The fact that he devoted himself to such a task indicates the depth of the influence of the ps.-Dionysian corpus; among Maximus's other voluminous writings are several important works on spirituality and asceticism in which it is obvious that he was writing very much in that tradition.[100] Maximus died in A.D. 662, mutilated and in exile, as a defender of orthodoxy against imperial Monothelitism; nevertheless, his later influence was enormous. It was Maximus who ensured ps.-Dionysius his place in later Orthodox theology, and who transmitted to later generations the emphasis on negative theology, that is on mystery, already strong in the Cappadocians and now reiterated by ps.-Dionysius. Maximus's work, too, included notable attempts at a synthesis of Christian knowledge. The same trend was continued by a further voluminous writer, the greatest theologian of the next century and the most famous defender of images, St. John Damascene, whose "Fount of Knowledge" included a synthesis of extracts from earlier writers constituting an exposition of the orthodox faith.[101] Each of these three writers concerned himself both with the definition of religious knowledge (*gnosis*), and the importance of revelation through signs; each, too, aimed at producing a type of synthesis or compendium of human and divine knowledge. The titles of their works are sug-

99. *PG* 4.16–432, 526–76; see Louth, *Denys the Areopagite*, 113–14.
100. Maximus's works are currently being edited for the *Corpus Christianorum* series; meanwhile see Beck, *Kirche und theologische Literatur*, 436ff., esp. 439–40; on the influence of ps.-Dionysius, see, e.g., M. de Gandillac, *Oeuvres complètes du Pseudo-Denys l'Aréopagite*, 2d ed. (Paris: Bibliothèque philosophique, 1943), 46–49.
101. See Beck, *Kirche und theologische Literatur*, 476ff.; cf. 301: "In Joannes triumphiert der Areopagite."

gestive enough—*Celestial Hierarchies, Mystagogia, Exposition of the Orthodox Faith.* It was a time for codification and for definition. As the Iconoclast and Iconophile councils of the seventh and eighth centuries fed on collections of proof texts, approved passages from the Fathers, statements of earlier councils, so too the leading orthodox theological writers sought to set down and define the essence of the orthodox faith, at the same time giving a new emphasis to the idea of the Christian faith as mystery and Christian knowledge as a matter of revelation. The ps.-Dionysius had not silenced theological discourse after all.

Moreover, even though such a theory underlined the very problems inherent in visual representation, it is not hard to see these writings as supporting an increased emphasis on religious art. In the *Celestial Hierarchy,* the ps.-Dionysius insists that the divine hierarchy must not be thought to correspond to the images with which it is represented in the Scriptures: images are necessary because "we lack the ability to be directly raised up to conceptual contemplations. We need our own upliftings that come naturally to us and which can raise before us the permitted forms of the marvelous and unformed sights," and also because "it is most fitting to the mysterious passages of scripture that the sacred and hidden truth about the celestial intelligences be concealed through the inexpressible and the sacred and be inaccessible to the hoi polloi." [102]

Two parallel thrusts in the theology inspired by the ps.-Dionysius both conduce toward an intensified attention to religious images: both the insistence on the mystery of God, revealed not through human reason but through God's own signs, and the consequent need to define the exact way in which those signs, among them religious images, represent reality. We see

---

102. *Celestial Hierarchy* 140A–B (trans. Luibheid and Rorem, 149).

here the technologizing of divine knowledge to which earlier Christian writings have been aspiring. It is, however, knowledge based on the conception of an ultimate truth, which can be reached only through contemplation, not through human means, or if so, only in the most imperfect way. The universe of the ps.-Dionysius is hierarchically structured in the extreme and has no capacity for deviation. Although the human search for God is defined as the search for the truth, even this takes place through God's initiative, which the ps.-Dionysius defines as "love," or rather, "desire."[103] The activity of the divine hierarchy, through which humans rise to union with God, is not reason but love; indeed, human reason is itself derived from divine wisdom.[104] The ideas are Platonizing, like the justification of religious images in terms of prototype and copy—and not surprisingly so, when the problems presented by religious knowledge and religious images were so close to the problems faced by Plato.

The Totalizing Discourse

Thus the conception of the relation between discourse and reality enunciated by the ps.-Dionysius and endorsed by later writers depended on the idea of absolute truth. It allowed no waver or dissent. The compendia produced by such authors as the ps.-Dionysius, Maximus, and John Damascene were meant as handbooks to the truth, not as guides to rational discussion. Whatever may have become of the seven philosophers from the Athenian Academy, and in particular Simplicius, who returned from Persia to compose a long series of Aristotelian commentaries,[105] the great names for the two hundred years after the

103. ἔρως in preference to ἀγάπη: *Divine Names*, 708Bff. The fact that in Greek there are two words both meaning "love" forces the author to discuss the difference, though for him God's love includes both types.
104. Ibid., 868B.
105. See above, note 21.

early seventh century are those of ecclesiastics. Stephen of Alexandria seems to have taught philosophy in Constantinople under Heraclius, but when Theophylact Simocatta under Heraclius prefaces his *History* with a dialogue between philosophy and history, he locates it under the patronage of the patriarch. Yet learning did not come to an end;[106] rather, it fell increasingly in the preserve of the church and was expressed in theological works and learned sermons, when it was not being deployed to polemical effect in the doctrinal battles of the seventh and eighth centuries. This is the society, forced back on itself militarily and economically, drastically reduced in geographical area, and threatened by a new enemy in the East in addition to the more familiar ones in the West, in which proliferating religious images offered an alternative discourse in place of what had been effectively lost, and themselves demanded a *logos* of increasing sophistication. The works of the ps.-Dionysius attracted a series of commentaries and scholia, and the various parties in the Christological disputes—Neochalcedonians, Monophysites, Monothelites, Nestorians—drew up armories of ingenious scholastic argument. Meanwhile, the great intellectuals of the church had inherited the prestige and authority that had formerly been bestowed on a traditional elite by a classical education. They monopolized the power of rhetoric. In the works of the theologians of the seventh century the theology of the image, designed to explain the mystery of the divine and its relation to man, had come to constitute the rational discourse of a Christian society. Eventually they were faced not only by new invasions and military defeat but also by the need to defend and explain the theory itself. They were to be successful, though only with great struggles; but that is, for the moment, another story.

106. See "Images of Authority," 24–25.

Envoi

Christian discourse presents a paradox: sprung from a situation of openness and multiplicity, its spread produced a world with no room for dissenting opinion. It was not an intrinsically more religious or more spiritual mentality that enabled Christianity to prevail in the medieval culture of Byzantium and the West, so much as the fact that the Christian church and Christian discourse had achieved the position of chief carriers and arbiters of culture. Though not the only possible mode of expression, Christian discourse came in practice to be exactly that; it provided both the framework within which most people looked at the world and the words that they used to describe it.

Whether this situation is to be termed "decline" is obviously a matter of opinion. Certainly old structures gave way. Secular culture, lacking the institutional strength and the purposeful thrust of Christian discourse, was in the end unable to resist. The former had remained an elite preserve; there was little or no incentive to literacy for secular purposes and no desire to teach by other means. Christians, by contrast, had both the will and the way. I have attempted to show how, and in part why, this might have happened. As a somewhat hostile critic has put it, "the true culture of Byzantium, i.e. the body of received doctrine and opinion that defined the outlook of a representative segment of the Byzantine public and filtered down to the ordinary folk, was dominated, not by classical antiquity as we understand it, but by a construct of the Christian and Jewish apologists built up in the first five or six centuries A.D."[1] The nature of that "construct" and the implications of its substitution for the existing classical models have been major concerns of this book.

The general adoption of Christian discourse brought major problems. The mixture of half-understood beliefs and prejudices held by the general population was only part of the difficulty. At an even more basic level the problem of Christian language was such that generations of the most powerful Christian thinkers had to wrestle with questions of representation, rationality, realism, and naming. Naturally these problems did not present themselves equally to all strata of society. Gregory of Nyssa and Augustine knew perfectly well that their philosophical difficulties would be of no interest to the majority. Yet the philosophical and theological problems that they, as well as later thinkers such as the ps.-Dionysius and Maximus Confessor, attempted to face did determine the framework within which more ordinary intellects could operate—just as today, without our understanding the technicalities of physics, our categories of thought are in practice dictated by what a journalist recently described as "the suffocating embrace of scientific materialism in modern culture." The adoption of a Christian worldview and with it a Christian discourse in the Roman Empire was hardly a "scientific revolution"; all the same, it represented a cultural shift of the most fundamental kind. It gave society new themes. At the same time, the problems of meaning, truth, and objectivity raised by the very notion of Christian discourse are also the ones with which the intellectual disciplines often called "the human sciences" continue to struggle in our own generation. It is this philosophical and intellectual dimension—re-

1. Mango, "Discontinuity with the Classical Past," 57.

inforced by our contemporary consciousness of the all-pervasiveness of rhetoric[2]—that needs to be reintroduced into the historian's approach to the Christianization of the Roman Empire.

The paradoxical result of the process we have been considering is that the steady diffusion of Christian discourse in late antiquity led both to the conclusion that God is unknowable and to the development of Christian religious images. How is this apparent contradiction to be explained?

I have argued that Christian discourse rested from its beginnings, and for whatever reasons, essentially on the figural. This statement is hardly new, though it is usually literary critics who make it. Strikingly, philosophers and students of religious language are increasingly sensitive to the role of metaphor, paradox, and imagery in Christian discourse, again with analogies with scientific language. But the observations are rarely given a historical application. I have tried to suggest here that the discursive and the historical should be brought together, and that this figural aspect of Christian language had profound implications for the society of late antiquity and the early medieval period.

Is it really likely that men and women became somehow more spiritual as the Roman Empire drew on? This is exactly what is often proposed: as life became more uncertain, as the state found itself in difficulties, its citizens turned to religion for comfort and in so doing inaugurated a religious age. It is the classic functional explanation, and like most explanations of this kind, it ignores the fact that the same or worse conditions in other

2. New books with "rhetoric" in their titles appear every day: e.g., to choose at random, J. S. Nelson, A. Megill, and D. McCloskey, eds., *Rhetoric of the Human Sciences: Language and Argument in Scholarship and Public Affairs;* S. A. Tyler, *The Unspeakable: Discourse, Dialogue, and Rhetoric in the Postmodern World* (both Madison: University of Wisconsin Press, 1987). Traditional rhetoric is defended again by Brian Vickers, *In Defence of Rhetoric* (Oxford: Oxford University Press, 1988).

periods of history, including our own, have failed to produce the same results. It is also an explanation which carries the implausible corollary that in times of public calm or success religion can be expected to flounder. And it implies a suspiciously naive assumption that we can appreciate without further ado the impact on contemporary consciousness of troubles perceived by us, the historians, with the benefit of hindsight, as life-threatening to their society.

No, whether religion is or is not important at a given time, whether people think it important to give up part or even most of their lives to practices that others may find absurd, what consolation they may derive from this behavior and what priority they give it has much more to do with how they are brought up, what they are told, how pervasive is the structure that supports such ideas, and how many or how few are their alternatives, than it does with their natural spirituality. Like that of medieval society, but in contrast with our own, the sign system of late antique society was "poised on God."[3] When a society adopts a different religious system—that is, a different system of signs—the reasons why its citizens accept it thereafter will be as multiple as those that led to its adoption in the first place. Naturally, however, the message it promulgates and the means by which it is promulgated will be central, and all the more so in the context of the limited alternatives on offer in a traditional society.

An emphasis on religious language helps us to understand some of the more puzzling aspects of the late antique period. Far from being marginal extravagances, the Christological disputes of the fourth to sixth centuries, for instance, emerge as lying at the very heart of the process of Christianization: it was critically important, if barely possible, to define in words the content of the faith. The church councils, from Nicaca I (A.D. 325) to Ni-

3. See J. Baudrillard, *La société de consommation* (Paris: Denoël, 1970), chap. 1.

caea II (A.D. 787), were no mere theological indulgences, but among the most dynamic historical factors in the period; and they were so precisely because of the intractable nature of the faith that was in need of definition.

The issue of representation was central: if Christianity could not be adequately expressed by logical means, resort must be had to image, and where words failed, to the visual image. Thus the religious image, justified in the early stages as a way of educating the ignorant and illiterate, became the staple of Christian society and attracted its own sophisticated theology of representation. Religious images—icons—stand at the logical end of Christian representation. From Christology—the attempt to define the nature of Christ—the passage of debate to the theory of the image was utterly predictable; and if images were to acquire such significance, the exact manner of their representation must be settled.

This then was a society in which attention was directed toward a particular set of problems implicit in the very concept of Christian discourse. Modern societies place their main attention elsewhere. But once the Christian church had reached a certain point of prominence in the Roman Empire, the problems of definition and of representation carried their own logic and their own dynamism. We should not be surprised if contemporaries pursued them to the limit, any more than we are surprised by the political, scientific, or academic discourses of our own society.

I have deliberately ended before the real disputes about religious images begin. The implications of writings like those of the ps.-Dionysius and, later, Maximus Confessor are very clear even so. For if the goal of the human spirit was to be defined as a process of divinization achievable only in contemplative union with God, if the human and divine worlds display the harmony of God through an all-embracing system of signs, the ultimate reality necessarily lay beyond words. A religious image—at best an image created by divine means, "not made with human hands"—

may reasonably have seemed to reach closer to God than any verbal definition could ever do. Among the many reasons that can be advanced for the rise of icons and the Iconoclastic movement, we should not forget to give prominence to those related to the problems of Christian representation.

It is no coincidence that it was in the Greek East that images and subsequently Iconoclasm, and then, we should not fail to remember, the permanent restoration of images, came to occupy such a central position in religious discourse and consciousness, for Greek rhetoric and Greek philosophical language had after all provided the "fleshly wrappings" in which the Christian message was presented. The Platonizing discourse of representation lent itself only too easily to Christian material. On this view, the Christological disputes of the first Christian centuries were actually the legacy of Greek logic and Greek philosophy. This book does not, being a set of lectures and limited in scope, have the conventional chapter on Augustine, who in his "refusal of *logos*," can now indeed be claimed as the founder of postmodernism.[4] His influence is indeed felt throughout; yet the continuity traced here is a continuity in the Greek half of the Roman Empire, the half that became Byzantium. This focus—in contrast to the more common one, which attempts to trace the transition from classical world to the Western middle ages—also has advantages in that it brings certain themes into relief, not merely the move toward religious images, but also the problematic of the idea of "decline" that has been adopted by so many modern historians.

It is a curious fact that so many of the same problems are confronting the human sciences today in their own struggles with questions of meaning and representation. Increased awareness of the effects of powerful rhetorical strategies, and especially of

4. As is done by Arthur Kroker, *The Post Modern Scene: Excremental Culture and Hyper-Aesthetics* (London: Macmillan, 1986), 28, 35 ff.

representation as essentially problematic, leads to the questioning of what can be thought to be real and to the attempt to define the relation between the representation and the object represented—or to the attempt to recapture the possibility of "real values" in criticism or objective knowledge in philosophy. Mimesis is again the center of attention.[5] And there is another resonance. The sign system of early Christianity did not, surprisingly perhaps, form itself either around eating (as in the Last Supper) or death (as in the Crucifixion) but, encouraged by the need to explain the union of bodily flesh and divinity in the Incarnation, around the body itself, and especially the mechanics and avoidance of carnal knowledge and procreation. Paradoxically, in the context of the discourse of abstinence, the true knowledge at which the signs pointed was defined in terms of desire. "Let him kiss me with the kisses of his mouth," reads the opening of the Song of Songs, signifying, in Origen's interpretation, the divine wisdom that comes from the mouth of Christ. So the ps.-Dionysius, following Origen's exegesis of the Song as relating to the union of the soul and God, makes love the key to that relationship. Now *eros,* desire, also occupies the center of poststructuralist poetics and is often seen as a key to theories of the subject. Whereas in modern intellectual circles Christian discourse is rarely acceptable as such, ironically *eros,* the discourse of desire, has filled the space left vacant.[6]

By the late sixth and seventh centuries in the Eastern Empire one can perceive, together with the enormous political and military difficulties of that period, an encroaching scholasticism and a closing in of intellectual horizons. As the city of Constanti-

5. See, e.g., A. D. Nuttall, *A New Mimesis: Shakespeare and the Representation of Reality* (London: Methuen, 1983); cf. R. Barthes: "the function of narrative is not to 'represent,' it is to constitute a spectacle still very enigmatic for us" ("Introduction to the Structuralist Analysis of Narratives," in *Image, Music, Text,* ed. and trans. S. Heath [London: Fontana, 1977], 123).

6. See further J. Kristeva, *Love Stories;* cf. Moi, ed., *Kristeva Reader,* 238.

nople shrank, the recourse to religious images and the eager embracing of the mysticism of a ps.-Dionysius may seem understandable. Yet I hope to have shown in this book that religious developments are never so simple. Christian discourse had a liberating as well as a totalizing influence; furthermore, whatever the impact of contemporary events may have been, the power of image and symbol manifested in early Byzantium, and seen by us as somehow characteristic of a "Byzantine" or in some sense medieval world-view, had been implicit in the very nature of Christian discourse and in the story of its long adaptation to and adoption in the Roman Empire. To understand the role of Christian words in the Christianization of the Roman Empire is also to understand in a profound sense the essence of the transition from Rome to Byzantium.

Bibliography

Achtemeier, P. J. "Jesus and the Disciples as Miracle-Workers in the Apocryphal New Testament." In Fiorenza (ed.), 149–86.

Albrecht, R. *Das Leben der heiligen Makrina auf dem Hintergrund der Thekla-Traditionen.* Göttingen: Vandenhoek & Ruprecht, 1986.

Alexandre, M. "Les nouveaux martyrs." In Spira (ed.), 33–70.

Alexiou, M. *The Ritual Lament in Greek Tradition.* Cambridge: Cambridge University Press, 1974.

Allen, P. "Some Aspects of Hellenism in the Early Greek Church Historians." *Traditio* 43 (1987): 368–81.

Alter, R., and F. Kermode, eds. *The Literary Guide to the Bible.* London: Collins, 1987.

Anderson, G. *Ancient Fiction: The Novel in the Graeco-Roman World.* London: Croom Helm, 1984.

Ariès, P., and G. Duby, eds. *A History of Private Life.* Vol. 1: *From Pagan Rome to Byzantium.* Ed. P. Veyne, trans. A. Goldhammer. Cambridge, Mass.: Harvard University Press, 1987.

Armstrong, A. H., ed. *Classical Mediterranean Spirituality.* London: Routledge & Kegan Paul, 1986.

Atkinson, C. W., et al., eds. *Immaculate and Powerful: The Female in Sacred Image and Social Reality.* Boston, Mass.: Beacon Press, 1985.

Aubineau, M. "Bilans d'une enquête sur les homélies de Proclus de Constantinople." *Revue des études grecques* 85 (1972): 572–96.

———. *Hésychius de Jérusalem, Basile de Seleucie, Jean de Béryte, Pseudo-Chrysostome, Léonce de Constantinople: homélies pascales (cinq homélies inédites).* Sources chrétiennes 187. Paris: Cerf, 1972.

———. *Les homélies festales d'Hésychius de Jérusalem.* 2 vols. Subsidia Hagiographica 59. Brussels: Société des Bollandistes, 1978–80.

Auerbach, E. *Literary Language and Its Public in Late Antiquity and in the Middle Ages.* Trans. R. Manheim. New York: Pantheon Books, 1965.

———. *Mimesis: The Representation of Reality in Western Literature.* Trans. Willard R. Trask. Princeton: Princeton University Press, 1953.

Ayers, R. H. *Language, Logic, and Reason in the Church Fathers.* Hildesheim: Georg Olms Verlag, 1979.

Baker, J. A. "The Myth of the Church: A Case Study in the Use of Scripture for Christian Doctrine." In Hooker and Hickling (eds.), 165–77.

Ball, J. "Anthropology as a Theological Tool, I: Culture and the Creation of Meaning." *Heythrop Journal* 28 (1987): 249–62.

Bammel, C. P. Hammond. "Products of Fifth-Century Scriptoria Preserving Conventions Used by Rufinus of Aquileia." *JThS,* n.s. 29 (1978): 366–91; 30 (1979): 430–62; 35 (1984): 347–93.

Bardenhewer, O. *Geschichte der altkirchlichen Literatur.* 2d ed. Vol. 1. Freiburg i. Breslau, 1913.

Barnes, T. D. "Angel of Light or Mystic Initiate?" *JThS,* n.s. 37 (1987): 353–68.

———. *Constantine and Eusebius.* Cambridge, Mass.: Harvard University Press, 1981.

———. "The Editions of Eusebius's *Ecclesiastical History.*" *GRBS* 21 (1980): 191–201.

———. "Panegyric, History, and Hagiography in Eusebius's Life of Constantine." In R. Williams (ed.), 94–123.

———. "Synesius in Constantinople." *GRBS* 27 (1986): 93–112.

Baynes, N. *Byzantine Studies and Other Essays.* London: Athlone Press, 1955; repr. 1974.

———. *Constantine the Great and the Christian Church.* London: British Academy, 1930; repr. 1972.

Beard, M. "Cicero and Divination: The Formation of a Latin Discourse." *JRS* 76 (1986): 33–46.

Beck, H.-G. *Kirche und theologische Literatur im byzantinischen Reich.* Munich: C. H. Beck, 1959.

Bellah, R., et al. *Habits of the Heart.* Berkeley and Los Angeles: University of California Press, 1985.

Benko, S. *Pagan Rome and the Early Christians.* London: Batsford, 1985.

Berger, P. L., and T. Luckmann. *The Social Construction of Reality.* Harmondsworth, Eng.: Penguin Books, 1967.

Bloch, H. "Medieval Misogyny: Woman as Riot." *Representations* 20 (Fall 1987): 1–24.

Bloch, M., ed. *Political Language and Oratory in Traditional Society.* London: Academic Press, 1975.

Blockley, R. C. *The Fragmentary Classicising Historians of the Later Roman*

Empire. 2 vols. Classical and Medieval Texts, Papers, and Monographs 6, 10. Liverpool: ARCA, 1981, 1983.

Blumenthal, H. J. "529 and After: What Happened to the Academy?" *Byzantion* 48 (1978): 369–85.

———. "Simplicius and Others on Aristotle's Discussions of Reason." In *Gonimos: Neoplatonic and Byzantine Studies Presented to Leendert G. Westerink at 75*, 103–19. Buffalo, N.Y.: Arethusa, 1988.

Blumenthal, H., and R. Markus, eds. *Neoplatonism and Early Christian Thought*. London: Variorum, 1981.

Booth, W. *The Rhetoric of Fiction*. Chicago: University of Chicago Press, 1961.

Bouffartigue, J. "Représentations et évaluations du texte poétique dans le Commentaire sur la République de Proclos." In Hoffmann, Lallot, and le Boulluec (eds.), 130 ff.

Bourdieu, P. *Outline of a Theory of Practice*. Trans. R. Nice. Cambridge: Cambridge University Press, 1977.

Bourdieu, P., and J.-C. Passéron. *Reproduction in Education, Society, and Culture*. Trans. R. Nice. London: Sage, 1977.

Bovon, F., et al., eds. *Les Actes apocryphes des apôtres*. Geneva: Labor & Fides, 1981.

Bowersock, G. W. "From Emperor to Bishop: The Self-conscious Transformation of Political Power in the Fourth Century A.D." *Classical Philology* 81 (1986): 298–307.

———. *Hellenism in Late Antiquity*. Jerome Lectures. Cambridge: Cambridge University Press, 1990.

———. "The Imperial Cult: Perceptions and Persistence." In Meyer and Sanders (eds.), 171–241.

Bowie, E. L. "The Greeks and Their Past in the Second Sophistic." *Past and Present* 46 (1970): 3–41.

Bregman, J. *Synesius of Cyrene: Philosopher-Bishop*. Berkeley and Los Angeles: University of California Press, 1982.

Brock, S. P. "Dramatic Dialogue Poems." *IV Symposium Syriacum: Literary Genres in Syriac Literature*. Orientalia Christiana Analecta 229 (1987): 135–47.

———. "From Antagonism to Assimilation: Syriac Attitudes to Greek Learning." In Garsoian, Mathews, and Thomson (eds.), 17–34.

———. *The Harp of the Spirit*. London: Fellowship of St. Alban & St. Sergius, 1975.

———. *The Luminous Eye*. Rome: ACIIS Publications, 1985.

———. "Syriac Dialogue Poems: Marginalia to a Recent Edition." *Le Muséon* 97 (1984): 29–58.

Brock, S., and S. A. Harvey. *Holy Women of the Christian Orient*. Berkeley and Los Angeles: University of California Press, 1987.

Brown, N. O. *Love's Body.* New York: Random House, 1966.

Brown, P. "Approaches to the Religious Crisis of the Third Century A.D." *EHR* 83 (1968): 542–58.

———. "Aspects of the Christianisation of the Roman Aristocracy." *JRS* 51 (1961): 1–11.

———. *The Body and Society: Men, Women, and Sexual Renunciation in Early Christianity.* New York: Columbia University Press, 1988.

———. "A Dark-Age Crisis: Aspects of the Iconoclastic Controversy." *EHR* 88 (1973): 1–34.

———. "Late Antiquity." In Ariès and Duby (eds.), 235–312.

———. *The Making of Late Antiquity.* Cambridge, Mass.: Harvard University Press, 1978.

———. *Religion and Society in the Age of St. Augustine.* London: Faber, 1972.

———. "The Rise and Function of the Holy Man in Late Antiquity." *JRS* 61 (1971): 81–101.

———. "Sexuality and Society in the Fifth Century A.D.: Augustine and Julian of Eclanum." In Gabba (ed.), 49–70.

Brown, R. E., et al., eds. *Mary in the New Testament.* London: Geoffrey Chapman, 1978.

Browning, R. "The 'Low-Level' Saint's Life in the Early Byzantine World." In Hackel (ed.), 117–27.

———, ed. *The Greek World: Classical, Byzantine, and Modern.* London: Thames & Hudson, 1985.

Bultmann, R. *History of the Synoptic Tradition.* 2d ed. Oxford: Basil Blackwell, 1968.

Burgess, Anthony. *The Kingdom of the Wicked.* New York: Arbor House, 1985.

Burke, K. *Language as Symbolic Action.* Berkeley and Los Angeles: University of California Press, 1966.

———. *The Rhetoric of Religion.* Berkeley and Los Angeles: University of California Press, 1962.

Burkert, W. *Ancient Mystery Cults.* Cambridge, Mass.: Harvard University Press, 1987.

Burnett, A., and S. Walker, eds. *The Image of Augustus.* London: British Museum, 1981.

Bury, J. B. "Cleopatra's Nose." *RPA Annual for 1916,* 16–23. Reprinted in *Selected Essays of J. B. Bury,* ed. H. Temperley, 60–69. Cambridge: Cambridge University Press, 1930.

Bynum, C. *Holy Feast and Holy Fast: The Religious Significance of Food for Medieval Women.* Berkeley and Los Angeles: University of California Press, 1987.

Calderone, S. "Eusebio e l'ideologia imperiale." In *Le trasformazioni della cultura nella tarda antichità. Atti del convegno tenuto a Catania, Università degli Studi, 27 sett.–2 ott. 1982*, 1–26. Rome, 1985.

———. "Teologia politica, successione dinastica e consecratio in età constantiniana." In *Le culte des souverains dans l'empire romain*, 215–61. Entretiens Hardt 19. Vandoeuvres, 1973.

Camelot, T. "Les traités *De virginitate* au IVe siècle." In *Mystique et continence: Travaux scientifiques du VIIe congrès international d'Avon*. Paris: Etudes carmélitaines, 1952.

Cameron, Alan. "The Empress and the Poet." *Yale Classical Studies* 27 (1982): 217–89.

———. "The Last Days of the Academy at Athens." *Proceedings of the Cambridge Philological Society* 195 (1969): 7–29.

———. "The Latin Revival of the Fourth Century." In Treadgold (ed.), 42–58.

Cameron, Averil. "Byzantine Africa: The Literary Evidence." In *Excavations at Carthage VIII*, ed. J. Humphrey, 29–62. Ann Arbor: University of Michigan Press, 1982.

———. "Byzantium in the Seventh Century: The Search for Redefinition." In Fontaine and Hillgarth (eds.), forthcoming.

———. "The Construction of Court Ritual: The Byzantine Book of Ceremonies." In Cannadine and Price (eds.), 103–36.

———. "Eustratius's Life of the Patriarch Eutychius and the Fifth Ecumenical Council." In Chrysostomides (ed.), 225–47.

———. "Gelimer's Laughter." In Clover and Humphreys (eds.), 171–90.

———. "The History of the Image of Edessa: The Telling of a Story." *Okeanos: Harvard Ukrainian Studies* 7 (1984): 80–94.

———. "Images of Authority: Elites and Icons in Late Sixth-Century Byzantium." *Past and Present* 84 (1979): 3–35.

———. *Procopius and the Sixth Century*. London: Duckworth, 1985.

———. "Rome and the Greek East: Imperial Rule and Transformation." In Browning (ed.), 203–14.

———. "Le società romano-barbariche e l'oriente bizantino: continuità e rotture." *Storia di Roma* 3. Turin: Einaudi, forthcoming.

———. "The Theotokos in Sixth-Century Constantinople: A City Finds Its Symbol." *JThS*, n.s. 29 (1978): 79–108.

———. "Virginity as Metaphor." In Cameron (ed.), 184–205.

———. "The Virgin's Robe: An Episode in the History of Early Seventh-Century Constantinople." *Byzantion* 49 (1979): 42–56.

———, ed. *History as Text*. London: Duckworth, 1989.

Cameron, Averil, and J. Herrin, eds. *Constantinople in the Eighth Century: The Parastaseis Syntomoi Chronikai*. Leiden: E. J. Brill, 1984.

Campenhausen, H. V. "Das Bekenntnis Eusebs von Caesarea." *Zeitschrift für die Neutestamentliche Wissenchaft und die Kunde der alteren Kirche* 67 (1976): 123–39.

Canevet, M. *Grégoire de Nysse et l'herméneutique biblique.* Paris: Etudes augustiniennes, 1983.
Cannadine, D., and S. Price, eds. *Rituals of Royalty: Power and Ceremonial in Traditional Societies.* Cambridge: Cambridge University Press, 1987.
Carroll, M. P. *The Cult of the Virgin Mary: Psychological Origins.* Princeton: Princeton University Press, 1986.
Cavallo, G. "La circulazione libraria nell'età di Giustiniano." In *L'imperatore Giustiniano: storia e mito. Giornati di Studio a Ravenna, 14–16 ott. 1976,* ed. G. G. Archi, 201–36. Circolo toscano di diritto romano e storia del diritto 5. Milan, 1978.
Chadwick, H. *Early Christian Thought and the Classical Tradition.* Oxford: Oxford University Press, 1966.
———. "John Moschus and His Friend Sophronius the Sophist." *JThS,* n.s. 25 (1974): 41–74.
Chitty, D. *The Desert a City.* Oxford: Oxford University Press, 1966.
Chrysostomides, J., ed. *Kathegetria: Essays Presented to Joan Hussey for Her 80th Birthday.* Camberley, Eng.: Porphyrogenitus, 1988.
Clark, E. A. "'Adam's Only Companion': Augustine and the Early Christian Debate on Marriage." *Recherches augustiniennes* 21 (1986): 139–62.
———. *Ascetic Piety and Women's Faith.* Lewiston, N.Y./Queenston, Ont.: Edwin Mellen Press, 1986.
———. *The Life of Melania the Younger: Introduction, Translation, and Commentary.* New York: Edwin Mellen Press, 1984.
———. "The Uses of the Song of Songs: Origen and the Later Latin Fathers." In Clark, *Ascetic Piety,* 386–427.
———. *Women in the Early Church.* Wilmington, Del.: Edwin Mellen Press, 1983.
Clark, G. *Iamblichus: On the Pythagorean Life.* Liverpool: Liverpool University Press, 1989.
Clover, F. M. "Le culte des empereurs dans l'Afrique vandale." *Bulletin archéologique du C.T.H.S.,* n.s. 15–16 (1984): 121–28.
———. "Emperor Worship in Roman Africa." In *Romanitas. Festschrift J. Straub,* ed. G. Wirth, 661–74. Berlin: Walter de Gruyter, 1982.
Clover, F. M., and R. S. Humphreys, eds. *Tradition and Innovation in Late Antiquity.* Madison: University of Wisconsin Press, 1989.
Coleiro, E. "St. Jerome's Lives of the Hermits." *Vigiliae christianae* 11 (1957): 161–78.
Consolino, F. E. "Modelli di comportamento e modi di santificazione per l'aristocrazia femminile d'occidente." In Giardina (ed.), 1:273–306.
———. "Σοφίης ἀμφοτέρης πρύτανιν: gli epigrammi funerari di Gregorio Nazianzeno (A.P. VIII)." *Athenaeum,* n.s. 65 (1987): 407–25.
Conte, G. B. *The Rhetoric of Imitation.* Ithaca, N.Y.: Cornell University Press, 1986.

Coulter, J. A. *The Literary Microcosm: Theories of Interpretation of the Later Neoplatonists.* Leiden: E. J. Brill, 1976.

Cox, P. *Biography in Late Antiquity.* Berkeley and Los Angeles: University of California Press, 1983.

———. "Pleasure of Text, Text of Pleasure: Origen's *Commentary on the Song of Songs.*" *Journal of the American Academy of Religion* 54 (1986): 241–51.

Croke, B., and A. Emmett, eds. *History and Historians in Late Antiquity.* Sydney: Pergamon Press, 1983.

Crossan, J. D. *The Dark Interval: Towards a Theology of Story.* Niles, Ill.: Argus Communications, 1975.

———. *Four Other Gospels.* Minneapolis: Winston Press, 1985.

Crouzel, H. *Origen.* Trans. A. S. Worrall. Edinburgh: T. & T. Clark, 1989.

Cullmann, O. *The Earliest Christian Confessions.* London: Lutterworth Press, 1949.

Dagron, G. *Constantinople imaginaire: études sur le recueil des "Patria."* Paris: Presses universitaires de France, 1984.

———. "L'empire romain d'orient au IVe siècle et les traditions politiques de l'hellénisme: le témoignage de Thémistios." *Travaux et mémoires* 3 (1968): 1–242.

———. *Naissance d'une capitale: Constantinople et ses institutions de 330 à 451.* Paris: Presses universitaires de France, 1974.

———. *Vie et miracles de Sainte Thècle.* Subsidia Hagiographica 62. Brussels: Société des Bollandistes, 1978.

Daniélou, J. *From Shadows to Reality.* Trans. Dom Wulstan Hibberd. London: Burns & Oates, 1960.

———. *Origen.* Trans. W. Mitchell. London: Sheed & Ward, 1955.

Datema, C., and P. Allen. *Leontii presbyteri Constantinopolitani homiliae.* Corpus Christianorum series graeca 17. Turnhout: Brepols, 1987.

Davies, S. L. *The Revolt of the Widows: The Social World of the Apocryphal Acts.* London: Feffer & Simons, 1980.

Dibelius, M. *A Fresh Approach to the New Testament and Early Christian Literature.* New York: Scribner's, 1936.

Dobschütz, E. von. "Der Roman in der altchristlichen Literatur." *Deutsche Rundschau* 111 (1902): 87–116.

Dodds, E. R. *The Greeks and the Irrational.* Berkeley and Los Angeles: University of California Press, 1951.

———. *Missing Persons.* Oxford: Oxford University Press, 1977.

———. *Pagan and Christian in an Age of Anxiety.* Cambridge: Cambridge University Press, 1965.

Dorey, T. A., ed. *Empire and Aftermath: Silver Latin.* Vol. 2. London: Routledge & Kegan Paul, 1975.

Dormeyer, D., and H. Frankemölle. "Evangelium als literarische Gattung und als theologischer Begriff. Tendenzen und Angaben der Evangelienforschung im 20. Jahrhundert, mit einer Untersuchung des Markus Evangeliums in seinem Verhältnis zur antiken Biographie." In *ANRW* II.25.2, ed. H. Temporini and W. Haase, 1543–1704. Berlin: Walter de Gruyter, 1984.

Dörrie, H. "Die griechischen Romane und das Christentum." *Philologus* 93 (1938): 273–76.

Douglas, M. *Natural Symbols.* London: Barrie & Rockcliff, Cresset Press, 1970.

Downey, G. "Julian and Justinian and the Unity of Faith and Culture." *Church History* 28 (1959): 339–49.

————. "Justinian's View of Christianity and the Greek Classics." *Anglican Theological Review* 40 (1958): 13–22.

Draguet, R. *La vie primitive de S. Antoine conservée en syriaque.* Corpus Scriptorum Christianorum Orientalium 417–18, Script. Syr. 183–84. Louvain, 1980.

Drake, H. A. *In Praise of Constantine.* Berkeley and Los Angeles: University of California Press, 1976.

Dreyfus, H. L., and P. Rabinow. *Michel Foucault: Beyond Structuralism and Hermeneutics.* Chicago: University of Chicago Press, 1982.

Drijvers, H. J. W. *East of Antioch.* London: Variorum, 1984.

————. "Hellenistic and Oriental Origins." In Hackel (ed.), 25–33.

Dummer, J., ed. *Text und Textkritik. Eine Aufsatzsammlung.* Berlin: Akademie Verlag, 1987.

Dumont, L. *Essays on Individualism.* Trans. L. Dumont and P. Hockings. Chicago: University of Chicago Press, 1986.

Dvornik, F. *Early Christian and Byzantine Political Philosophy.* 2 vols. Washington, D.C.: Dumbarton Oaks, 1963.

Ebersolt, J. *Constantinople.* Paris: Adrien-Maisonneuve, 1951.

Elshtain, J. B. *Public Man, Private Woman.* Princeton: Princeton University Press, 1981.

Engelhardt, I. *Mission und Politik in Byzanz. Ein Beitrag zur Strukturanalyse byzantinischer Mission zur Zeit Justins und Justinians.* Miscellanea Byzantina Monacensia 19. Munich, 1974.

Ennabli, L. *Les inscriptions funéraires chrétiennes de la basilique dite de Sainte-Monique à Carthage.* Coll. de l'Ecole française de Rome 25. Rome, 1975.

Esbroeck, M. van. "Les textes littéraires sur l'Assomption avant le Xe siècle." In Bovon et al. (eds.), 265–86.

Finley, M. I. *The Ancient Economy.* Berkeley and Los Angeles: University of California Press, 1973; 2d ed., with supplementary notes, Harmondsworth, Eng.: Penguin Books, 1985.

Fiorenza, E. Schussler. *In Memory of Her: A Feminist Theological Reconstruction of Christian Origins.* New York: Crossroads, 1983.

———. "Miracles, Mission, and Apologetics: An Introduction." In Fiorenza (ed.), 1–25.

———, ed. *Aspects of Religious Propaganda in Judaism and Early Christianity.* Notre Dame: University of Notre Dame Press, 1976.

Flusin, B. *Miracle et histoire dans l'oeuvre de Cyrille de Scythopolis.* Paris: Etudes augustiniennes, 1983.

Fontaine, J., and J. Hillgarth, eds. *The Seventh Century: Change and Continuity.* London: Warburg Institute, forthcoming.

Forbes, C. "Comparison, Self-Praise, and Irony: Paul's Boasting and the Conventions of Hellenistic Rhetoric." *New Testament Studies* 32 (1986): 1–30.

Fornara, C. *The Nature of History in Ancient Greece and Rome.* Berkeley and Los Angeles: University of California Press, 1983.

Fortin, E. L. "Christianity and Hellenism in Basil the Great's Address *Ad Adulescentes.*" In Blumenthal and Markus (eds.), 189–203.

Foucault, M. *The Archeology of Knowledge.* Trans. A. Sheridan-Smith. New York: Harper & Row, 1972.

———. *The Order of Things.* Trans. A. Sheridan-Smith. New York: Random House, 1970.

———. *Le souci de soi.* Paris: Gallimard, 1984.

Fowden, G. "Between Pagans and Christians." *JRS* 78 (1988): 173–82.

———. "The Pagan Holy Man in Late Antique Society." *JHS* 102 (1982): 33–59.

———. "The Platonist Philosopher and His Circle." *Philosophia* 7 (1977): 359–83.

Frank, K. S., ed. *Askese und Mönchtum in der alten Kirche.* Darmstadt: Wissenschaftliche Buchgesellschaft, 1975.

Frye, N. *The Great Code: The Bible and Literature.* London: Routledge & Kegan Paul, 1982.

Gabba, E., ed. *Tria Corda. Scritti in onore di Arnaldo Momigliano.* Biblioteca di Ateneo 1. Como: Edizioni New Press, 1983.

Gager, J. "Body-Symbols and Social Reality: Resurrection, Incarnation, and Asceticism in Early Christianity." *Religion* 12 (1982): 345–64.

———. *Kingdom and Community: The Social World of Early Christianity.* Englewood Cliffs, N.J.: Prentice-Hall, 1975.

Garnsey, P., K. Hopkins, and C. R. Whittaker, eds. *Trade in the Ancient Economy.* London: Chatto & Windus, 1983.

Garsoian, N. G., T. F. Mathews, and R. W. Thomson, eds. *East of Byzantium: Syria and Armenia in the Formative Period.* Washington, D.C.: Dumbarton Oaks, 1982.

Gay, P. *The Enlightenment: An Interpretation.* 2 vols. London: Weidenfeld & Nicolson, 1967–70.

Geanokoplos, D. "Church Building and 'Caesaropapism,' A.D. 312–565." *GRBS* 7 (1966): 167–86.

Geertz, C. *The Interpretation of Cultures.* London: Hutchinson, 1975.

———. "Religion as a Cultural System." In *Anthropological Approaches to the Study of Religion,* ed. M. Banton, 1–45. New York: Praeger, 1966.

Gellner, E. *Nations and Nationalism.* Oxford: Basil Blackwell, 1983.

Georgi, D. "The Records of Jesus in the Light of Ancient Accounts of Revered Men." *Society of Biblical Literature, Proceedings of the 108th Annual Meeting,* 2:527–42. Philadelphia, 1972.

Gero, S. "The True Image of Christ: Eusebius's Letter to Constantia Reconsidered." *JThS,* n.s. 32 (1981): 460–79.

Gerostergios, A. *Justinian the Great: The Emperor and Saint.* Belmont, Mass.: Institute for Byzantine and Modern Greek Studies, 1982.

Giardina, A., ed. *Società romana e impero tardoantico.* 4 vols. Rome: Laterza, 1986.

Girard, R. *Des choses cachées depuis la fondation du monde.* Paris: B. Grasset, 1978.

———. *Violence and the Sacred.* Trans. P. Gregory. Baltimore: Johns Hopkins University Press, 1977.

Goodspeed, E. J. *History of Early Christian Literature.* Rev. R. M. Grant. Chicago: University of Chicago Press, 1966.

Goody, J. *The Interface Between the Written and the Oral.* Cambridge: Cambridge University Press, 1987.

———. *The Logic of Writing and the Organization of Society.* Cambridge: Cambridge University Press, 1986.

Graef, H. *Mary: A History of Doctrine and Devotion.* London: Sheed & Ward, 1963–65; repr. 1985.

Grant, R. M. *The Earliest Lives of Jesus.* London: SPCK, 1961.

———. *The Letter and the Spirit.* London: SPCK, 1957.

Gray, P. "The 'Select Fathers': Canonizing the Patristic Past." *Studia Patristica* 23 (1989): 21–36.

Grégoire, H. "La vision de Constantin 'liquidée.'" *Byzantion* 14 (1939): 341–51.

Gregory, T. E. "The Survival of Paganism in Christian Greece: A Critical Survey." *American Journal of Philology* 107 (1986): 229–42.

Griffith, S. H. "Ephraem, the Deacon of Edessa, and the Church of the Empire." In *Diakonia: Studies in Honor of Robert T. Meyer,* ed. T. Halton and J. P. Williman, 22–52. Washington, D.C.: Catholic University of America Press, 1986.

Habicht, C. *Pausanias's Guide to Ancient Greece.* Berkeley and Los Angeles: University of California Press, 1985.

Hackel, S., ed. *The Byzantine Saint.* Studies Supplementary to Sobornost 5. London: Fellowship of St. Alban & St. Sergius, 1981.

Hadas, M., and M. Smith. *Heroes and Gods: Spiritual Biographies in Antiquity.* New York: Harper & Row, 1965.

Hadot, I. "La vie et l'oeuvre de Simplicius d'après des sources grecques et arabes." In *Simplicius: sa vie, son oeuvre, sa survie. Actes du colloque international de Paris (28 sept.–1er oct. 1985)*, ed. I. Hadot, 3–39. Berlin: Walter de Gruyter, 1987.

Hägg, T. *The Novel in Antiquity*. Berkeley and Los Angeles: University of California Press, 1983.

Hanson, R. P. C. *Allegory and Event: A Study of the Sources and Significance of Origen's Interpretation of Scripture*. London: SCM Press, 1959.

Harl, M. "Les trois livres de *Salomon* et les trois parties de la philosophie dans les Prologues des Commentaires sur le *Cantique des Cantiques* (d'Origène aux chaines exégétiques grecques)." In Dummer (ed.), 249–69.

Harpham, G. G. *The Ascetic Imperative in Culture and Criticism*. Chicago: University of Chicago Press, 1987.

Harris, W. V. *Ancient Literacy*. Cambridge, Mass.: Harvard University Press, 1989.

Harrison, V. E. F. "Word as Icon in Greek Patristic Theology." *Sobornost* 10 (1988): 38–49.

Harvey, S. A. "The Politicisation of the Byzantine Saint." In Hackel (ed.), 37–42.

Hennecke, E. *New Testament Apocrypha*. Ed. W. Schneemelcher; Eng. trans. ed. R. M. Wilson. 2 vols. London: Lutterworth Press, 1963–65.

Hepburn, R. W. *Christianity and Paradox*. London: Watts, 1958.

Herrin, J. *The Formation of Christendom*. Oxford: Basil Blackwell, 1987.

———. "Women and the Faith in Icons in Early Christianity." In Samuel and Stedman Jones (eds.), 56–83.

Hick, J., ed. *Faith and the Philosophers*. London: Macmillan, 1964.

Hobsbawm, E., and T. Ranger, eds. *The Invention of Tradition*. Cambridge: Cambridge University Press, 1983.

Hodges, R., and D. Whitehouse. *Mahomed, Charlemagne, and the Origins of Europe*. London: Duckworth, 1983.

Hoffmann, P., J. Lallot, and A. le Boulluec, eds. *Le texte et ses représentations*. Etudes de littérature ancienne 3. Paris: PENS, 1987.

Holum, K. *Theodosian Empresses: Women and Imperial Dominion in Late Antiquity*. Berkeley and Los Angeles: University of California Press, 1982.

Honigmann, E. *Évêques et évêchés monophysites de l'Asie antérieure au VIe siècle*. Louvain: Corpus Scriptorum Christianorum Orientalium, 1951.

Honoré, T. *Tribonian*. London: Duckworth, 1978.

Hooker, M., and C. Hickling, eds. *What About the New Testament? Essays in Honour of Christopher Evans*. London: SCM Press, 1975.

Hopkins, K. *Death and Renewal*. Cambridge: Cambridge University Press, 1983.

Houlden, J. L. *Connections*. London: SPCK, 1986.

Hunger, H. "Romanos Melodos, Dichter, Prediger, Rhetor—und sein Publikum." *JÖB* 34 (1984): 15–42.

Hunt, E. D. *Holy Land Pilgrimage in the Late Roman Empire, A.D. 312 to 460.* Oxford: Oxford University Press, 1982.

Jackson, B. D. "The Theory of Signs in St. Augustine's *De doctrina christiana.*" In Markus (ed.), 92–147.

Jaeger, W. *Early Christianity and Greek Paideia.* Cambridge, Mass.: Harvard University Press, 1961.

James, M. R., ed. and trans. *The Apocryphal New Testament.* Oxford: Oxford University Press, 1924.

Jeffreys, E., M. Jeffreys, R. Scott, et al., eds. *The Chronicle of John Malalas.* Melbourne: Australian Association for Byzantine Studies, 1986.

Judge, E. A. "Paul's Boasting in Relation to Contemporary Professional Practice." *Australian Biblical Review* 16 (1968): 37–50.

Jugie, M. *La mort et l'assomption de la Sainte Vierge.* Studi e testi 114. Vatican City, 1944.

Kaestli, J.-D. "Les principales orientations de la recherche sur les Actes apocryphes des Apôtres." In Bovon et al. (eds.), 49–67.

Kantorowicz, E. *The King's Two Bodies.* Princeton: Princeton University Press, 1957.

Kazhdan, A., and A. Cutler. "Continuity and Discontinuity in Byzantine History." *Byzantion* 52 (1982): 429–78.

Kee, A. *Constantine Versus Christ: The Triumph of Ideology.* London: SCM Press, 1982.

Kee, H. C. "Aretalogy and Gospel." *Journal of Biblical Literature* 92 (1973): 402–22.

Kelly, J. N. D. *Jerome.* New York: Harper & Row, 1975.

Kennedy, G. *The Art of Rhetoric in the Roman World, 300 B.C.–A.D. 300.* Princeton: Princeton University Press, 1972.

———. *Greek Rhetoric Under Christian Emperors.* Princeton: Princeton University Press, 1983.

Kermode, F. "The Canon." In Alter and Kermode (eds.), 600–610.

———. *The Genesis of Secrecy: On the Interpretation of Narrative.* The Charles Eliot Norton Lectures, 1977–78. Cambridge, Mass.: Harvard University Press, 1979.

———. *The Sense of an Ending: Studies in the Theory of Fiction.* New York: Oxford University Press, 1967.

Kerr, H. T. *Preaching in the Early Church.* New York: Fleming H. Revell, 1942.

Kitzinger, E. *Byzantine Art in the Making.* Cambridge, Mass.: Harvard University Press, 1977.

———. "The Cult of Images in the Period Before Iconoclasm." *Dumbarton Oaks Papers* 8 (1954): 85–150.

Kleinberg, A. M. "*De agone christiano:* The Preacher and His Audience." *JThS*, n.s. 38 (1987): 16–33.

Klock, C. *Untersuchungen zu Stil und Rhythmus bei Gregor von Nyssa. Ein Beitrag zum Rhetorikverständnis der griechischen Väter.* Beiträge zur klassischen Philologie 173. Frankfurt a. Main: Athenaeum, 1987.

Koester, H. *Introduction to the New Testament.* 2 vols. Philadelphia: Fortress Press, 1982.

Krautheimer, R. *Three Christian Capitals.* Berkeley and Los Angeles: University of California Press, 1983.

Kretschmar, G. "Ein Beitrag zur Frage nach dem Ursprung der frühchristlichen Askese." In Frank (ed.), 129–80.

Kristeva, J. *Love Stories.* Trans. L. S. Roudiez. New York: Columbia University Press, 1987.

Kroll, J. *Gott und Hölle. Der Mythos vom Descensus-Kampf.* Studien der Bibliothek Warburg 20. Leipzig, 1932; repr. Darmstadt: Wissenschaftliche Buchgesellschaft, 1963.

Kuhn, T. S. *The Structure of Scientific Revolutions.* Chicago: University of Chicago Press, 1962; 2d, enlarged ed., 1970.

Kundera, M. *Laughable Loves.* Trans. S. Rappaport. Harmondsworth, Eng.: Pelican Books, 1985.

Kustas, G. A. *Studies in Byzantine Rhetoric.* Thessalóniki: Patriarchal Institute for Patristic Studies, 1973.

Kyrtatas, D. "Prophets and Priests in Early Christianity: Production and Transmission of Religious Knowledge from Jesus to John Chrysostom." *International Sociology* 3 (1988): 365–83.

La Capra, D. *History and Criticism.* Ithaca, N.Y.: Cornell University Press, 1985.

Laeuchli, S. *The Language of Faith.* London: Epworth Press, 1965.

———. *The Serpent and the Dove.* Nashville: Abingdon Press, 1966.

Laistner, M. L. W. *Christianity and Pagan Culture in the Later Roman Empire.* Ithaca, N.Y.: Cornell University Press, 1951.

Lane Fox, R. *Pagans and Christians in the Mediterranean World from the Second Century A.D. to the Conversion of Constantine.* Harmondsworth, Eng.: Viking Press, 1986.

La Piana, G. *Le rappresentazioni sacre nella letteratura bizantina dalle origine al secolo IX.* Grottaferrata, 1912.

Laporte, J. *The Role of Women in Early Christianity.* New York: Edwin Mellen Press, 1982.

Leeman, A. *Orationis Ratio.* Vol. 1. Amsterdam: A. M. Hakkert, 1963.

Lemerle, P. *Le premier humanisme byzantin.* Paris: Presses universitaires de France, 1971.

Leroy, F. J. *L'homilétique de Proclus de Constantinople.* Studi e Testi 247. Vatican City, 1967.

Liebeschuetz, J. H. G. W. *Barbarians and Bishops: Army, Church, and State in the Age of Arcadius and Chrysostom.* Oxford: Clarendon Press, 1990.

———. "Synesius and the Municipal Politics of Cyrenaica in the Fifth Century A.D." *Byzantion* 55 (1985): 146–64.

———. "Why Did Synesius Become Bishop of Ptolemais?" *Byzantion* 56 (1986): 180–95.

Lizzi, R. *Il potere episcopale nell'oriente romano. Rappresentazione ideologica e realtà politica (IV–V sec. d.C.).* Rome: Edizioni dell'Ateneo, 1987.

———. "Significato filosofico e politico dell'antibarbarismo sinesiano. Il *De Regno* e il *De Providentia.*" *Rendiconti dell' Accademia di archeologia, letteratura e belle lettere di Napoli* 56 (1981): 49–62.

Lloyd-Jones, H. *The Justice of Zeus.* 2d ed. Berkeley and Los Angeles: University of California Press, 1983.

Lossky, V. *In the Image and Likeness of God.* Ed. J. W. Erikson and T. E. Bird. Crestwood, N.Y.: St. Vladimir's Seminary Press, 1974.

———. *The Mystical Theology of the Eastern Church.* Trans. members of the Fellowship of St. Alban & St. Sergius. Cambridge: James Clarke, 1957; repr. 1973.

Louth, A. *Denys the Areopagite.* London: Geoffrey Chapman, 1989.

Lowenthal, D. *The Past Is a Foreign Country.* Cambridge: Cambridge University Press, 1985.

Luibheid, C., and P. Rorem, trans. *Pseudo-Dionysius: The Complete Works.* Classics of Western Spirituality. London: SPCK, 1987.

Maas, M. "Roman History and Christian Ideology in Justinianic Reform Legislation." *DOP* 40 (1986): 17–31.

McClendon, J. W., Jr. *Biography as Theology.* Nashville: Abingdon Press, 1974.

MacCormack, S. "Christ and Empire: Time and Ceremonial in Sixth-Century Byzantium and Beyond." *Byzantion* 52 (1982): 287–309.

———. "Latin Prose Panegyrics: Tradition and Discontinuity in the Later Roman Empire." *Revue des études augustiniennes* 22 (1976): 29–77.

McCormick, M. *Eternal Victory.* Cambridge: Cambridge University Press, 1986.

MacDonald, D. *The Legend and the Apostle.* Philadelphia: Fortress Press, 1983.

McFague, S. *Metaphorical Theology: Models of God in Religious Language.* Philadelphia: Fortress Press, 1982.

———. *Speaking in Parables: A Study of Metaphor and Theology.* Philadelphia: Fortress Press, 1975.

Macintyre, A. "Is Understanding Religion Compatible with Believing?" In Hick (ed.), 115–33.

MacMullen, R. *Christianizing the Roman Empire, A.D. 100–400.* New Haven: Yale University Press, 1984.

———. "Constantine and the Miraculous." *GRBS* 9 (1968): 81–96.

———. *Corruption and the Decline of Rome.* New Haven: Yale University Press, 1988.

———. "Judicial Savagery in the Roman Empire." *Chiron* 16 (1986): 147–66.

———. *Paganism in the Roman Empire.* New Haven: Yale University Press, 1981.

———. "What Difference Did Christianity Make?" *Historia* 35 (1986): 322–43.

Macquerie, J. *God-Talk.* London: SCM Press, 1967.

Macrides, R., and P. Magdalino. "The Architecture of *Ekphrasis:* Construction and Context of Paul the Silentiary's *Ekphrasis* of Hagia Sophia." *BMGS* 12 (1988): 47–82.

Maguire, H. *Art and Eloquence in Byzantium.* Princeton: Princeton University Press, 1981.

Mahoney, J. "The Ways of Wisdom." Inaugural Lecture, King's College London. 1987.

Man, P. de. *Allegories of Reading.* New Haven: Yale University Press, 1979.

———. *Blindness and Insight.* New York: Oxford University Press, 1971.

Mango, C. A. "Antique Statuary and the Byzantine Beholder." *DOP* 17 (1963): 53–75.

———. *The Art of the Byzantine Empire, 312–1453.* Englewood Cliffs, N.J.: Prentice-Hall, 1972.

———. "The Availability of Books in the Byzantine Empire, AD 750–850." In *Byzantine Books and Bookmen,* 29–45. Washington, D.C.: Dumbarton Oaks, 1975.

———. *Byzantium: The Empire of New Rome.* London: Weidenfeld & Nicolson, 1980.

———. *Le développement urbain de Constantinople.* Paris: Boccard, 1985.

———. "Discontinuity with the Classical Past in Byzantium." In Mullet and Scott (eds.), 48–57.

Mann, M. *Sources of Social Power: A History of Power from the Beginning to A.D. 1760.* Vol. 1. Cambridge: Cambridge University Press, 1986.

Maraval, P. *Lieux saints et pèlerinages d'orient: histoire et géographie des origines à la conquête arabe.* Paris: Cerf, 1985.

Marcos, N. Fernando. *Los "Thaumata" de Sofronio. Contribución al estudio de la "Incubatio" cristiana.* Madrid: Consejo superior de investigaciones científicas, 1975.

Markus, R. A., ed. *Augustine.* New York: Anchor Books, 1972.

Mathews, T. F. "The Early Armenian Iconographic Program of the Ejmiacin Gospel (Erevan), Matenadaran MS. 2374, *olim* 229." In Garsoian, Mathews, and Thomson (eds.), 199–216.

Mazzarino, S. *The End of the Ancient World.* Trans. G. Holmes. London: Faber, 1966.

Meeks, W. *The First Urban Christians: The Social World of the Apostle Paul.* New Haven: Yale University Press, 1983.

Meredith, A. "Asceticism—Christian and Greek." *JThS*, n.s. 27 (1976): 313–22.

Merkelbach, R. *Roman und Mysterium in der Antike.* Munich: C. H. Beck, 1962.

Merquior, J. G. *Foucault.* London: Fontana, 1985.

Meyer, B. F., and E. P. Sanders, eds. *Jewish and Christian Self-Definition.* Vol. 3. Philadelphia: Fortress Press, 1982.

Miles, M. "The Evidence of Our Eyes: Patristic Studies and Popular Christianity in the Fourth Century." *Studia Patristica* 18 (1985): 59–63.

Millar, F. "Condemnation to Hard Labour in the Roman Empire, from the Julio-Claudians to Constantine." *Papers of the British School at Rome* 52 (1984): 124–47.

———. "Politics, Persuasion, and the People Before the Social War (150–90 B.C.)." *JRS* 76 (1986): 1–11.

Mitchell, W. J. T., ed. *On Narrative.* Chicago: University of Chicago Press, 1980.

Moi, T., ed. *The Kristeva Reader.* Oxford: Basil Blackwell, 1986.

Momigliano, A. "The Life of St. Macrina by Gregory of Nyssa." In Ober and Eadie (eds.), 443–58.

———. "Pagan and Christian Historiography in the Fourth Century A.D." In Momigliano (ed.), 79–99.

———. "Popular Religious Beliefs and the Late Roman Historians." *SCH* 8 (1971): 1–18.

———. "Religion in Athens, Rome, and Jerusalem in the First Century B.C." *Annali della Scuola Normale di Pisa,* 3d ser., 14 (1984): 873–92.

———. "The Theological Efforts of the Roman Upper Classes in the First Century B.C." *Classical Philology* 79 (1984): 199–211.

———, ed. *The Conflict Between Paganism and Christianity in the Later Roman Empire.* Oxford: Basil Blackwell, 1963.

Moretti, F. *Signs Taken for Wonders: Essays in the Sociology of Literary Forms.* Trans. S. Fischer, D. Forgacs, and D. Miller. London: Verso Books, 1988.

Morgan, J. R. "History, Romance, and Realism in the *Aithiopika* of Heliodorus." *Classical Antiquity* 1 (1982): 221–65.

Mortley, R. "The Title of the Acts of the Apostles." *Cahiers de Biblia Patristica* 1 (1987): 105–12.

———. *From Word to Silence.* Vol. 1: *The Rise and Fall of Logos.* Theophaneia 30. Vol. 2: *The Way of Negation, Christian and Greek.* Theophaneia 31. Bonn: Habelt, 1986.

Mudge, L. S., ed. *Essays on Biblical Interpretation.* Philadelphia: Fortress Press, 1980.

Mullett, M., and R. Scott, eds. *Byzantium and the Classical Tradition.* Birmingham: Centre for Byzantine Studies, 1981.

Murgia, C. E. "The Date of Tacitus' *Dialogus.*" *HSCP* 84 (1980): 99–125.

———. "Pliny's Letters and the *Dialogus.*" *HSCP* 89 (1985): 171–206.

Murphy, J. J. *A Synoptic History of Classical Rhetoric.* New York: Random House, 1972.

Murray, C. "Art in the Early Church." *JThS*, n.s. 28 (1977): 303–45.

———. "History and Faith." In Cameron (ed.), 165–80.

Murray, R. *Symbols of Church and Kingdom: A Study in Early Syrian Tradition.* Cambridge: Cambridge University Press, 1975.

Nau, F. "L'histoire ecclésiastique de Jean d'Éphèse." *Revue de l'orient chrétien* 2 (1897): 481 ff.

Neusner, J., ed. *Christianity, Judaism, and other Greco-Roman Cults. Part 1: New Testament.* Leiden: E. J. Brill, 1975.

Newman, J. H. *Apologia pro vita sua.* Ed. Maisie Ward. London: Sheed & Ward, 1976.

Nietzsche, F. *The Twilight of the Idols and the Anti-Christ.* Trans. R. J. Hollingdale. Harmondsworth, Eng.: Penguin Books, 1968.

Nock, A. D. *Conversion.* Oxford: Clarendon Press, 1933.

Norden, E. *Die antike Kunstprosa vom VI. Jarhundert v. Chr. bis in die Zeit der Renaissance.* 2 vols. Leipzig: B. G. Teubner, 1909.

Nuttall, A. D. *A New Mimesis: Shakespeare and the Representation of Reality.* London: Methuen, 1983.

Obelkovitch, J., L. Roper, and R. Samuel, eds. *Disciplines of Faith: Studies in Religion, Politics, and Patriarchy.* London: Routledge & Kegan Paul, 1987.

Ober, J., and J. W. Eadie, eds. *The Craft of the Ancient Historian.* Lanham, Md.: University Press of America, 1985.

Ong, W. *Orality and Literacy: The Technologizing of the Word.* London: Methuen, 1982.

Otto, R. *The Idea of the Holy.* Trans. J. W. Harvey. London: Oxford University Press, 1929.

Overbeck, F. *Über die Anfänge der patristischen Literatur.* Repr. Basel: B. Schwabe, 1954.

Overing, J., ed. *Reason and Morality.* Association of Social Anthropologists Monographs 24. London: Tavistock, 1985.

Pagels, E. *Adam, Eve, and the Serpent.* London: Weidenfeld & Nicolson, 1988.

———. *The Gnostic Gospels.* New York: Random House, 1979.

Palmer, A.-M. *Prudentius on the Martyrs.* Oxford: Clarendon Press, 1989.

Palmer, A., with L. Rodley. "The Inauguration Anthem of Hagia Sophia in Edessa: A New Edition and Translation with Historical and Architectural Notes and a Comparison with a Contemporary Constantinopolitan Kontakion." *BMGS* 12 (1988): 117–69.

Palmer, R. "Allegorical, Philological, and Philosophical Hermeneutics: Three Modes in a Complex Heritage." In *Contemporary Literary Hermeneutics and Interpretation of Classical Texts*, ed. S. Kresic, 15–38. Ottawa: University of Ottawa Press, 1981.

Parkin, D. "The Rhetoric of Responsibility: Bureaucratic Communications in a Kenya Farming Area." In M. Bloch, (ed.), 113–39.

Partridge, L., and R. Starn. *A Renaissance Likeness: Art and Culture in Raphael's Julius II.* Berkeley and Los Angeles: University of California Press, 1980.

Pasquali, G. "Die Composition der *Vita Constantini* des Eusebius." *Hermes* 45 (1910): 369–86.

Patte, D., ed. *Semiology and Parables*. Pittsburgh: Pickwick Press, 1976.

Patlagean, E. *Pauvreté économique et pauvreté sociale à Byzance (4e au 7e siècles)*. Paris: Mouton, 1977.

Pépin, J. *Mythe et allégorie*. Paris: Editions Montaigne, 1958.

Perkins, J. "The Apocryphal Acts of the Apostles and Early Christian Martyrdom." *Arethusa* 18 (1985): 211–30.

Perrin, N. *What Is Redaction Criticism?* Philadelphia: Fortress Press, 1969.

Perry, B. E. *The Ancient Romances*. Berkeley and Los Angeles: University of California Press, 1967.

Pope, B. C. "Immaculate and Powerful: The Marian Revival in the Nineteenth Century." In Atkinson et al. (eds.), 173–200.

Poupon, G. "L'accusation de magie dans les actes apocryphes." In Bovon et al. (eds.), 71–93.

———. "Les Actes apocryphes des apôtres de Lefèvre à Fabricius." In Bovon et al. (eds.), 25–47.

Price, S. R. F. *Rituals and Power: The Roman Imperial Cult in Asia Minor.* Cambridge: Cambridge University Press, 1984.

Rabello, A. M. *Giustiniano, Ebrei e Samaritani alla luce delle fonti storico-letterarie, ecclesiastiche e giuridiche*, vol. 1. Milan: Giuffrè, 1987.

Ramsey, I. T. *Religious Language*. London: SCM Press, 1957.

Rawson, E. *Intellectual Developments in the Late Roman Republic*. London: Duckworth, 1984.

Reardon, B. *Courants littéraires des IIe et IIIe siècles après J.-C.* Paris: Belles Lettres, 1971.

Rees, B. *Pelagius: A Reluctant Heretic*. Bury St. Edmunds, Eng.: Brydell Press, 1988.

Richard, M. "Florilèges spirituels grecs." In *Dictionnaire de Spiritualité*, 5:475–86. Paris: Beauchesne, 1962.

Ricoeur, P. *The Conflict of Interpretations: Essays in Hermeneutics.* Ed. D. Hide. Evanston, Ill.: Northwestern University Press, 1974.

———. *History and Truth*. Trans. C. A. Kelbley. Evanston, Ill.: Northwestern University Press, 1965.

———. *The Rule of Metaphor*. Trans. R. Czerny with K. McLaughlin and J. Costello. Toronto: University of Toronto Press, 1977.

———. *Time and Narrative*. Trans. K. McLaughlin and D. Pellauer. 2 vols. Chicago: University of Chicago Press, 1984–85.

Roberts, C. H. *Manuscript, Society, and Belief in Early Christian Egypt*. London: Oxford University Press for the British Academy, 1979.

Roberts, C. H., and T. C. Skeat. *The Birth of the Codex*. London: Oxford University Press for the British Academy, 1983.

Robinson, J. M., and H. Koester. *Trajectories Through Early Christianity*. Philadelphia: Fortress Press, 1971.

Roques, D. *Synésios de Cyrène et la Cyrénaïque du Bas-Empire*. Paris: CNRS, 1987.

Roques, R. *L'univers dionysien: structure hiérarchique du monde selon le Pseudo-Denys*. Paris: Cerf, 1983.

Rosenfeld, L. W. "The Practical Celebration of Epideictic." In E. White (ed.), 131 ff.

Roueché, C. M. "Acclamations in the Roman Empire." *JRS* 74 (1984): 181–88.

———. *Aphrodisias in Late Antiquity*. London: Society for the Promotion of Roman Studies, 1989.

Rousseau, P. *Ascetics, Authority, and the Church in the Age of Jerome and Cassian*. Oxford: Oxford University Press, 1978.

Rousselle, A. "Parole et inspiration: le travail de la voix dans le monde romain." *History and Philosophy of the Life Sciences*, sec. 2, 129–57. Pubblicazioni della Stazione zoologica di Napoli 5.2. Naples, 1983.

———. *Porneia*. Paris: Presses universitaires de France, 1983.

Ruether, R. R. *Gregory of Nazianzus: Rhetor and Philosopher*. Oxford: Clarendon Press, 1969.

Ruggini, L. C. "Il miracolo nella cultura del tardo impero: concetto e funzione." In *Hagiographie, cultures et sociétés, IVe–XIIe siècles*, 161–204. Paris: Etudes augustiniennes, 1981.

Russell, D., and M. Winterbottom. *Ancient Literary Criticism*. Oxford: Oxford University Press, 1972.

Russo, E. "L'affresco di Turtura nel cimitero di Commodilla, l'icona di S. Maria in Trastevere e le più antiche feste della Madonna a Roma." *Bollettino dell'Istituto storico italiano per il medio evo e archivio muratoriano* 89 (1980–81): 71–79.

Said, E. *Orientalism*. London: Routledge & Kegan Paul, 1978.

———. *The World, The Text, and the Critic*. Cambridge, Mass.: Harvard University Press, 1983.

Ste. Croix, G. E. M. de. *The Class Struggle in the Ancient Greek World.* London: Duckworth, 1981.

———. "Early Christian Attitudes to Property and Slavery." *SCH* 12 (1975): 1–38.

Saller, R. *Personal Patronage Under the Early Empire.* Cambridge: Cambridge University Press, 1982.

Samuel, R., and G. Stedman Jones, eds. *Culture, Ideology, and Politics.* London: Routledge & Kegan Paul, 1982.

Sanders, E. P. *Jesus and Judaism.* Philadelphia: Fortress Press, 1985.

———. *Paul, the Law, and the Jewish People.* Philadelphia: Fortress Press, 1983.

Schoedel, W. R., and R. Wilken, eds. *Early Christian Literature and the Classical Intellectual Tradition: In Honorem R. Grant.* Berkeley and Los Angeles: University of California Press, 1979.

Scholes, R. T. *Textual Power: Literary Theory and the Teaching of English.* New Haven: Yale University Press, 1985.

Scholes, R. T., and R. Kellogg. *The Nature of Narrative.* London: Oxford University Press, 1966; repr. 1976.

Schuler, E. L. *A Genre for the Gospels: The Biographical Character of Matthew.* Philadelphia: Fortress Press, 1983.

Segal, E., and F. Millar, eds. *Caesar Augustus: Seven Aspects.* Oxford: Clarendon Press, 1984.

Seiber, J. *Early Byzantine Urban Saints.* British Archaeological Reports, Supplementary Series 37. Oxford, 1977.

Seidel, G. "Ambiguity in Political Discourse." In M. Bloch (ed.), 205–26.

Setton, K. M. *Christian Attitudes to the Emperor in the Fourth Century.* New York: Columbia University Press, 1941.

Ševčenko, I. "Levels of Style in Byzantine Prose." *JÖB* 31 (1981): 289–312.

Ševčenko, I., and N. P. Ševčenko, eds. *The Life of St. Nicholas of Sion.* Brookline, Mass.: Hellenic College Press, 1984.

Showalter, E. *The Female Malady: Women, Madness, and English Culture, 1830–1980.* New York: Pantheon Books, 1985.

Sider, R. D. *Ancient Rhetoric and the Age of Tertullian.* London: Oxford University Press, 1971.

———. *The Gospel and Its Proclamation.* Wilmington, Del.: Edwin Mellen Press, 1983.

Smith, J. Z. "Good News Is No News: Aretalogy and Gospel." In Neusner (ed.), 21–38.

Smith, M. "Prolegomena to a Discussion of Aretalogies, Divine Men, the Gospels, and Jesus." *Journal of Biblical Literature* 90 (1971): 181–84.

Smith, R. C., and J. Lounibos, eds. *Pagan and Christian Anxiety: A Response to E. R. Dodds.* Lanham, Md.: University Press of America, 1984.

Smith, R. R. R. "The Imperial Reliefs from the Sebasteion at Aphrodisias." *JRS* 77 (1987): 88–138.

———. "Simulacra gentium: The *Ethne* from the Sebasteion at Aphrodisias." *JRS* 78 (1988): 50–77.

Smith, R. W. *The Art of Rhetoric in Alexandria: Its Theory and Practice in the Ancient World.* The Hague, 1974.

Söder, R. *Die apokryphen Apostelgeschichten und die romanhafte Literatur der Antike.* Stuttgart: Kohlhammer, 1932; repr. 1969.

Soldati, J. "Talking Like Gods: New Voices of Authority." In R. C. Smith and Lounibos (eds.), 169–90.

Soskice, J. M. *Metaphor and Religious Language.* Oxford: Clarendon Press, 1985.

Spawforth, A. J., and S. Walker. "The World of the Panhellenion" (parts 1 and 2). *JRS* 75 (1985): 78–104; 76 (1986): 88–105.

Sperber, D. *Rethinking Symbolism.* Cambridge: Cambridge University Press, 1975.

Spira, A., ed. *The Biographical Works of Gregory of Nyssa.* Philadelphia: Philadelphia Patristic Foundation, 1984.

———. "Volkstümlichkeit und Kunst in der griechischen Väterpredigt des 4. Jahrhunderts." *JÖB* 35 (1985): 55–73.

Stanton, G. N. "Form Criticism Revisited." In Hooker and Hickling (eds.), 13–27.

———. "Interpreting the New Testament Today." Inaugural Lecture, King's College London. 1978.

———. *Jesus of Nazareth in New Testament Preaching.* Cambridge: Cambridge University Press, 1974.

Starn, R. "Meaning-Levels in the Theme of Historical Decline." *History and Theory* 14 (1975): 1–31.

Stein, E. *Histoire du bas-empire.* Vol. 2. Ed. J.-R. Palanque. Paris, 1949; repr. Amsterdam: Hakkert, 1968.

Stock, B. *The Implications of Literacy: Written Language and Models of Interpretation in the Eleventh and Twelfth Centuries.* Princeton: Princeton University Press, 1983.

Sykes, S. W. "The Role of Story in the Christian Religion: An Hypothesis." *Journal of Literature and Theology* 1 (1987): 19–26.

Syme, Sir Ronald. *Ammianus and the Historia Augusta.* Oxford: Clarendon Press, 1968.

Talbert, C. H. "Biographies of Philosophers and Rulers as Instruments in Religious Propaganda in Mediterranean Antiquity." In *ANRW* II.16.2, edited by H. Temporini and W. Haase, 1619–51. Berlin: Walter de Gruyter, 1978.

Tardieu, M. "Sabiens coraniques et 'Sabiens' de Ḥarrān." *Journal asiatique* 274 (1986): 1–44.

Theissen, G. *The Miracle Stories of the Early Christian Tradition*. Edinburgh: T. & T. Clark, 1983.

———. *The Social Setting of Pauline Christianity*. Ed. J. H. Schutz. Philadelphia: Fortress Press, 1982.

———. *Studien zur Soziologie des Urchristentums*. Tübingen: Mohr, 1979.

Tiede, D. "Religious Propaganda and Gospel Literature of the Early Christian Mission." In *ANRW* II.25.2, ed. H. Temporini and W. Haase, 1705–29. Berlin: Walter de Gruyter, 1984.

Tissot, Y. "Encratisme et Actes apocryphes." In Bovon et al. (eds.), 109–20.

Topping, E. C. "On Earthquakes and Fires." *Byzantinische Zeitschrift* 71 (1978): 22–35.

———. "Romanos, on the Entry into Jerusalem: A Basilikos Logos." *Byzantion* 47 (1977): 65–91.

Torjesen, K. J. *Hermeneutical Procedure and Theological Method in Origen's Exegesis*. Patristische Texte und Studien 28. Berlin, 1986.

Treadgold, W., ed. *Renaissances Before the Renaissance*. Stanford: Stanford University Press, 1984.

Trible, P. *God and the Rhetoric of Sexuality*. Philadelphia: Fortress Press, 1978.

Trombley, F. "Paganism in the Greek World at the End of Antiquity: The Case of Rural Anatolia and Greece." *Harvard Theological Review* 78 (1985): 327–84.

Trypanis, C. A. *Fourteen Early Byzantine Cantica*. Wiener byzantinische Studien 5. Vienna, 1968.

Van Dam, R. "Hagiography and History: The Life of Gregory Thaumaturgus." *Classical Antiquity* 1 (1982): 272–308.

Van den Ven, P. "S. Jérome et le moine Malchus." *Le Muséon*, n.s. 1 (1900), 413–55; 2 (1901), 208–326.

Van Esbroek, J. "Jalons pour l'histoire de la transmission manuscrite de l'homélie de Proclus sur la Vierge (BHG 1129)." In Dummer (ed.), 149–60.

———. "Les textes, littéraires sur l'Assomption avant le Xe siècle." In Bovon et al. (eds.), 265–86.

Vermes, G. *Jesus the Jew*. London: Fontana, 1976; 2d ed., 1983.

———. *Jesus and the World of Judaism*. London: SCM Press, 1983.

Veyne, P. "The Roman Empire." In Ariès and Duby (eds.), 5–234.

———. "La famille et l'amour sous le haut empire romain." *Annales E.S.C.* 33 (1978): 35–63.

———. *Le pain et le cirque*. Paris: Seuil, 1976.

Via, D. O., Jr. *The Parables*. Philadelphia: Fortress Press, 1967.

Votaw, C. W. *The Gospels and Contemporary Biographies in the Greco-Roman World*. Philadelphia: Fortress Press, 1970.

Waddell, H. *The Desert Fathers*. London: Fontana, 1962.

Wallace-Hadrill, A. "Greek Knowledge, Roman Power." *Classical Philology* 83 (1988): 224–33.

——. *Suetonius: The Scholar and His Caesars.* London: Duckworth, 1983.

——, ed. *Patronage in Ancient Society.* London: Routledge & Kegan Paul, 1989.

Walker, A. *In Search of Our Mothers' Gardens.* San Diego/New York: HBJ/ Harvest Press, 1983.

Walsh, M. *The Apparitions and Shrines of Heaven's Bright Queen.* 4 vols. New York, 1904.

Ward, B. *Miracles and the Medieval Mind: Theory, Record, and Event, 1000–1215.* London: Scolar Press, 1982.

——, ed. *Sayings of the Desert Fathers.* London: Mowbrays, 1975.

Ward-Perkins, B. *From Classical Antiquity to the Middle Ages: Urban Public Building in Northern and Central Italy, A.D. 300–850.* Oxford: Oxford University Press, 1984.

Warner, M. *Alone of All Her Sex: The Myth and Cult of the Virgin Mary.* London: Weidenfeld & Nicolson, 1976.

Weitzmann, K., ed. *The Age of Spirituality: Catalogue of the Exhibition at the Metropolitan Museum of Art, November 19, 1977, Through February 12, 1978.* New York: Metropolitan Museum of Art, in association with Princeton University Press, 1979.

Wenger, A. *L'assomption de la Très Sainte Vierge dans la tradition byzantine du VIe au Xe siècle.* Archives de l'orient chrétien 5. Paris, 1955.

Wheeldon, M. "'True Stories': The Reception of Historiography in Antiquity." In Cameron (ed.), 36–63.

Whitby, Mary. "Eutychius, Patriarch of Constantinople: An Epic Holy Man." In Whitby, Hardie, and Whitby (eds.), 297–307.

——. "The Occasion of Paul the Silentiary's Ekphrasis of S. Sophia." *Cambridge Quarterly* 35 (1985): 215–28.

Whitby, Michael, P. Hardie, and Mary Whitby, eds. *Homo Viator: Classical Essays for John Bramble.* Bristol: Bristol University Press, 1987.

White, E. E., ed. *Rhetoric in Transition.* New York: Praeger, 1980.

White, H. *Metahistory.* Baltimore: Johns Hopkins University Press, 1973.

——. "The Question of Narrative in Contemporary Theory." *History and Theory* 23 (1984): 1–33.

——. *Tropics of Discourse.* Baltimore: Johns Hopkins University Press, 1978.

White, L., Jr., *The Transformation of the Roman World: Gibbon's Problem After Two Centuries.* Berkeley and Los Angeles: University of California Press, 1966.

Wicker, K. O. "First Century Marriage Ethics: A Comparative Study of the Household Codes and Plutarch's Conjugal Precepts." In *No Famine in the*

Land, ed. J. W. Flanagan and A. W. Robinson, 141–53. Claremont, Calif.: Scholars Press for the Institute of Antiquity and Christianity, 1975.

Wilder, A. *Early Christian Rhetoric: The Language of the Gospel*. London: SCM Press, 1964.

———. *Jesus' Parables and the War of Myths: Essays on Imagination in the Scriptures*. London: SPCK, 1982.

Wilken, R. L. *The Christians as the Romans Saw Them*. New Haven: Yale University Press, 1984.

Williams, G. *Change and Decline: Roman Literature in the Early Empire*. Berkeley and Los Angeles: University of California Press, 1978.

Williams, R. *Arius: Heresy and Tradition*. London: Darton, Longman & Todd, 1987.

———, ed. *The Making of Orthodoxy: Essays in Honour of Henry Chadwick*. Cambridge: Cambridge University Press, 1989.

Wilson, A. M. "Biblical Imagery in the Preface to Eustratios' Life of Eutychios." *Studia Patristica* 17 (1985): 303–9.

Wilson, B. R., ed. *Rationality*. New York: Harper & Row, 1970.

Wilson, N. G. *St. Basil on the Value of Greek Literature*. London: Duckworth, 1975.

———. *Scholars of Byzantium*. London: Duckworth, 1983.

Winkelmann, F. "Zur Geschichte des Authentizitätsproblems der *Vita Constantini*." *Klio* 40 (1962): 187–243.

Winkler, J. J. *Auctor et Actor: A Narratological Reading of Apuleius's "The Golden Ass."* Berkeley and Los Angeles: University of California Press, 1985.

———. "Lollianus and the Desperadoes." *JHS* 100 (1980): 155–66.

Winterbottom, M. "Quintilian and Rhetoric." In Dorey (ed.), 79–97.

Witherington, B., III. *Women in the Earliest Churches*. Cambridge: Cambridge University Press, 1988.

———. *Women in the Ministry of Jesus*. Cambridge: Cambridge University Press, 1984.

Wuellner, W. "Greek Rhetoric and Pauline Argumentation." In Schoedel and Wilken (eds.), 177–88.

Yarborough, A. "Christianisation in the Fourth Century: The Example of Roman Women." *Church History* 45 (1976): 149–65.

Young, F. *From Nicaea to Chalcedon*. London: SCM Press, 1983.

———. "The God of the Greeks and the Nature of Religious Language." In Schoedel and Wilken (eds.), 45–74.

Zanker, P. *The Power of Images in the Age of Augustus*. Ann Arbor: University of Michigan Press, 1988.

General Index

acclamation, 83
Acts of Andrew, 95
Acts of John, 175
Acts of Paul, 95, 97, 147
Acts of Peter, 94
Acts of Pilate, 101
Acts of Thomas, 117
Adam, 163, 164, 171
Aelius Aristides, 125
Alexandria, 127
allegory, 65
ambiguity, in political discourse, 130–31
Ambrose, 73, 87
  on virginity, 172
Ammianus Marcellinus, 126, 131, 140
anthropology, 18
Antioch, 136–37, 184
  sack of (A.D. 540), 210
Antony, 127. See *Life of Antony*
Apocryphal Acts, 90–98. See also entries
    under *Life of . . .*
  as "popular literature," 107–8
  and narrative, 113–19
apologetic, 79, 86, 109, 119
Apophthegmata Patrum, 153
art, visual, 57
  early Christian, 59, 150–52
  as theme in Christian writing, 64
ascetic, 57
asceticism, 69–71, 115–16. See also
    Harpham, G.
Athanasius, 169

Augustine, 15, 35, 42–43, 45–46, 47,
    59, 189
  on Christian discourse, 186
  on individual, 186
  on preaching, 186
  on sexuality, 172
  City of God, 139, 141
  Confessions, 139, 157
  De Doctr. Christ., 66–67, 157
author, 46, 47–48

Basil, 130, 145, 158, 206
Bible, 7, 48
  bridal imagery in, 68, 72
  language of, 65–66
biography, 57, 91–92. See also *Lives*
bishops, 30, 127
  role of, 130, 185
Blesilla, 178
body, 57, 58
  metaphor of, 68–72, 150
bridal imagery. See Bible
Brown, Peter, 10, 115
building, imperial, 63–64
Burgess, Anthony, 24
Bury, J. B., 12
Byzantine, 59, 60, 103, 104, 162, 167,
    189
Byzantium, 18, 83, 189, 222–24, 229

Cappadocians, 138, 156, 205
Cassius Dio, 75

255

Rome, 61, 76–77, 167, 182
old and new Rome, 198
Rufinus, 140
rulers, praise of, 125–26. *See also*
panegyric

Sallust, model for Jerome, 184
scriptural, 48
Scriptures, 45, 55, 59, 65, 66–67, 79,
150, 178, 215, 217
Sebasteion, 78
Second Sophistic, 82–83
Senate, 74
senatorial, 76, 81, 148, 153
senators, 76
Seneca, *De Clementia*, 126
sexual continence, 41
sexual relations, 72
sexuality, 72
Shepherd of Hermas, 50
signs, 47, 48–49, 61, 86
discussed in *De Doctr. Christ.*,
66–67
language of, 55, 64–65
lists of, 209, 217, 219, 225–26, 227
visual and verbal, 63
Simon Magus, 96
"simplicity," 179. *See also* Christian
discourse
Simplicius, 220
Solomon, 204
Song of Songs, 65, 175, 228
Sophronius, 212
speech, 15, 19
story, 89–119
Suetonius, 74
symbolism, 68
symbols, 48, 215–16
Synesius, 125, 127–29
De Regno, 129
Syriac literature, 103–4, 161–62, 203

Tacitus
Annals, 74
Dialogus de Oratoribus, 73–74, 81
Tertullian, 85, 115
text, 47

textuality, 6, 21, 43. *See also* Christian,
texts
Thecla, 95, 115, 117, 147, 166
in Methodius's *Symposium*, 177
Theissen, G., 37
Themistius, 126, 131–33
Theodosius I, emperor, 126, 136, 152,
191
Theophylact Simocatta, 221
Thessalonica, 49
time, 116
totalizing (discourse), 31, 58, 123,
220–22
Tricennalian Oration, 55–56
Trinity, 68
truth, 57, 66. *See also* Christian, truth
and falsehood, 111–12
and fiction, 92, 118
religious, 49
typology, 48, 55, 167
Tyre, 64

Vegetius, 135
Virgin. *See also* Mary; *Protevangelium*
as mystery, 165–70
in homilies, 165
in late sixth century, 201, 209–10
in miracle stories, 212–13
mourning, 106, 167
rhetoric of, 98
Virgin Birth, 68, 209
virginity
as theme in apocryphal Acts, 97, 117
discourse of, 171–80
in Christian writing, 72–73
visions, 50–51, 54, 61
of children, 213
of Virgin, 212

wisdom, 57–58, 67
women, 97
Christian women and learning,
147–48, 178–79
in Christian *Lives*, 148
objects of discourse of virginity,
176–77
word, 48–49
Word, 15, 32, 40, 157, 169

Index of
Scriptural Citations

Compositor:	G & S Typesetters, Inc.
Text:	11 x 14 Sabon
Display:	Trump Medieval
Printer:	Braun-Brumfield, Inc.
Binder:	Braun-Brumfield, Inc.